In Transition

Also by Judith M. Bardwick
THE PSYCHOLOGY OF WOMEN

IN
TRANSITION

HOW FEMINISM, SEXUAL LIBERATION, AND THE SEARCH FOR SELF-FULFILLMENT HAVE ALTERED OUR LIVES

JUDITH M. BARDWICK

Holt, Rinehart and Winston   New York

To Jennifer, Peter, Deborah, and Ted

301.412
B23ʳ
112306
Jan. 1980

Published by Holt, Rinehart and Winston, 383 Madison Avenue, New
York, New York 10017.

Published simultaneously in Canada by Holt, Rinehart and Winston
of Canada, Limited.

Library of Congress Cataloging in Publication Data
Bardwick, Judith M., 1933-
In transition.

Bibliography: p.
Includes indexes.
1. Feminism–United States. 2. Women–
United States–Social conditions. 3. United
States–Social conditions–1970-   4. Sex
role. I. Title.
HQ1426.B29   301.41'2'0973   78-14168
ISBN College Paperback edition: 0-03-043061-5
ISBN General Book Hardcover edition: 0-03-043046-1
First Edition
Printed in the United States of America
10 9 8 7 6 5 4 3 2 1

Excerpt from "Rough Times" reprinted from Marge Piercy, Living in
the Open, *© 1976 by Alfred A. Knopf, Inc.*

ROUGH TIMES

We are trying to live
as if we were an experiment
conducted by the future,

blasting cell walls
that no protective seal or inhibition
has evolved to replace.

—Marge Piercy

CONTENTS

In Transition

Introduction:
A Decade
of Change

Since I am a professor of psychology, most of my writing has appeared in journals or in books intended for professionals and students. This book is different because I am writing for laypeople as well as colleagues. I decided to write this book in 1974, on returning to the United States after a year spent wandering in Latin America. While I was away I was a tourist who did not read or think about the psychology of women, changing roles, or any of the other material that had preoccupied me since 1962.

Within a week after I returned home, the phone began ringing. I was shoved back into the role of professor, or perhaps "expert," because the calls were mostly from women, many of whom were strangers, and all of whom were asking for information and help. I remember some of the questions: "I don't know what I want to do. What should I do?" "What will happen to my children if I go back to school? Will I flunk if I try it?" "How can I get my husband to do his share?" "Is my husband the worst one?"

Partly because I had spent such a long time away and now saw things more sharply, but mostly because enormous shifts in values seemed to have occurred between 1973 and 1974, I was struck both by the amount of change and the apparent frequency of people feeling confused, frightened, or angry. This book is an attempt to explain why people are feeling the way they are.

I will examine the changes we have undergone and their effects. Changes in our values have resulted in new attitudes about work, parenting, sex, marriage, and divorce. Enough change has occurred so that we can ask how much has taken place and what solutions, conflicts, and problems have resulted. My focus is on the amount and direction of the changes as they have been shaped by the major movements of the seventies. The explanation of our current uncertainty or confusion involves three major themes: (1) the effects of changes in basic values; (2) the emergent priority of egocentric gratification; and (3) sexism, the conscious or unwitting assumption that anything associated with men is superior to what is thought of as feminine.

We are a society continuously transformed by technology, and we are a people now continuously exposed to reversals in fundamental, traditional values. In this decade, shifts in basic values have profoundly altered what many people expect from themselves, from others, and from life. We are all affected by the changes, or the appearances of change, because their visibility in the media makes awareness unavoidable.

The media create instant and universal awareness of social movements and upheavals in values. On television and in films, books, and newspapers, in established magazines and brand new ones, we were promised paradise in open marriage, we were warned of entrapment created by parenthood, and we learned of the delights of swinging. Most importantly, we were exposed to feminist demonstrations and women's anger.

In turn, the media visibility of successful movements became the impetus for the development of counter-revolutionary movements equally determined to resist change. While the majority of us became aware of value changes because they permeated the media, our awareness did not simplistically generate acceptance of them. Some felt relief, joined consciousness-raising groups or the National Organization for Women, and embraced the new values. Others, equally certain, rejected the new values and turned to *Total Woman* and *Fascinating Womanhood.* Perhaps most of us vacillated because we felt confused and uncertain as we posed questions where we had asked none and confronted choices where we had not known we had them.

The visibility of change increases its pace. Visibility creates awareness and lets people label their previously vague discontent. When specified, vague discontent can become focused anger and the impetus for change. Insofar as media visibility creates the sense that many others feel the same way, individuals' anger and desire for change become legitimate. When shared awareness is coupled with organization, and there really is widespread discontent, the potential for significant and real social change is great.

Irrespective of content, the sheer rate of change has become significant. Tremendous changes in attitudes and in laws are now occurring in periods from three to ten years. We are therefore experiencing upheavals in basic values in units of years instead of decades. Because visibility in the media is so potent and widespread, awareness of value change is inescapable. Whether people react to such permeating awareness by embracing and participating in new values or by rigidly clinging to traditional values, at the least large numbers of people are being forced to appraise assumptions and perspectives they had taken for granted. Many have been and will continue to be forced, by changes in their values or changes in the values of others, to significantly alter how they behave. Shifts in basic values have created profound dislocations for the large number of people whose lives have become very different from what they expected when they were growing up.

In addition to the effects of the extraordinary rate, breadth, and visibility of change in fundamental values and assumptions, the content of the changes has been equally unsettling. The content primarily reflects the characteristics of the feminist movement, which has been significantly influenced by the human potential movement, the sexual revolution, and the pervasive sexism of this culture.

In Colonial America women were accorded far more respect than they had had in the Old World. By the 18th century many women were engaged in business, and at least some were in the professions. Their domestic responsibilities were economically significant. But by the end of the 18th century and the beginning of the 19th there was a trend toward loosening family ties, largely because the young left home to seek their fortunes elsewhere. In reaction to this break-up of the family, a cultural idealization developed, in which "The Family," embodied in "Woman", was the source of all love and expressions of a higher morality.[1] Once a competent partner, woman was now given a new ideal—to be a saint. Women in the rapidly expanding middle class who were affluent enough to hire help could now adopt the model of the upper class and become "Ladies." In either case, in the ideal, women lost their robustness and became sexless. In all events, their competence was trivialized.

With the Industrial Revolution in the 19th century and the enormous growth of the middle class, the world of work became increasingly separated from the home. Men left the hearth to wrest the family income from an impersonal world, while women remained at home to grace it. The lives of women and men were thus disconnected; and, in turn, ideas about differences in what men and women were like and what each could do became exaggerated. All of this led to the familiar sharp divisions in the norms we now hold for male and female—to the polarized distinctions in the personality qualities each sex is expected to exhibit and the types of work each sex is supposed to do in order to fulfill its "essential nature."

The three movements—feminism, the human potential movement, and the sexual revolution—are all reactions against the even more extraordinarily rigid and exaggerated social rules that evolved in the United States after World War II. After 1945 we returned to a "normalcy" that had never been. In the postwar period almost everyone married, had children, and adhered to a single scenario of what was the right—that is, the adult and moral—life. It was assumed that all psychologically healthy people married, were monogamous, and became parents. Not to marry and not to have children were judged to be obvious expressions of neurosis, selfishness, and inadequacy. If we examine the data it is very clear that the assumption that it was natural for everyone to marry and have children was a postwar phenomenon. In 1920, the rate of first marriage per 1000 single women was 97. In the Depression year of 1930 it fell to approximately 73. The rate of first marriage rose sharply through the war and peaked around 1945, when it reached 150. The next two decades showed a decline and leveling off to 105, the rate from 1958 to 1971.[2] The compelling marital norms paralleled those about having children. Among women born between 1900 and 1910, 26 percent were childless; among those born between 1930 and 1950, only 10 percent were childless (including a substantial number who were infertile).[3] By 1974, 95 percent of women aged 35 or older had been married at least once, and 90 percent of them had had at least one child.[4]

The social rules about women's family responsibilities, coupled with emerging ideas about child rearing which said that children were psychologically fragile but infinitely perfectible, led to motherhood becoming a full-time career based on total and selfless commitment. As a result of the norms and as a consequence of the actual numbers of those who married and became mothers, all women were perceived as actual or potential wives and mothers, to the exclusion of other roles. More than that, the image of what the ideal wife and mother was supposed to be—that is, warm, nurturant, and supportive—came to define what women in general were supposed to be. In spite of the relatively large number of women in professions in the 1930s and despite women's full participation in the economy during World War II, women were seen as having neither the personality qualities nor the skills that would enable them to be competent and successful in the impersonal, competitive world of work. Women were defined solely in the image of their domestic responsibilities. Yet even within the sphere of the home, there was no acknowledgment of competence. Indeed, the notion of competence did not even enter into the perception of woman's role, so restricted to nurturance had it become.

The potential for widespread unhappiness occurred not only because the traditional norms were so coercive but also because postwar society exaggerated the creativity of homemaking and especially the joys of maternity. Unachievable expectations of happiness in the traditional roles were created.

Nonetheless, the domestic roles have been sufficient for some women. For many other women, these roles have provided a certain gratification, but not enough. For others, domesticity has come to be judged as a trap in which they lose their sense of self. Women's traditional responsibilities are seen by feminists as the crucial impediment to women's independence and self-respect because these roles keep women economically and psychologically dependent, if not subservient.

Feminism is an explicit rejection of the lifestyle created by strongly coercive norms that define and restrict what women are and can do. With the caveat that there are important differences even within any feminist group, we can distinguish three kinds of feminists.* There are conservative feminists who are content with a modestly altered division of housework or who want equal pay for equal work. They have become sensitized to the ways in which their lives have been affected by sexist custom, but, essentially content with the status quo, they are interested primarily in making some changes in their personal lives.

Mainstream feminists are now the most visible part of the movement. They have been effective in changing the law and influencing judicial decisions; they appeal to a far greater percentage of the population than do the radicals; and they are the group most people now think of when the terms "feminist" and "the movement" are used. They are the group I am referring to when I use these terms. Mainstream feminists include, for example, the majority of those in the National Organization for Women, Women's Equity Action League, and women's professional organizations and political caucuses. They are essentially reformist groups which want to retain and modify the institutions of the country.

Radical feminists have significantly different political, economic, and social objectives from the mainstream feminists. The radicals want to transform or eliminate many American institutions. Radical groups see society as needing basic changes, not simple reforms. However, both radical and mainstream feminists look beyond individual goals; both are concerned with institutional or cultural sexism.

Sexism is popularly described in terms of male attitudes and behaviors. I will argue that all members of a sexist culture, women as well as men, operate on the conscious or unconscious assumption that whatever is "masculine" is intrinsically better than anything "feminine." The most prevalent solutions offered by mainstream feminists to the

*We should note that there are significant errors of simplification when we use such terms as "the movement" or "feminism," because these terms imply a unified ideological or political position. There is a great range of values and objectives and, indeed, a significant amount of divisiveness, within feminism. But in order to focus on important themes we must emphasize consistency. In order to make things clear we make distinctions that are as reasonable as they are arbitrary.

confinement of women's lives—indeed, the primary goals of the dominant sector within feminism—have become the integration of women into the mainstream of the American economy and Establishment power. Without necessarily saying so, most feminists have accepted the male model of the good life in sex, work, marriage, and parenthood. The most visible goals of mainstream feminism are status, power, money, and autonomy—all historically associated with men. The most visible goals of feminism have been derived from an image of what men's lives were imagined to be like—along with an explicit rejection of what women's lives were really like.

The human potential movement proliferated at roughly the same time as the contemporary feminist movement and, like feminism, was a response to our realization of how we had made "normalcy" a limited, rigid set of experiences. In some ways an outgrowth of the beat and countercultures, the human potential movement reversed values, rejecting any rules that imposed constraint. Encounter groups, T-groups, and places such as Esalen generated hopes and expectations that people could expand infinitely and feel continuously alive if only they would get rid of their old tapes of cultural conditioning. The underlying assumption was that people are infinitely perfectible; the promise was that not only the individual self but the self within a relationship could achieve heightened levels of "feeling" and "being," expanded awareness and consciousness, to an extent never before imagined.

Since "potential" is by definition infinite, people sought unlimited, unconfined, intense stimulation within themselves and with others. This led to a search for painfree growth experiences; for relationships that would be nondefensive, nonmanipulative, not hung up on old rules, liberating; for an expanded self that would know no limits and recognized none of the constraints imposed by the routines of ordinary coping.

The human potential movement shifted the emphasis from conformity to creativity, from the family to the self. With feminism, it was an important influence in legitimizing the pursuit of gratification of one's own individual needs. The most important question became, "What's in it for me?" At about this time, a third movement, the sexual revolution, was arising in response to the confinement imposed by our rigid social rules. The model for successful liberation from archaic sexual regulations became the ability to engage in sexual intercourse without hangups or entanglements in heterosexual or homosexual encounters. The sexual revolution added more fuel to the new hedonism and to the goal of egocentric gratification. Now the question became, "Does this feel good? Am I happy?"

Our traditional values and our expectations about what life would be like had emphasized duty, discipline, hard work, and commitment to the family. The focus was on satisfaction rather than happiness. Now, for more than a decade, feminism, the human potential movement, and the sexual revolution have come together to generate a search for egocentric hedonism. Moreover, this goal has become the essential criterion by which we measure whether we are getting enough out of work, parenthood, marriage, any experience or relationship, all commitments. Whether or not we subscribe to the philosophies expressed in the three movements, we are all influenced by the changes in values they have generated because they are inescapably visible.

While unfettered self-expansion and self-pleasure have become major priorities in the media ideology of our culture, the costs of commitment and obligation to others have been exaggerated. The new ideology dictates that the self is to become magnificently independent; in the extreme view, anything less is seen as inadequacy. Especially in male–female relationships, many people view an inability to be truly autonomous, to be free from old rules and old relationships, as a clear demonstration of being "unliberated."

It seems fair to say that today the contracts we have made with ourselves and with others are in a state of disequilibrium. It is hardly surprising that almost anyone who presents a simple solution, a painless prescription that promises happiness, finds eager followers. It was logical, probably inevitable, that new ideas would develop about what life ought to be like, and that they would be essentially reversals of the rigid and duty-laden rules so many of us grew up with. But uncontaminated by reality, these new expectations in their extreme, are, unachievable. The social changes today are a reaction to old problems and solutions to some of them. But, in turn, these new values create new problems.

Today we are experiencing the inevitable anxiety that occurs during any period of major transition, when old and new values exist at the same time. But we are also experiencing anger and depression when we act according to new values and discover that no lifestyle is painless.

Those who define all change as progress and judge the past to have been without merit grab on to a new set of rules. Others respond by idealizing the past, mourning its passing, and clinging tenaciously to old values. For many, besieged and bewildered by convulsions in values, the bedrock of certainty has been replaced with a sense of alienation, the feeling that nothing is secure, nothing has meaning, and we are powerless.

Most of us, though, respond ambivalently because we recognize that former values and lifestyles provided gratification as well as frustration; we understand that change solves old problems and simultaneously creates new, unpredicted ones. Most of us learned the old norms, but we are adapting our lives to new rules that are still evolving, not yet certain.

This book is mainly about the middle class and especially the college educated. That is partly because we know much more about this group than about either the working class or upper class, and because middle-class people are both most aware of social change and most willing—if not eager—to experiment.[5] It is also because this is the group I belong to. When topics are as personal as these—for few in this society are unaffected by these great shifts in values—it is dishonest to pretend to be objective and uninvolved. When the material is so close, analyses and judgments are inevitably influenced by one's own experiences and the person one is. I am middle aged, a feminist, a scientist, an academic, and a divorced mother of three. All of the value changes I describe, I have experienced. I have no prescriptions for happiness.

The Effects
of Change

1

Within roughly the last 15 years we have experienced the drug revolution, the sexual revolution, gay liberation, students' rights, children's rights, and the civil rights and Native American and Latino movements. We have reversed attitudes about the effectiveness of centralizing power in government, the legitimacy of the Vietnam war, and the value of continuous economic growth. Our historic preference for large families has given way to zero population growth. We have seen the beginning of detente and the end of the Cold War; the rise of OPEC and the establishment of formal relations with the People's Republic of China. We have become concerned with ecology and consumers' rights.[1] We have threatened the sanctity of religion by pressuring for basic reforms, and we have created political adults out of 18-year-olds by lowering the legal voting age through the Twenty-Sixth Amendment to the Constitution.

Some changes have involved fundamental moralities: pornography became a matter of local sentiment; rape laws were reformed; abortion was decriminalized nationally and prostitution locally in some Nevada counties; some states adopted no-fault divorce laws; courts began to give some divorced fathers custody of their children; and numerous state statutes now make affluent or working women just as responsible for spousal support as their husbands.[2] In many areas sex education is routinely taught in school and the Bible is not. In 1977 the U.S. Supreme Court declared unconstitutional state regulations prohibiting distribution of contraceptives to those under 16, and some high schools have nurseries for the young children of pupils. Homosexuality has been removed from the list of neuroses by both the American Psychological Association and the American Psychiatric Association. Radical therapists insist that psychosis is just another way of seeing the world.

More than anything else, the 1970s have been the decade of the women's movement. From federal guidelines for equal educational and employment opportunities, to significantly increased percentages of women in the graduate professional schools, to feminist books on the bestseller lists and feminist TV specials, to the enormous publicity accorded the few women who have risen high in politics or professions, the movement has spilled out of the confines of narrow objectives. Some churches, including Reform Judaism, the United Methodists, African Methodist Episcopal, and Unitarian Universalist, have ordained women. Among Roman Catholic nuns, a militant faction want to be ordained and participate as equals in running the church. In 1977 President Carter appointed two women to his Cabinet. In the same year, women were able to compete, for the first time, for Rhodes scholarships. Women are joining ROTC on campuses, while experimental groups of female GIs are undergoing basic training with male recruits. The Air Force Academy, West Point, Annapolis, the Coast Guard Academy, and the U.S. Merchant Marine Academy are now coed.[3] In 1975 there were 331 legal abortions for every 1000 live births.[4] Lesbian mothers have sued for custody of their children. Feminist therapists insist that nonfeminist therapists' ideas about what psychologically healthy women and men are like are sick. Judy K. Hartwell, accused of murdering her husband, offered the defense that she feared he was about to perform certain sex acts on her forcibly. She was acquitted after the judge instructed the jury that a married woman has the legal right to use force to resist her husband's unwanted sexual advances.

By 1975 awareness of women's issues was so great that California passed the Displaced Homemakers Equal Opportunity Act.

> The Legislature hereby finds and declares that there is an ever-increasing number of persons in this state who, having fulfilled a role as homemakers, find themselves "displaced" in their middle years through divorce, death of spouse, or other loss of family income. As a consequence, displaced homemakers are very often without any source of income; they are ineligible for categorical welfare assistance; they are subject to the highest unemployment rate of any sector of the work force; they face continuing discrimination in employment because they are older and have no recent paid work experience; they are ineligible for unemployment insurance because they have been engaged in unpaid labor in the home; they are ineligible for social security because they are too young, and for many, they will never qualify for social security because they have been divorced from the family wage earner; they have often lost their rights as beneficiaries under employers' pension and health plans through divorce or death of spouse, despite many years of contribution to the family well-being; and they are most often ineligible for Medi-Cal, and are generally unacceptable to private health insurance plans because of their age.

> The Legislature further finds and declares that homemakers are an unrecognized part of the work force who make an invaluable contribution to the welfare of the society as a whole. . . .

In the late 1960s and early 1970s radical feminists called for the end of marriage and capitalism, and advocated homosexuality and test-tube conceptions. The radicals were especially visible because they had learned how to shock us and therefore how to assure widespread coverage in the media. While such exposure led many to dismiss all feminists as crazy or irrelevant, its conspicuousness made the existence of a women's movement impossible to ignore. Equally important, the demands of mainstream feminist groups such as NOW (National Organization for Women) seemed tame in contrast; such goals as ending sex discrimination in social benefits and in employment, granting tax deductions for child care costs to working parents, establishing more child care centers, providing equal educational opportunities, giving housing and family allowances to women at the poverty level—all of which would be revolutionary in effect—appeared rational, even tame.

It is hard to measure the impact of the radicals, since their accomplishments do not lend themselves to an easy accounting. We cannot ask, for example, How many legislators have they put into office? How many reforms have they been responsible for? Yet they seem to have provided much of the initial crucial energy of the movement.

But every movement must organize and set goals so that accomplishments and impediments are clear and concrete. The radicals, in general, did not do this, and that became the mission of the mainstream feminists. A movement may become less radical when its objectives have to be specified with realistic means to achieve them. It may also be true that a movement becomes less radical as its anger is dissipated by the energy required to organize.

Because both radical and mainstream feminists articulated the frustration and latent motivation for change that already existed among a significant percentage of women, feminism could and did become a major movement. It was led by women who had been educated to participate as individuals and as equals in the work world and who found themselves unable to do so. Their education prepared them to achieve and compete in the world outside the home. That women were being trained to work outside their traditional confined roles itself signified that an important social change had already occurred, but it had not been recognized or responded to by society. Victimized and angered, feminists transformed their individual frustrations into an ideology of change.

More than anything else, feminism is a psychological revolution based on women's insistence that they have a basic right to make choices and to be judged as individuals. The movement is a statement that women are not whatever their marital status is. Feminism is a statement by those whose lives had been organized by their responsibilities to others that they have the right to self-expression, to individual achievement, to independence. Since individualistic gratification—as well as economic independence—can be gained directly by success in an occupation, mainstream feminists have directed their major efforts to achieving parity in careers. As radical feminism declined and mainstream feminism became dominant, media portrayal of the movement became increasingly sympathetic. The emphasis on work success unwittingly lowered the status of women's traditional roles even further. As a result of the extraordinary success of feminism and its visibility, resistance to the movement was an inevitable secondary development. Between the pro-and anti-feminist efforts, how much change has actually taken place?

Social Change and Backlash

For every revolution we can predict a counter-revolution. The greater the surge for change, the greater the search for tradition. A movement whose objectives are to force society to reconceptualize what women and therefore men are, and to profoundly alter what men and women do, threatens everyone. Such a movement involves a serious disruption in our lives or provokes a disturbing evaluation of who we are and what we have become. Feminists and their opponents are both very visible. The question we need to answer, therefore, is how much change has really occurred in people's values, in their acceptance of mainstream feminist goals.

Some resistance is independent of the issues of feminism and comes from persons who resist all social change. These people tend to be politically conservative, religious, and less educated. Most resistance, however, is specific to the content of the movement. Since feminism has emphasized economic parity, a backlash from white men is predictable, since the economy is not generating jobs that can absorb female and minority workers. The economy is essentially static, so that the implementation of equal opportunity goals means that a choice must be made between white males and minority males and women.

> We know of specific cases where excellent white male candidates lost out in job opportunities to women as departments scurry to keep HEW off their backs. The advantage for women and minority groups is the fear of

employing institutions that they will lose federal funds if they do not meet certain quotas. We are in a situation where there is some reverse discrimination. Hiring for white males has been radically delayed this year as institutions bargain over the small pool of female and minority applicants.[5]

In spite of the fact that federal law requires most businesses and schools with federal government contracts to establish goals for the number of women and minority people they hope to employ or enroll, opponents of affirmative action claim that the government is requiring rigid quotas. In the last several years white men have sued on the basis of "reverse discrimination," and some have had success. In 1976 the District Court of Washington, D.C., informed Georgetown University's law school that its plan to give 60 percent of its first-year scholarships to members of minority groups discriminated illegally in that it gave favored treatment not justified under the banner of affirmative action. The U.S. District Court, Eastern District of Virginia, ruled in the same year that a state university's preferential hiring of females violated the equal protection clause of the Fourteenth Amendment and Title VII of the Civil Rights Acts of 1964, even if it were done to implement an affirmative action program. The court made these rulings despite earlier decisions in other circuit courts in 1971, 1972, and 1973 holding that prohibitions against preferential hiring could be overridden by affirmative action programs. In 1977, a white male named Allen Bakke, who had twice applied and twice been denied admission to the University of California Medical School, claimed he had been unjustly discriminated against by the university's special admissions program for disadvantaged students and took the case to the Supreme Court. The court ruled in 1978 that he had indeed been discriminated against by the university's rigid quota system and, although upholding race as a legitimate determinant in admissions, said the school had to admit him. In 1976 the Supreme Court ruled that General Electric was not discriminating on the basis of sex when the company excluded sick-pay benefits because of illnesses related to pregnancy—even though it paid for cosmetic surgery including hair transplants. (I, for one, have seen very few bald women or pregnant men.)

In fact, there has been so little real change that affirmative action and "reverse discrimination" are impressive largely as psychological phenomena. Thus far the numbers attest that the confrontation is vastly more philosophic than economic. Academic institutions, for example, have been under heavy pressure in the last several years to increase the women on their faculty. Data on 88 percent of all institutional units shows that the percentage of women on the faculty increased from 25.2 to 25.5 from 1976 to 1977, for a whopping gain of .3 percent. For those who would point to large gains in entry level positions, let the data speak. In 1976 the number of full professors who were women was 9.6 percent; in 1977, it was 9.7 percent. For associate professors, the 1976 figure was 17.7 percent, compared to 18.0 percent in 1977. Women assistant professors were 30.4 percent in 1976, 31.7 percent in 1977; instructors, 50.6 percent in 1976 and 50.0 percent in 1977; lecturers, 40.8 percent in 1976 and 42.8 percent in 1977; and women of no academic rank, 34.8 percent in 1976 and 34.7 percent in 1977.[6] For those who might protest that the base year of 1976 is misleading because great change would have occurred after the passage of Title IX of the Education Amendments in 1972, we can add a comparison between women faculty in colleges and universities in 1974 and in 1959 to 1960. The figure for women professors in 1959–1960 was 10 percent, compared to 9 percent in 1974; associate professors, 17.5 percent in 1959–1960 and 15 percent in 1974; and women were 24 percent of the assistant professors and 45 percent of instructors in 1974.[7] If this is change, what would be a static situation?

The women's movement appears to threaten men most as it forces them to share their traditional power and privileges. Insofar as masculinity has been associated with male dominance over some other men and (theoretically) over all women, the reality or even the possibility of female equality can generate anxiety in men about their masculinity. Even men who hold liberal values in other areas may feel challenged by sexual parity, especially when it takes the form of women and men having identical roles. Thus, although more and more men as well as women say they support changing the status of women, men are more inclined to adhere to traditional views of gender and thus of role differences.[8] While, on the whole, women and men are essentially equal in their liberalism or conservatism, today liberal women tend to diminish gender distinctions while liberal men show some tendency toward an "equal but different" viewpoint.

Among men who are really opposed to significant changes in the gender roles, there seem to be two groups. One group is conservative and idealizes women's fulfillment in the traditional roles. The second group is hostile and devalues women who take on nontraditional responsibilities. The latter are cynical rather than idealistic about women's traditional responsibilities and may view women as not being satisfied or effective in any role. Men who favor innovations in women's responsibilities tend to be educated and believe that women are discriminated against.[9]

Men who are confronted by angry wives will predictably feel resentment and then anxiety when their wives want to change the contract of their relationship, often after several years of marriage. Some men's resistance expresses both conscious fears that new demands will be made on them or that they will lose support, and less conscious anxieties that the changes their wives want have as much to do with their own inadequacy as with their wife's ambition.

A more complicated form of resistance stems from women having internalized the traditional norms. In this case women feel a conscious anger at their husbands, who, they insist, bound them to the home and prevented them from doing what was important to them. While these women are often aware of being scared about whether they could succeed in work or in school, they are not aware of the extent to which their choices in the past were governed by their own traditional values. Wives may therefore demand and want their husbands' attitudes and behavior to change, but at an unconscious level neither expect nor desire what they are requesting.[10] We see this, for example, when a wife insists on the opportunity to earn money, the husband agrees, and the wife is then upset because she feels he is not willing to support her anymore.

Another source of resistance to feminist goals is the conservatism of children. They seem very resistant to changing ideas about what the sexes are supposed to do and be like. This is probably because their gender is the only thing about them that does not change as they grow up. In one experiment, for example, psychologist Marcia Guttentag attempted to change sexist attitudes in schoolchildren. Guttentag designed a six-week program intended to increase awareness of sexist issues. The program was given to over 1000 children aged 5, 10, and 14 in three school districts in Boston. The focus was on sexual stereotypes in personality, work, and family responsibilities. The program emphasized the ideas that women can do any sort of work that men can, that men should enjoy their families, and that both sexes ought to have the personality qualities we admire.

Tests given before the experimental curriculum established that the majority of the children knew from the age of 5—from television, their peers, and what they saw at home—that boys and men are strong and do interesting things and girls and women are weak and silly and are best kept at home. These views were held by children of diverse ethnic, social, and economic backgrounds, and it made no difference whether their mothers were employed.

At the end of the program the researchers found that 10-year-old boys whose mothers worked and all 14-year-old boys, with employed or unemployed mothers, became notably more stereotyped, rigid, and outspoken about what women's roles ought to be. In contrast, many of the girls moved closer to feminist views, accepting the ideas that women can do a wide variety of jobs and can combine marriage and work.[11]

In another effort to reduce children's sexism, Gale Mitchell designed a curriculum which she used with eigth- and ninth-grade students. She made up a country called Ruritania, in which two groups, the Schleeps and Greeps, lived. Her charts showed that Schleeps were 49 percent of the population, made up 50 percent of the college graduates and 60 percent of those working, held 97 percent of the major government jobs, controlled 82 percent of the money invested in business, earned almost double what Greeps did, could have almost any kind of job they wanted, and could get the training they needed for the employment they chose. The students were asked to describe what they would feel like if they were a Schleep or a Greep and what their life would be like.

The students were very angry about the enormous inequities—until the groups were described as male and female and the data as true for the United States. The girls either tended to become angrier or to back down, apparently because they were afraid of alienating the boys. Boys said it changed things to know the data referred to real sex differences. This was the way things ought to be. Mitchell found that the boys who expressed the strongest sexist prejudices were the poorer students, the "tough guys," and the athletes. Boys who were successful academically were much more flexible about sex roles.[12]

Another significant source of resistance to the women's movement, especially toward its focus on achievement in work, is many women's experience of the traditional roles as significant and creative. While many mothers of young children would welcome some help, most continue to want major responsibility in rearing their own small children. As long as this continues to be true (and as long as women are expected to raise their own children), women will reduce their work involvements at precisely the time when ambitious men are most fully involved in their careers.

Some women may therefore choose to remain within the traditional roles, at least for part of their adult life, because they find the responsibilities important and the work at least sometimes creative and pleasurable. Other women may limit their activities to a *confined* version of the traditional role for the negative reason that they are afraid to venture out of it. Thus, for diverse reasons, some women and men who are successful according to traditional criteria will not want these measures of successful adulthood changed.

While men have been the primary and obvious target of feminist *anger,* some women believe that traditional women have been the primary target of feminist *contempt*. This is because the most visible feminist position is that real parity will be achieved through success in work. This position implies the judgment that the roles of wife and mother are of less value than roles which are paid, and therefore that wives and mothers are of less value than employed women. While the mainstream feminist position is actually that everyone has the right to make choices and develop self-esteem in different ways, the focus is on increasing opportunity for career success. Many women who are unwilling to take this route and engage in this risk, many misunderstand the feminist message to be, "You are worthless and you have wasted your life."

Earlier expressions of a counter-revolutionary conservatism had little effect: MOM (Men Our Masters); HOW (Happiness of Womanhood); The Pussycats ("The lamb chop is mightier than the karate chop"). But Helen Andelin's *Fascinating Womanhood* has now sold over 400,000 hardback copies since it was published in 1965, and 11,000 teachers have given the author's eight-week course to 300,000 women in the past 14 years. *The Total Woman* by Marabel Morgan sold 370,000 hardback copies in 1974 alone, and Pocket Books paid $750,000 for the paperback rights.[13]

The counter-revolutionary movement developed when feminist accomplishments and values were so visible that they were impossible to ignore. The counter-movement formed when the success of feminism created a large number of disturbed, anxious people.* Much of the focus of the anti-feminist movement has been the fight against ratification of the Equal Rights Amendment (ERA). While anti-ERA forces coach their arguments in terms of threats to the family, the end of alimony, the possibility of women being drafted into the military, and the fascinating specter of unisex toilets, they are also expressing rejection of a movement they perceive as elitist, preoccupied with the goals of the career-oriented middle class, and contemptuous of housewives and the working class. When women vote against the ERA they may also be voting against a movement that they believe characterizes them as people who have been duped by society, who are brainless, passive, incompetent, and frightened. They are voting against values and heroines that make them feel unintelligent and unsophisticated. They are

---

*There has been resistance to specific goals of the movement. The anti-abortion movement, for example, has become organized and important. But the anti-abortionists are only incidentally anti-feminist. Since the sanctity of human life is a preeminent value in all our religions, the anti-feminist stance derives from the fact that abortion was and remains a feminist goal. But antagonism to abortion is based on a moral principle and not on anti-feminism per se.

saying, "I am affirming the value of my life. The hell with you and your ERA."[14]

Passage of the ERA would, in fact, be an explicit recognition of the need for such an amendment. It would then be hard to escape the interpretation that women need the protection of an amendment because they are significantly discriminated against. In this sense the ERA specifically acknowledges women's minority status as women, that is, as they have been discriminated against and confined to the traditional roles.

While anti-ERA groups express opposition to feminism, such books as *Fascinating Womanhood* and *Total Woman* go further. These books and the classes based on them purport to provide a solution to the anxiety provoked by the feminists' questions, giving women clear instructions on how to find happiness through subservience to their husbands. These specific and detailed programs provide scenarios to play and sentences to say, in which adult women are asked to pretend to be dumb, absentminded, childish, submissive but seductive, diffident, deferential, passive, weak, and opinionless. How acting out such roles can lead to self-esteem is unclear to me. I have equal difficulty imagining that men can respond to this contrived playacting with a surge of masculine confidence.

Many women apparently do find solace in these programs, which assure and support traditional women by saying that the choices they have made and the values they hold are correct, even moral, and sanctioned by God. In fact, these programs assert, the path to joy lies in following the old rules—but more strictly and extremely than before. In addition to the comfort gained from simple rules that deny social change, the essential message is sustaining, since it proclaims that if man is a king, his wife is a queen.

It seems absurd but understandable that a movement devoted to upgrading the status of women is perceived as liberating by women ready to act on the new options and as sexist and denigrating by women who are not. To the latter, feminism appears to be a movement that scorns them and despises the central values of their lives. Imagine how threatening that is, since feminist values appear to them to be the dominant values in the media, in the nation. They are correct: profeminist values have become the majority opinion.

While the feminist movement has been enormously visible, there is still the question of the extent to which feminism has altered society. We do not yet have artificial wombs; the nuclear family limps but lives; capitalism still thrives. But the movement, especially the mainstream sector, has wrought great changes in legislation, in judicial decisions, and especially in people's awareness. In less than one decade over 50 percent of both women and men have become sensitive to sexist presumptions and discriminatory practices where ignorance and insensitivity existed before. The speed of change is highlighted when we realize how shockingly recent are the organizational beginnings of contemporary feminism. In 1966 Betty Friedan and a small group of others met in Washington and organized NOW, the National Organization for Women. WEAL, the Woman's Equity Action League, filed its first complaint of sex discrimination against the academic community on January 31, 1970. In October 1972 the jurisdiction of the U.S. Commission on Civil Rights was extended to include discrimination based on gender.

In 1974, for the first time in the history of the survey, the Roper Poll for Virginia Slims found that the majority of women—57 percent of the 3000 polled—were in favor of most efforts to improve women's status.[15] Four years earlier, the figure had been 40 percent. The results of five national surveys conducted between 1964 and 1974 showed a striking shift in attitudes—especially between 1970 and 1973 and particularly among women who had finished college and were employed. In 1970, 80 percent of the population agreed that it was better for a husband to achieve outside of the home and for the wife to remain within it. In 1973 the number who still felt this way had fallen to 60 percent. By 1973 two-thirds of the women believed that men should share in housework, that women should be considered as seriously as men for executive or political positions, that a woman could be President. Almost unanimously, 98 percent of the women believed that equal work deserves equal pay.[16] The Harris survey of December 1975 found that 63 percent of those interviewed favored "most of the efforts to strengthen and change women's status in society"; in 1970 the figure had been 42 percent. It is interesting to note that this was the first time in the history of the Harris survey that the percentage of women favoring a change in women's status (63 percent) was greater than the percentage of men (59 percent).[17]

The movement plays not only in New York, Berkeley, and Ann Arbor but also in Peoria. It is not only to be found in the radical press but in the most domestic of magazines, *Family Circle*. It has altered the objectives of the University Christian Movement as well as university academics. It has influenced the Women's Christian Temperance Union to send a delegation to the International Women's Year meeting in Mexico City. The League of Women Voters, the American Association of University Women, and the Federation of Business and Professional Women have made passage of the ERA a major goal. The National Council of Catholic Women and the Girls Clubs of America are increasingly concerned with feminist issues. The U.S. National Women's

Agenda was written by the Future Homemakers of America, the National Black Feminist Organization, the National Council of Negro Women, the National Gay Task Force, the National Organization for Women, the Association of Junior Leagues, Hadassah, Church Women United, the Young Women's Christian Association, Lesbian Mothers, the National Defense Fund, Camp Fire Girls, and the Girls Clubs of America.[18]

All of the data are consistent, showing a rising percentage who accept reformist, mainstream feminist goals along with a significant but minority percentage who cleave to conservative, traditional sex-role divisions. People are asking questions, assessing priorities, altering relationships, and setting goals in ways that no one could have imagined 10 years ago. Feminism has disrupted any complacent sense that tradition guides us; it has accelerated change and created awareness of the transformations that remain necessary.

Values and Sexual Identity

Values, transformed into norms, are society's rules and expectations. When values change and options are introduced, choice becomes possible and anxiety becomes probable. Today, I think, expressions of ambivalence reflect psychological health, because only those who have a sense of the changes which have happened to them, and thus of the contradictions within themselves, have a sense of what is real.

When there are no clear messages of what we ought to be, when there are no restrictions on what we can be, when the rate of change is very swift and what we say today is very unlike what we said five years ago and totally unlike what we learned as children, and when we know that the values of today will surely not be those headlined five years from now—then uncertainty must be the basic reality.

Profound changes in social values result in changed norms. Changing norms result in a loss of certainty about what are society's rules. We respond to this uncertainty in ways that often reflect our need for certainty—that is, either by embracing the old rules exaggeratedly or fervently, or by accepting the new rules unquestioningly, even if they are the exact reverse of the old.

At the popular level, feminism seems to have generated a simple rule: In the future each sex will participate in the work or emotional roles traditionally assigned to the other. But since traditional norms defined acceptable behavior and desirable qualities as proper to one sex and prohibited to the other, this simple rule has raised the complex and fundamental question of what is feminine or masculine.

Earlier in this chapter we asked how much change has actually taken place. The answer is that significant changes in attitudes and values have occurred within this decade and especially in the last five years. Thus, the second question must be, What are the effects? What happens to people when they undergo fundamental changes in values, especially when the changes relate to sexual identity?

Sexual identity, that is, the sense of being or feeling appropriately feminine or masculine, is earned in society according to whatever age and sex expectations that society has. Sexual identity is not given and it is not lightly donned. It is a core part of our sense of self. It influences how we feel about ourselves and it is influenced by the ways that others respond to us. Sexual identity is therefore not only individual and internal but also interactive and reciprocal. It is a core part not only of an individual's identity but also a core part of how society is structured. Our expectations about how the sexes behave as female or basic to our ideas about what normal people do and what normal men and women are like.

The feminist movement, like many other movements, is clearest about what it is rejecting from the past. But the movement is not clear about what norms will replace those which have been rejected; new norms are hard to imagine. If the new norm is that henceforward each sex will do what it had previously been forbidden to do, thereby making gender irrelevant, this ostensible solution ignores the fact that changes in gender roles involve not simply changes in what people do but also changes in concepts of femininity and masculinity. It is hard to conceive of a more profound change.

Of course people do not experience the uncertainties and conflicts that stem from changing sexual identity in an abstract way. They wonder whether or not to marry, go to medical school, have children. Even simpler, they become concerned about who does the laundry or picks up the kids after school. While we can think of the latter as purely logistical decisions based on who has the time or the interest to do it, even discussion of what choices to make and who is to do what could not have arisen until people accepted the idea that women have a right to make important commitments outside the family because they have a right to a more egocentric sense of themselves. The effect of the new attitudes—especially as they jolt our sense of what is appropriately feminine or masculine or provoke us to perceive sexism where we were once blind to it—is the subject of the rest of this book.

But we have not finished answering the second question. Aside from issues of gender, what happens to people when the changes in social values are so fundamental that their commitments necessarily change?

The Loss of Existential Anchors

When there is extraordinary value change, the security that people gain from conforming to the expectations of their culture is endangered and identity crises are predictable. I mean this simply and concretely. When social values are changing, much less reversing, it becomes increasingly difficult to know what we may expect from others and they from us. It becomes more difficult to know what we should want and what we should become. In a period of profound social change people lose their existential anchors.*

"Existential anchors" are the commitments and responsibilities that give life direction and meaning. Anchorage is found in the efforts, and tasks which come from commitment. In primitive economies anchorage comes from unending efforts to survive—to eat, to be warm, to cope with the violent onslaught of the elements. Freed by our affluence, we have sought commitment in the extended family, marriage, parenting, and work.

Sex roles have defined responsibilities in work, marriage, and parenthood. The roles of husband and wife, father and mother, have been one source of sexual identity. The specific tasks of the roles can be thought of as existential anchors. Anchors are commitments that tie us to reality because they force us to act on problems and tasks which are real. Grappling with the responsibilities of these roles, which have provided many of our most significant and permanent commitments, gave us our major routes toward achieving adulthood. Coping with these jobs gave us the feeling that we had secured an identity and earned maturity.

In societies that do not change rapidly people know what life was like and what their life will be. Their anchors are specific tasks—to build a house, kill a lion, have a child—and they are safeguarded by the essential stability of a society where rules are not changing and people have certain responsibilities that are known and accepted.

A short decade ago most women's identities were anchored in the stereotyped ideal of their family roles. In today's new extreme ideal this anchor is specifically rejected in favor of anchoring within one's self, as though one can have a self independent of relationships. The anchor of parenthood may be rejected for the anchor of work, that is, an identity based upon occupational success.

*This is one explanation for the current explosive embracing of religion, including fundamentalist Christianity, Hasidic Judaism, and diverse Eastern faiths. It also explains the extraordinary popularity of messianic gurus.

In their most exaggerated form, these ideals may contain a new danger. At least some existential anchors must be permanent to ensure that people have some sources of a stable identity. This occurs most easily if among the responsibilities the society defines as permanent commitments there are some tasks that need be accomplished only once because that achievement or commitment cannot be undone. Parenthood is probably the most permanent of the anchors; marriage once was. In some societies, belonging to a family is a significant anchor, but in our mobile society it has lost some of its importance. Can we find a stable anchor for our identities in work success? I cannot imagine any area more filled with risk. Success in work involves the fluctuating economy, bureaucracies, changing technology, competition—a myriad of factors over which we have no control. Work success involves risk. In work we are as good as the last thing we accomplished. That means that we may be successful and then again we may not. Identity based on work success cannot be a stable, once-accomplished, settled thing. It is always contingent.*

Some find their most crucial anchors in their family. This is where they know who they are and what they must do. Part of their identity is secure in the role of wife, husband, child, mother, father. They do not have to recreate these relationships. While family responsibilities may be psychologically draining—and we have all had times when we wanted to get rid of such responsibilities—still, if we sense that these bonds are permanent, we have a crucial source of identity. Especially because the competitive and risky work milieu is so unstable, the stability of reciprocal, permanent relationships, in which we know our responsibilities, makes them a crucial source of most people's anchorage. It is therefore not surprising that while people are divorcing at record-breaking rates, they are remarrying at extraordinary rates. People are seeking anchorage, hoping for permanence, if not in this relationship, perhaps in the next.

It should be clear that values have not simply changed; in some instances they have reversed. All of us who are trying to adapt to the new values need to create anchorage when the blueprints have not yet been drawn.

Where, then, are our anchors? This is no idle question. I think it is a central issue, the most imperative question in a society that is a maelstrom of changing technologies, ideals, and moralities. Technologi-

*This point was dramatically illustrated by the men who lost their jobs during the severe recession of the mid-seventies. The effects were basically the same for line workers and executives: depression, anxiety, loss of self-esteem, and marked uncertainty.

cal societies are threatening by dint of the sheer rate of change which is their characteristic; change itself creates uncertainty because the future is not like the past. Thus people in rapidly changing societies are most in need of anchors. If our world is in a vortex of change, our identity cannot remain stable because as values change, so do roles and therefore so do commitments. And if there are no rules except "do your own thing," then the ideal person becomes someone who can float on the latest air currents of fashion, shifting direction like a dandelion seed.

Where Shall We Go?

We achieve an identity and self-esteem when we accomplish what everyone agrees is important. It is easier the more specific the goal or task is. When old norms are given up, we are freed from the restrictions of their obligatory responsibilities, but we are not freed from our need to construct an identity. A society without defined roles creates anxiety because responsibilities are not clear and we are deprived of the security gained from coping with what we know we have to do.

I am certainly not proposing a return to *Kinder, Kirche, Küche*. But lately we have tended to deny rewards from the traditional roles, with their permanent commitments and stable existential anchors. What new hazards are created when we romanticize what we expect from relationships and work and deny the inevitable constraints and frustrations that are part of reality? If egocentric pleasure becomes the most important goal, does that create that profoundly desolate posture where we engage in commitments only as long as they gratify us, so that nothing can be assumed to be permanent? Can we really reverse the earlier rule that some commitments are unalterably permanent? What would it be like if the anchorages of identity and self-esteem became accomplishments or relationships that had to be endlessly negotiated or achieved and achieved again?

In some ways we are approaching this situation. For example, divorce is now so frequent that impersonal statistics have become personal as our friends and colleagues and relatives and neighbors end their marriages. This reality makes divorce a vividly salient choice, increasing the probability that we will examine the satisfactions and frustrations we experience within our own marriage. The frequency of divorce, in combination with the visibility of egocentric and hedonistic values, legitimizes our feeling that we are justified in continuing a marital commitment only if we are sufficiently satisfied. But what are the effects on the individuals and the relationship itself when marriage becomes a bargaining alliance in which each partner negotiates for individual advantage? Or, we might wonder, what happens when sexual gratification becomes the chief symbol of egocentric hedonism—does every act of coitus become a sexual test? What is the outcome for those who get A+ and advanced standing—and for those who fail?

What happens to relationships when we bring the conditional mentality of the work place to them? Are people to be demoted or promoted, hired or fired, depending on whether or not they make us feel good? Basically, what if we are overestimating the gratifications which are possible? What might be the effects if the fantasized rewards are so exaggerated and unrealistic that they are unattainable, and we are making the continuation of a commitment conditional upon gaining what is in reality unachievable?

While it was absolutely necessary to reject the most constrictive aspects of the traditional sex roles, we are now in danger of embracing false anchors based on competition in employment, on continuously changing relationships, on unbounded egocentricity. We cannot go back, ignoring the new values and realities, but we will have to create new norms, with specified responsibilities, to serve as anchors.

I anticipate that many of the norms that will evolve in the near future will be asexual, unrelated to gender in any way. But as long as social change continues to be so threateningly swift and its effects so pervasive, some of the new norms that develop will probably be attached to gender simply because sex is a characteristic that does not change. And anchorages based upon sex may lend themselves most easily to being permanent. For example, we can reasonably expect an increased emphasis on paternity, because it is a permanent locus of identity. If this occurs, the status of maternity will also rise.

This era is a revolt against the limitations we imposed upon ourselves when we created an insane "normalcy." The movements of this decade express our yearning for the things we have not done, the opportunities we have not had, the experiences we have not known. There is an illusion that lifting limitations will make us free and there is a denial that freedom is really the responsibility to decide what we will do. There is very little awareness that things are lost and things are gained in every commitment.

We are feeling the anxieties of anomie and meaninglessness as well as the exhilaration of new formulations and extraordinary beginnings. The dangers of tradition, especially the truncation of experience and growth and feeling, are very familiar. The danger of the new exaggerated ideal is that it has replaced the Protestant debt with the free lunch, has defined progress as the simple reverse of tradition, has generated fantasy untouched by the compromises imposed by reality. To grow, to change in important ways, requires courage. Today we need the courage not to conform to narrow rules of "liberation," but to recall that traditional roles provided fulfillment as well as frustration. There are costs and profits to every lifestyle.

Contemporary feminism reflects our culture's general drift toward the legitimacy, even the priority, of egocentric hedonism. This means that we want to be free to choose what we do, to narcissistically dictate the extent of our commitments, and to continue a commitment only as long as it gives us a sense of pleasure or fulfillment. But it is not possible to create existential anchors when commitment is really only to oneself. Commitment and thus anchorage involve long-term responsibilities for and involvement with others. Not only is unalloyed egocentric hedonism unachievable, it also leads to conditional commitment or, more extremely, to noninvolvement—to the drifting, spinning, free-floating anxiety of the unengaged, uninvolved life.

We have to make new rules. We need commitments based on consensual values which have yet to evolve. It will not be surprising if, in some ways, we seem to go back, associating some responsibilities with gender, accepting some responsibilities as permanent. If this happens, there will still have been a major change. Earlier we conformed to norms and accepted responsibilities because we did not question them. Now we are likely to formulate rules and accept obligation knowing that we do have options. We have learned that we do not have to accept unnecessary and arbitrary confinement; but we must also learn that we need the security created by commitment and belonging. We will then give up some freedom because we have learned that in order to be free from existential anxiety we need existential anchors.

There is nothing small here. Even so apparently literal and modest a demand as equal pay for equal work involves a reevaluation of women as workers, of women as mothers, of mothers as workers, of work as suitable for one gender and not for the other. The demand implies equal opportunities and thus equal responsibilities. It implies a childhood in which girls are rewarded for competence, risk taking, achievement, competitiveness, and independence—just like boys. Equal pay for equal work means a revision in our expectations about women as equal workers, and it involves the institutional arrangements to make them so.

This is a period of awareness of change, of hope for liberation, and of feelings of uncertainty—if not fear. This is a time of demands for radical transformations, of a responding surge of counter-revolutionary intransigence, and of inevitable evolutionary changes.

The feminist movement is like a tsunami, the great wave that accumulates power and smashes distant shores far from the epicenter of an underwater disturbance. The ultimate effect of even apparently minor changes is awesome: it is the potential restructuring of the net-work of interlocking responsibilities upon which society has been based. Fortunately, social change tends to be less extreme than rhetoric. While the extreme change of reversed values increases the likelihood that existential anchorage is lost, a reformist change may create new op-tions. And while reform is unsettling, it still allows us to retain some sense that we know who we are and that what we did in the past was of some merit.

Feminist Goals and Sexist Judgments

2

A team of psychologists led by Inge Broverman set out to explore the relationship between a woman's sense of competence and the number of children she had. "Competence" was defined as a cluster of traits including independence, rationality, leadership ability, and assertiveness. From previous work they knew these traits were primarily associated with males and were considered socially desirable.

Reflecting society's general point of view and perhaps their own professional frame of reference, the researchers began their study with the assumption that women who scored high on a measure of competence would describe themselves in terms of their occupations and would be far less likely than noncompetent women to accept an exclusively traditional role. Because they assumed that competent women would be less involved with the traditional role in any of its aspects, they researchers expected competent women to have fewer children than women who scored as less competent.

They found, instead, that competent women modified their reproductive behavior to accommodate their circumstances and their psychological needs. When conditions were favorable, competent women had more rather than fewer children. Competent women had more children when their financial situation was good. Competent women who were warm—that is, concerned and involved with children—had the greatest number of children; whereas competent women who were cold had the fewest. Competent women who worked more had fewer children, and those who worked less had more. In summary, competent women adjusted the number of children to their reality situation and their internal inclinations in an adaptive and rational way. Women who were not competent did not alter their reproductive behavior in any consistent way.

The most significant finding of this study was that its basic assumption—that feelings of competence can be developed in work achievement, but not in raising children or other aspects of the traditional female role—was simply not true.[1]

Competence is a set of skills, an attitude, a judgment one makes about oneself that can be developed, to the extent that one respects what one does, within either feminine or masculine roles. Yet there is a widespread and insidious belief that qualities associated with competence—being able to do a task well, to cope, to lead, to assert, to decide —can only be developed through paid employment. Because the stereotype of their traditional responsibilities excludes these desirable qualities, even women who are markedly competent in specific traditional roles may not perceive that they are also *generally* competent. This misperception makes them afraid to venture seriously into the competitive world of work.

I recently visited a brilliant woman whom I had known in college. Twenty years ago she graduated from an Ivy League school with highest honors. The mother of three, she had had part-time jobs and major responsibilities as a leader and policymaker in important volunteer organizations in the large city in which she lives. Since her youngest child is now in school, we got to talking about what she would do with her extra time. I could not believe how terrorized she was when she imagined taking a full-time job. When I reminded her of her past 20 years of accomplishments, she said, "They don't count. They weren't paid. I'm not trained for anything in particular." She continued, "If you think I'm bad, let me tell you about a friend of mine. She's in her fifties and has been important as a community and political leader in this city for 25 years. Well, she finally decided that she should get paid for her efforts, so she took the big plunge. She got a job as a saleswoman in a dress store. The whole week before she began the job, she couldn't sleep. She was sure she would never learn the stock. 'Hell,' she told me, 'it takes a goddamn Ph.D. to run the cash register.' "

After we talked, my friend had to go to a meeting of a city committee. She came back glowing and said, "I can make policy. I can do what those men do!" Then she hesitated and added, "If only I can get across the street."

The anxiety, the sense of incompetence, and the certainty of failure are pathologically irrational, given my friend's and similar women's histories of real and significant accomplishments. At the same time, these pathological fears are rational and predictable as long as paid employment, especially at the career level, is seen as the only arena in which coping counts and competence can be demonstrated. Even women who accomplish significantly in an objective sense often discount their success if it is not within paid employment.

The Self-Esteem of Housewives

In this decade we have become very familiar with the powerful data that achievement strivings in girls are blunted because of their anticipation of or later immersion within the traditional roles. While we have examined these negative consequences, we have rarely explored how some women create self-esteem in the traditional roles when most seem unable to do so.

What are the characteristics of women in the traditional roles who hold themselves responsible, initiate and accomplish goals, make decisions, have strong, healthy egos, and relate to others while maintaining a clear sense of themselves? How do they create their sense of competence? If we look closely, we find that they believe their responsibilities are important and their work holds the potential for creativity as well as drudgery. Many have extended their commitments into the community. They say they have real responsibilities and they know they have to cope, improvise, and learn a variety of tasks, many of which they have initiated.[2] Seen this way, women's traditional commitments—whether in the home or out in the community—hold at least as much potential and challenge as ordinary jobs and some careers.

But as long as the constrained and impoverished image of the homemaker prevails, it will be difficult for women to develop self-esteem and confidence. The powerful stereotyped images belie the easy observation that most people lead lives far more complex than any stereotype can describe. One effect of the socialization process is that even when one's life is vastly different from the stereotype, one still tends to judge others and to a lesser extent oneself according to the stereotype.

Our cultural stereotype describes the American housewife as passive, chained to domestic drudgery, and unconcerned with events outside the cozy cottage. Even housewives who are leading active lives in their community and the larger society describe women's traditional roles negatively and stereotypically. In her book *Occupation: Housewife,* Helena Lopata reports that she found that almost all the housewives she studied (only some of whom were working) led complex lives; belonged to a variety of groups; were knowledgeable about world affairs; and, when the demands of their families lessened in their middle age, increased their involvements outside. Many went back to school, got jobs, or worked in voluntary associations.

Nonetheless, even those women who were significantly involved in outside activities still tended to describe the roles that women play as restricted to family obligations. In spite of their own active and complex lives outside the home, they described women's roles as being married and having children and devoting themselves to such family activities, to the exclusion of anything else, forever.

Lopata found that American housewives are increasingly competent and creative, especially in the ways they combine different roles in their lifetime. Yet the image persists—without debate even from housewives whose lives contradict it—that creativity, autonomy, and competence cannot develop within the traditional roles because they are limited, unrewarding, and routine.

These negative judgments are shared by feminists and nonfeminists, by women and men alike. Since Americans tend to base their self-esteem on what they do, it is exceedingly difficult for women to earn self-respect as long as they are primarily involved in their traditional roles. The issue is even more complicated because until very recently, the norms of marriage and maternity—also very powerful— have meant that few women could achieve self-esteem if they did not marry and have children. The double bind is obvious.

While marriage and motherhood can provide significant pleasure, the roles also involve a lot of drudgery, repetition, and frustration, that is also true of most jobs and careers. When Abraham Maslow was studying creativity, he unconsciously associated being creative with certain professions such as painting, composing, and writing. To his surprise one of his subjects, a poor and uneducated woman who was a full-time housewife and mother, was not only superb in all usual aspects of her roles but was also original, inventive, and creative. From her he learned that a first-rate soup is more creative than a second-rate painting and that making a home and being a parent can be more creative than working in the arts.[3]

Besides the fact that women are not officially paid for their traditional work, does something else differentiate women's roles from all others? Most crucially and very simply, these particular tasks are defined as women's work. That, by itself, is likely to be the most significant source of the degrading stereotype.

Because the work men do is held in significantly higher esteem than the work women do, the work that only women do is held in lower esteem than the work that both sexes or only men do.[4] Therefore, it is too painfully logical that the role of housewife, a set of responsibilities usually limited to women, is an exceedingly low-status role. This is true in spite of the fact that until very recently women who did not achieve the role—who remained "old maids" or "spinsters"—had the lowest status of all.

This psychological bind is simple and obvious; it is also enormously complicated. It is tragically difficult for a woman to achieve a sense of her own worth when one of her major commitments or her primary set of responsibilities is esteemed neither by the society she lives in nor— because she is a member of that society—by herself. At the same time, if she does not achieve the status of wife and mother she runs the risk of having no status at all.

Whether a role is self-affirming or psychologically crippling depends in good part on whether or not one thinks it is worth doing, can be creative, and has the potential for accomplishing something and giving one pleasure. The first flush of angry anti-traditionalism in the early phase of the feminist movement seemed to say that there is rarely anything good or even modestly tolerable in women's traditional roles. More than that, the feminist preference for career and paycheck has tended to further devalue the roles of wife and mother and simultaneously to increase the crucial importance of career success as the way women can achieve self-respect. This is a reversal of values. In the traditional values women created an identity through connecting, that is, by marrying and having children. In the new values, unless or until women achieve some success of their own, their identity derives from their family and they have no individual identity. This value reversal is the basis of the sense of pressure to be employed, which is now felt even by affluent women. Not surprisingly, some psychologists have observed that among young married liberal college-educated women those who were not employed had low self-esteem.[5]

Feminist values have been enormously important in clarifying the negative judgments of society. Feminism has enabled women to see how external social values lead to internal feelings of low self-esteem and a lack of confidence. But when we discuss only what is negative, we increase the predisposition for seeing only what is negative. It is frightening that feminists focus almost exclusively on the negative, because the great majority of women will continue in the traditional roles even if they work, and some women, either because they are satisfied or because they are afraid, will confine themselves solely to traditional commitments.

The feminist judgments could not have had the impact they did unless a great number of women had been dissatisfied or felt ambivalent. People are unhappy when their lives are routine, their accomplishments ephemeral, and their achievements taken for granted. While these feelings are also experienced by many men, the status and nature of women's traditional work makes depression especially likely. Aside from the physical confinement imposed by the care of young children, women's traditional roles involve repetitive routines in which something is accomplished and then is undone in the same day: the clean room is messed up, dinner is eaten. It becomes easy for a woman to feel that she has not done anything, nothing has happened, and, horrifyingly, as far ahead as she can see, the future is made up of endless cycles of busywork. When our present and our future seem to be made up of endless nonevents, there is the danger of feeling that not just our work, but our selves, have no significance. Such negative feelings are increased when our world tells us that our accomplishments are not important.

Feminist descriptions of women's traditional roles verge on caricature insofar as they cite no gratifications, only oppressive burdens that prevent women from pursuing masculine accomplishments. The focus is on men; the bias is androcentric. If most of our attention is directed toward the ways in which women's traditional roles preclude significant career success or toward the means by which the traditional responsibilities can be circumvented in order to succeed, less attention will be paid to the idea that women are worthy of esteem in their capacities, qualities, and contributions as women.

Because most women will continue to marry and have children, women must be able to feel pride in their feminine roles as well as their work identity. We cannot return to the postwar Disney image of happy, happy homemakers, but we can remember that there is real gratification in these roles, as well as frustration. At this time we are underestimating the extent to which some aspects of women's traditional activities help women develop a feeling of confidence. With our focus on occupational success and on paid roles, we are also underestimating the contribution of the roles of husband and father in the development of men's feelings of masculinity, self-esteem, and competence.

In order for women to respect themselves they will have to center in the self. That is, they need a healthy, moderate level of egocentricity which is very different from the dependent, reactive, adaptive, selfless stereotype of the traditional helpmate. This ego strength can be developed within the family as well as in a job. What is crucial is for women to think that what they are doing is worth doing and to see that they are people who can plan, decide, act, and be responsible. But the evolution of self-esteem in women is always complicated by sexism, the preference or reverence for whatever is masculine.

Sexism

Psychologists are prone to speak glibly about the daughter's uncomplicated identification with her mother. They describe it as a simple process compared with that of a son because the daughter is never charged with the task of shifting her identification from the maternal to the other parent, as her brother has to. I am increasingly convinced that the process is not at all simple. The mother who incorporates the values of her culture does not regard her own femininity highly or unambivalently. The message is unconsciously transmitted to the daughter and made concrete by the mother's preference for her son. A mother cannot love her daughter's femininity more than she loves her own. According to clinician Esther Menaker at an unconscious level many women reject their mother as the model of what they would like to become. This rejection does not stem from anger because their mother has not give them a penis, as some psychiatrists have concluded, but because their mother does not convey a sense of really loving them.[6]

Sexism, or contempt for women, is not restricted to male judgments in a patriarchal culture or to an arbitrary phallocentric theory of psychological motivation or to the judgments of conformist clinicians. Those are value judgments which are external to one's self. Much more decimating is the recognition of one's own sexism, especially if one is a feminist and a woman. But when the values of a culture are sexist— as ours seem to be—then it is very difficult for individuals to avoid learning sexist values because those values permeate and are intrinsic to the society.

We seem to find in the male image, or in our projections of it, rocklike security and strength, and we seek these qualities in men. We may love traditionally feminine women, but we do not respect them in that we do not look to them for leadership, accomplishment, innovation, and independence. We do not expect women to show leadership in the acts that we most esteem or in the responsibilities that we judge most significant.

Psychologist Jeanne Block investigated ideal self-descriptions by asking college students to answer "What I would like to be like," in Norway, Sweden, Denmark, Finland, England, and the United States. There was considerable consistency in the ideals of what is masculine and feminine in the six nations. The sex differences were, in general, the sort with which we are familiar. Of all of the countries, American males most emphasized qualities of adventurousness, self-confidence, assertiveness, restlessness, ambition, self-centeredness, shrewdness, and competitiveness in their masculine ideal. More than any other group of women, American women, like American men, emphasized being practical, adventurous, assertive, ambitious, self-centered, shrewd, and self-confident as ideal qualities.[7]

These findings imply that while people who combine feminine and masculine qualities may feel most fulfilled and be highest in self-esteem, the major route to self-esteem for Americans still lies in success in competitive achievement and in being assertive, ambitious, self-centered, and confident. That is, Americans have higher self-esteem the more they can perceive themselves as having the characteristics that we label masculine. Without success in the "masculine" style, it is very difficult for Americans to esteem themselves or for others to esteem them. Moreover, women who describe themselves as high in masculine qualities and low in feminine ones have higher self-esteem than women who score high on the feminine and low on the masculine scales. In part, this relates to the fact that competence items form part of the masculine scale, and feeling competent is a crucial part of self-confidence; and, in part, it is because the male role and masculine characteristics have higher status.[8]

Sexist judgments are deeply internalized by women. To a grave extent, women, whether feminists or traditionalists, do not esteem those of their characteristics and contributions they perceive as feminine. It is not plausible to imagine that one can develop a sense of one's worth at the same time that one holds oneself in contempt. The disdainful regard for homemaking and mothering is based not just on the citation of boredom, tedium, and no pay. That withering judgment is also the expression of sexism.

Sexism and Ideas of Mental Health

Sexist values are so pervasive and fundamental that we are only beginning to really see them. In its most obvious form sexism refers to roles; we already know that the work associated with men is considered the most important work in this and most other societies.

A more subtle form of sexism exists; and because it is insidious, it is more dangerous. We are beginning to understand that our ideas of what is normal, what is psychologically healthy—indeed, our basic ideas about what is really human—are sexist. Sexism is not only disparagement of what women do but also disparagement of what women are. It is not merely that the roles of women have lower status—women have lower status in all the ways in which they differ from men. This occurs because the sexes are characterized by their differences. Since the standard of normalcy or psychological maturity and health is unconsciously male, females are stereotypically described in terms of what men supposedly are and women presumably are not.

Psychological theorists and therapists, who are called upon to define normalcy, are generally middle-class people who are well socialized into the values of their culture and who, in their professional lives, analyze and elaborate upon these accepted beliefs of their time. Therapy has thus been based upon what was believed to be the natural roles of both women and men. As the culture was stereotypically divided in terms of sex roles, so were the assumptions of the professionals. Women who wanted careers and were ambitious and assertive were presumed to be castrating and unnatural. Until recently, the therapist's task was to undo the patient's neurosis and create a psyche that could find fulfillment in *Kinder, Kirche,* and *Küche.*

The most insidious assumption of the professionals has been that men are psychologically healthier than women. When judgments are based on criteria of mental health and maturity in which male behavior is the standard, women must suffer in comparison with men.

In a famous study, Inge Broverman[9] asked 49 male and 33 female clinicians to identify from a list the personality traits that describe healthy men or healthy women or healthy adults. The answers showed basic agreement among the clinicians, regardless of their sex. Both male and female clinicians defined the healthy man and the healthy mature adult identically. There was, however, a significant difference between these descriptions and that of a psychologically healthy woman. The healthy woman was, first of all, supposed to be very different from the healthy man. Healthy women were also described as more submissive, less independent, less adventurous, more easily influenced, less aggressive, less competitive and objective, and more emotional than men. This definition implies that women who are not emotional, submissive, dependent, or passive are not healthy.

If healthy people are described in the same terms as healthy men, and women have to be different from men in order to be called healthy, then women can never, by these criteria, be healthy people. The accusation that women are psychopathic or inferior seems inevitable.

A few years after the Broverman study, Benjamin Fabrikant conducted a follow-up. Replicating Broverman, Fabrikant asked therapists to "respond to an adjective checklist describing Sex Role Characteristics as applied to either the male or female. These characteristics, or traits, are comparable to the lists found in the earlier studies."[10] Because the Broverman study became so famous, it seems safe to assume that Fabrikant's respondents were familiar with the earlier data and its shocking implications. Great changes seemed to have occurred. Now, both female and male therapists agreed, women could have a full life without being married; and if women did marry, they should be equal partners. The therapists also agreed that women cannot be totally satisfied if limited to the roles of wife and mother, and women should exercise their right to participate in additional roles. They even agreed that the wife's sexual satisfaction is very important and she can have a fulfilling sexual relationship with someone other than her husband. The therapists seemed to have been radicalized in a very short time.

When it came to the checklist of adjectives describing male sex-role characteristics or traits, both female and male therapists checked *aggressive, assertive, bold, breadwinner, chivalrous, crude, independent,* and *virile.* Male therapists also checked *achiever, animalistic, attacker, competent, intellectual, omnipotent, powerful,* and *rational;* female therapists added *exploiter, ruthless, strong, unemotional,* and *victor.*

Describing women, both male and female therapists cited *chatterer, decorative, dependent, dizzy, domestic, fearful, flighty, fragile, generous, irrational, nurturing, overemotional, passive, subordinate, temperamental,* and *virtuous.* Male therapists also checked *manipulative* and *perplexing;* females added *devoted, gentle, kind, sentimental, slave,* and *yielding.* (While it might sometimes be nice to be perceived as empathic, gentle, and kind, it is very difficult to find virtue in being a chattering, dependent, dizzy, fearful, flighty, irrational, overemotional, passive slave. The quality of liberalism is barely skin deep.)

This study reveals another source of the negative judgments about women. It is *hard* to be too competent, rational, able, active, rigorous, and effective; but it is *easy* to be too personal, emotional, cautious, fragile. Psychological theories reflect the values of the culture. Not only therapists but also our entire culture sees women as understanding, tender, generous, loving, moral, nurturant, kind, and patient—as well as incapable of responsibility, dependent, inconsistent, emotionally unstable, weak, intuitive (rather than intelligent), anxious, fearful, and childish.

Thus professional contempt is not simply in the judgment that both the traditionally supportive woman and the nontraditional competitive woman are not psychologically healthy. The professional judgment, consistent with those of the culture, expresses contempt for both the traditional roles and the personality qualities of women. It is a classic no-win situation: what women have traditionally valued most is not esteemed, and when women compete successfully they are not esteemed. Even more basically, women are not esteemed because they are not men. Low levels of esteem for large numbers of women are normative and very frightening. It is instructive as well as depressing that whenever I ask groups to list the characteristics of females and males, the initial list is always composed of positive qualities for men and negative ones for women. I often have to ask, "Isn't there anything positive about women?"

Psychologist Elizabeth Douvan has been more encouraging in describing characteristics which are more feminine than masculine. According to her studies, females are intraceptive; that is, they have a tendency to look inward and to be concerned with their internal world of feelings and esthetic judgments. They move relatively easily be-

tween the boundaried divisions of past and present, conscious and pre-
conscious. Females are better able to stop active striving and adapt a
quiescent, passive, and receptive attitude. Because they are not so
preoccupied with imposing their own styles and expectations, women
can attend more sensitively to internal and interpersonal processes.
The feminine style is empathic in its use of the self as an instrument to
understand another.[11]

As masculine independence is typically regarded as healthier than
feminine dependence, so a masculine ego—which has strong self-definitions and clear boundaries between the self and others, and is relatively
impermeable to others—is considered healthier than the feminine ego.
The boundaried self has been regarded as confident and assertive; but
since the unboundaried mode is associated with women, it has always
been regarded as a weakness.

Somehow no one ever asked what men missed by not being able
to use fantasy and imagination fluently, by not being empathic or sensitive to the feelings of themselves and others, by not being able to
synthesize intuitively. Stated in this way it becomes obvious that those
whose selves are rigidly boundaried are as impoverished as are those
whose vulnerable egos have an inadequate boundary.

It is a testimony to the normalcy of sexism that until feminist psychologists looked closely at the judgments of clinicians, we did not see
and could not understand how women have been damned by the criteria of psychological health.

Women achieve, in effect, a psychological minority status when we
accept the dominant, middle-class judgments about our differences
from the dominant group. Getting free of this self-denigration requires
examining our own traditions and characteristics without the coloring
influence of the major traditions and values of the society in which we
are unequal members. In order to become liberated, women have the
extraordinarily hard task of undoing their unconscious acceptance of
their minority status. Like all other groups that occupy an inferior
status, women will have to create their own respect for who and what
they are. This is a crucial task because, until they respect themselves,
people are too vulnerable to others' judgments. Self-respect for women
must include their specifically feminine qualities as well as their individuality and their competence in public achievements.

Since our society reveres successful competition, achievement, and
the acquisition of money and power—and has limited the right to
scramble for these payoffs to men—it was inevitable that in women's
first attempts to gain parity they would look at what men have and push
to get it too. This goal was chosen partly because occupational or political goals are objectifiable and have obvious rewards. It was also appeal-

ing because of women's own unconscious sexism, their acceptance of the belief that male styles and accomplishments are more worthwhile than those historically associated with women.

The move to broaden the bases of human worth is overdue. But to constrain emergent goals toward achievement in the competitive marketplace would finally and irrevocably tell traditional women that they are not as worthy as those who succeed in the marketplace; they are not as worthy as men and more "masculine" women. And ultimately, it would tell all women that their work, their contributions, their traditions, their empathy and style, are worth less. This would be a chilling and dangerous message.

The initial feminist analysis was preoccupied with the negative: what women had *not* become. Happily, within feminism and academia we have begun to focus on our selves. What *have* we become? What are women's strengths, insights, and priorities? What is our history? What are our contributions? What is our tradition? Where have we found our sense of honor? In addition to parity in the governing, educational, and economic spheres of this nation, women's equality requires that we center on ourselves rather than on men. When we feel pride in the qualities, values, and accomplishments that have historically been ours, we will have finally given up our psychological minority status.

Women must not profane themselves. It was necessary and constructive that a feminist leadership arise to attack trivial femininity as a lifestyle or a hallmark of normalcy. But while we reject an exaggerated and cruel idealization of a vapid femininity, we seem to be moving toward a rejection of everything that is biologically and historically unique to women. Such a thorough rejection would be an expression of self-contempt. If women persist in this direction, they will prolong their own victimization and their own sexist contempt for who they are. The existential anchorage of gender identity for women must involve not only a broader base of acceptable roles but also the security of self-esteem based on gender itself.

Work:
The Need
for Fulfillment

3

Only half a decade ago the idea that women had a basic right to work was radical. In the brief time since then we have seen attitudes change drastically. Now more women are employed and more men are glad that their wives earn money. Today, in such places as Ann Arbor (a college town), well-educated women whose children are old enough to be in school no longer have much of an option about work. For these women, values have reversed. It is not only assumed that they are employed; it is considered abnormal if they are not.

There have been two great interrelated changes in attitudes about work. First, people increasingly feel that work provides or should provide the opportunity for self-fulfillment. More than any other commitment, work is perceived as the way creativity, responsibility, and self-actualization can be achieved.[1] Second, women are actively seeking work in order to develop their potential.

About half of American women are in the labor force. The percentage has been increasing steadily. The federal government's 1976 employment report said that "The labor force has grown by 1.5 million over the past year, with adult women accounting for 1.1 million of this increase." The labor force is defined as everyone aged 16 and older who is employed or looking for work. In the years from 1947 to 1975, the female population increased 52 percent; the female labor force, 123 percent.[2] While there has been a continuing rise in the percentage of women in the labor force, the largest increases have been in the number of working wives and mothers.[3] The most startling change is in the increase in working mothers, especially those with preschool children. In 1970, in families where the husband was present, one-quarter of the mothers of children younger than 3, one-third of those whose youngest child was between 3 and 5, and half of the mothers whose children were school aged, were employed.[4]

When half a population does something, that behavior can no longer be considered deviant. It is, instead, normal. Until the 1970s it may have been "normal" for women to have a job, but not a career; and it was acceptable for women to work only if there were no small children at home or if their income was really necessary. With constrained job opportunities and limiting conditions, most women who worked—the majority of them married and with children—did so in order to improve the economic level of their family. Work for women was thus an extension of their traditional supportive role, moved out of the house and into the labor force. Until very recently, the continuously increasing percentage of employed women did not represent a significant change in women's values or self-perceptions.

As long as women have jobs and not careers, derive their status primarily from their husband's and their identity from being a wife and mother, think their husband's work is more important than their own, and feel guilt or worry about the effect on their family if they work at a career, then women's working is not based on new values, but on traditional ones. This is changing. A great number of women now want to work in order to develop *their* potential. Furthermore, they are insisting that work is their *right*. This is a reversal of older values.

As they demand the opportunity to earn success, to acknowledge ambition, to develop competence, to assume leadership, to acquire power, to try, to risk in the ways that men have, women are making a bold statement that they also, like men, are individuals. Women's commitment to a career reflects their desire to fulfill their own potential; it is a specific rejection of derived status, of identity based on being in a relationship.

Angered by the confinement imposed by their traditional roles in a culture preoccupied with work, women have swung to an idealization of it. The grass is necessarily greenest where one has not trod. It is easy to romanticize something when one has little experience with it. In the new myth work is supposed to provide fulfillment and creativity, but never the tedium of drudgery or the sweat of discipline. Work is idealized: gratifications are exaggerated and costs ignored. In contrast with our earlier view, which essentially defined work as what one *has* to do (an unpleasant connotation), women are choosing to work because they are looking for egocentric gratification.*

Half of all women work. Many want influential careers. To attain them requires forging new lifestyles with clear gains and costs, some of which are predictable and some of which are unknown. Fulfillment and stress, gratification and conflict, success and anxiety—all are predictable. These emotional by-products are clearest when we look at extremes of ambition, at those who want to lead in careers rather than work at jobs or be content with professional competence. While the payoffs are vastly greater, careers are enormously more costly in terms of commitment than are jobs. For many women, the crucial question has changed and is no longer, Are you employed? It is, How ambitious are you?

Changes in How Women See Themselves

As woman have decided that they have the same right as men to choose what they will do, they have shifted from constructing a self within roles of giving and relating, to building a self through independent achievement. When one has usually thought of oneself in terms of what one does for others and how one relates to them, it is enormously difficult to think of oneself outside of such relationships. It is hard and it is stressful to unlearn old lessons and say, "I am entitled to an appropriate egocentricity." Many women are now learning that the freedom to become whatever they can involves making demands upon others, as well as not doing as many things for them. It is uncomfortable. Most women, whether they work or not, have rarely had the heady sensation of thinking of themselves as *Me!*—that experience of oneself as initiating and choosing objectives because they feel right. Underlying questions of choice or role conflict, there is a push–pull for most women; they are torn between thinking of themselves traditionally, within relationships, and thinking of themselves in an ego-affirming *Me!* way.

The roles of wife and mother are narrow and leave little room for individualism. Within the family the roles of husband-father-provider

---

*While I am talking about reversals in psychological attitudes, I hasten to note that these are much more likely to occur and be important as a motivational factor for people who are affluent. The statistical reality is that the great majority of women work because they need the money, often desperately. Work is an *option* only for those who do not have to work. Thus these psychological changes are particularly important for and characteristic of the educated, upper-middle-class woman who is married. In this sense, mainstream feminism has been preoccupied with work-related issues important to an elite group.

are equally constrained. The image of men as individuals comes from their occupational roles. Work, especially a career, has been the sphere in which individuality is expected, expressed, and rewarded. Insofar as women did not participate in that sector, they were prevented from developing an individualistic, egocentric sense of themselves.

In addition, by college age if not before, most young men have developed the idea that their life will be largely determined by the work they will do. Middle-class males especially have the sense that, notwithstanding the state of the economy or luck, their successes in school and work will depend on their ambition, ability, and discipline. As a result, men tend to feel that they can or will be able to control what their life will be like, at least to a significant degree.

In contrast, the lives of most women have not reflected their history of achievement, their success or failure in school or at work. Although large numbers of women succeed in the individual and competitive world of school, especially in college, most have not developed an egocentric sense of themselves. This is because they expect and want to marry, and assume that the direction their lives take will be determined by marriage. If the most important commitment in a woman's future is marriage, then her future has little, if any, relationship to how much she has achieved in the past. If a woman's future is essentially determined by marrying (something over which she has only partial control) and marriage is her crucial source of identity, then success or failure in school or work will not determine what she will become. Nor will her history of achieving be a major determinant of her self-esteem.

Another reason why women do not attend to their past successes is that their traditional responsibilities are not defined as achievements in the same way that paid work is. That is, either they do not pay appropriate attention to past successes or they do not define what they are doing as an achievement. As a result women rarely see themselves as competent people who can generally expect to be successful. If competence is not part of your gender definition or acknowledged as a part of your roles, it is very difficult to learn to see yourself as competent. Most women see each success as specific and limited; they do not develop a generalized sense of their own competence. Women have to literally be taught that they are competent. To accomplish significantly, women will have to learn that they can cope, make decisions, set priorities, enjoy taking initiative, and accept the responsibilities of power. Most of all, they will have to develop a healthy sense of *Me!* They will have to realize that they are individuals who have some significant control over what they do with their lives.

Sexism in Employment

Organizational employment practices frequently reflect blatant sexism. For instance, the assumption that only someone with an all-out, single-minded commitment to ambition and achievement is worth hiring is often accompanied by a presumption that such an attitude is character-istic of men, never of women. Blatant sexism is evident in the denial that experience in child care, household logistics, and volunteer orga-nizations has anything to do with management, making decisions, di-recting people, or solving problems. When men are reluctant to act as mentors to women, we can see obvious sexism. It is manifest in a nearly unanimous preference to work with men and earn respect and rewards from men. It is transparent in the compliment that "You did it just like a man."

Sexist stereotypes influence people's expectations, so that they see and remember behaviors and attitudes which agree with the stereo-type. While individual women may be seen as exceptions and may know that they are very different from the stereotype, the stereotype works to always label capable women as exceptions. Without a quantum num-ber of successful women who are not at all like the stereotype, everyone classifies the few whom they meet as exceptional, so that the stereotype remains unchallenged. "Quantum" is not a specific number. It means, instead, as many as are necessary to achieve a certain effect. Until it has a quantum number of women, any organization will expect women to be like the stereotype and will unwittingly elicit stereotypical behavior from female employees.

Organizational sexism is also based on the fact that most of the gatekeepers and decision-makers are men. Men are reared with the initial idea that they must not be sissies, and with the crucial distinction that they are not female. They are taught that they are separate from, different from, and implicitly better than women. Since men generally hold positions of control, these attitudes are rarely challenged. Since there are so few outstandingly successful women, most men do not meet women who are their peers, much less their superiors. Few men learn that competence is asexual. Few learn that if women succeed, castration is not inevitable.

Sexist expectations become self-fulfilled prophecies. People who feel or know that they are marginal employees are anxious and likely to react at work in ways considered inappropriate or undesirable. Peo-ple who are on the outside of the organizational establishment and know they have no entrance into it are scared or belligerent or without ambition. Being too sensitive to what people with power say or do; being evasive, manipulative, and covertly aggressive; refusing more

responsibility or seeing how little work one can get away with—these
are rational responses when people, *of either gender,* feel they are
vulnerable and insignificant and their actions have little effect on their
position in the organization. For obvious reasons, this situation and
these responses will be characteristic of more women than men. What
the organization does is not only based on sexist assumptions but also
elicits stereotyped behavior which confirms the original assumptions.

Carolyn Bird, in *Born Female: The High Cost of Keeping Women
Down,* has written that women are least accepted where work involves
large sums of money, travel, risk, profit, machinery, and negotiations.[5]
I would add that women are also least accepted where the work involves being independent, making decisions, innovating, taking risks,
being assertive, assuming leadership, and having power. The expectation that women lack such qualities and skills is perhaps the most potent
and injurious form of sexism because the essential assumption is that at
work, "masculine" qualities are really best.

Because of our stereotypic views of the work situation, we make
assumptions about what behavior is appropriate. Keeping women out
of positions of responsibility and power is based on a rejection of the
personality characteristics women are supposed to have. It is a "Catch-
22." When their qualities are perceived to be like those of men, women
run the risk of being judged as castrating. When women have qualities
considered feminine, they run the risk of not being seen as competent.
Clearly, it is better to be a son of a bitch than a bitch.

This sexist bias is obvious in contemporary ideas about corporate
management. In the last several decades the emphasis in management
has changed to include a new sensitivity to handling people as well as
profits and production. Much of what managers do obviously involves
motivating, manipulating, supporting, punishing, encouraging, directing . . . people. Far more corporate attention is given to classes in which
women learn to be assertive—to develop qualities considered masculine—than to efforts to increase men's skills in handling people—a skill
considered feminine. The moral is clear: each sex needs to expand, to
learn skills or develop qualities historically associated with the other
sex. But sexism makes women's need to change vastly more visible and
seemingly more appropriate.

Deviance from Gender

I work both in an academic department and in an administration office
at a university. The situation in the administrative office is one in which
very little upward mobility is possible. While many of the men and

women who work there have advanced academic degrees, most are not ambitious or occupationally successful to a significant degree. They tend to be passive in that they seem content to remain at their jobs and do not actively search for promotion possibilities. They also tend to be preoccupied with concrete details of the work and to personalize exchanges about work. These are characteristics stereotypically attributed to women. When I see these qualities displayed by women, I find myself reacting with disappointment but not surprise. But because of the stereotype of men, I am disconcerted when they too lack ambition, personalize the work place, and appear to be content to repeat their familiar responsibilities.

While we might realize that such behavior is a response to the situation of work in a routine job with no upward mobility, our reaction of comfort or discomfort is directly influenced by the gender stereotypes which make the response deviant or congruent with our expectations.

In a situation in which decisiveness and assertiveness are appropriate and women act appropriately, they are likely to be seen as aggressive because being assertive and making decisions are so dissonant with traditional definitions of the feminine. The same behavior is consonant with definitions of masculinity, so that people are not jarred when these qualities are displayed by men. Instead of provoking a feeling of discomfort, such behavior in men confirms expectations; and that, in itself, is reassuring.

Two factors are involved in this case. One is that we associate gender with some behaviors or qualities and not with others. The second is that we define certain behavior depending on the situation—we assign masculine qualities to the marketplace, for instance, and permit more feminine characteristics to both sexes within the home.

We become uncomfortable, especially at work, when men expose their emotional vulnerability and let us see their dependence and uncertainty. When men do this, they have crossed the gender demarcation. That is, they have behaved in ways we think of as feminine. But as more women move into career slots where the most appropriate behavior is assumed to be "male," it is women who will much more often seem to behave in gender-dissonant ways. The stereotype of women's roles tends to prevent our seeing how decisive, assertive, and independent woman can be within them. In the work situation, where the same qualities are crucial and highly valued, they are forbidden to women to the extent that women are perceived as women. While male characteristics at work include confidence, assertiveness, decisiveness, and power, women who display these qualities risk being perceived as aggressive, authoritative, didactic, cold, and vindictive.

It is therefore understandable that we can more easily accept women who are assertive and decisive in such jobs as nursing supervisor or school principal than when they are bankers or corporate presidents. Nursing and education are "women's fields," in which power is exerted largely over other women and children.

In spite of new liberal values, traditional gender definitions are very powerful. Most men and women still tend to think of people who are intellectual, independent, and ambitious as masculine, and people who are supportive, emotional, and interdependent as feminine. Women who have been able to achieve significant work success have diverged from our basic ideas of appropriate role choices, motives, and styles. Until competitive success involves large enough numbers of women to be considered normal for women, our responses to the few achievers will be based on expectations from traditional norms as well as modern ones. Competent, independent, ambitious, and assertive women will continue to jar us.

What does it take to succeed in a competitive situation? Steven Goldberg, in his book *The Inevitability of Patriarchy,* cites qualities exuberantly opposed to our images of what is feminine: willingness to compete, a single-minded purpose, willingness to give up affection for the possibility of control and supra-familial power, a need to assert one's ego and impose one's will, a resistance to doing what one has been told to do, and a tendency to dominate others.[6] It is very difficult to imagine these as the qualities of the hand that rocks the cradle. We are more comfortable when women do not bare their ambitions so overtly nor display their enjoyment of power so clearly. We may resent men's ambition and power because they intrude into our lives, but we are startled by women's ambition and resentful of their power because of gender itself. Women are not supposed to have power. That most women are not yet comfortable with their ambition nor experienced in using power is to be expected. People who become visible as leaders cannot avoid confrontation and criticism, competition and conflict. These are heavy burdens at any time, but they are especially difficult for those who do not feel legitimate in the position. Of course, we know that power and leadership are antithetic to women's traditional roles. Because of gender discordance, women usually encounter less resistance when they use their power to influence others to be more effective than when they attempt to improve their own position.

Indeed, all of the qualities Goldberg cites as necessary to succeed in competitive situations are unfamiliar to women as a group. Not only are women generally inexperienced in handling power, they are similarly inexperienced in acting angrily even when anger is appropriate. In the stereotype, women are not entitled to anger. Anger, except in some girlish tantrum, is unfeminine. Direct, bold, eyeball-to-eyeball, confronting, dominating, resisting, insisting anger has been tradition- ally forbidden to women. When anger cannot be expressed directly it tends to be expressed indirectly or to be inhibited until there is an explosion of rage.

I knew this from theory, but in the circles in which I grew up and in which I live, a woman unfamiliar with her own anger and unwilling or unable to express it was a fantasy figure I never saw. Not until I attended an intensive weeklong encounter group which attracted many different kinds of women did I see women who were literally speechless when angry. Arms folded, heads jutting forward, their bod- ies expressing fury, they could not *say* anything. Another expression of anxiety about aggression was seen in women whose appearance and demeanor was totally passive, whose every movement was a request for help, who sought support from anyone, and then unpredictably flailed out, expressing inappropriate anger against those who had helped.

Stereotypically described as passive and dependent, women as a group are similarly inexperienced in being assertive. When people are assertive they are direct. They state their position, declaring areas of agreement and disagreement. When people are assertive they state what they think and take responsibility for their opinion. Women have tended to avoid the risks of confrontation that result from using power, expressing anger, or behaving assertively. Like all low-status people, for whom personal rejection is a real and terrifying threat, women have had too little acquaintance with the idea that their anger and opinions are legitimate and too little acquaintance with the idea that their anger and opinions are legitimate and too little experience in expressing them.

At work especially, people are trusted when they overtly declare their stance in a way that is objective and focused on the problem. At work we expect and are more comfortable when the style is impersonal. But women's style is personal. Women learn to be especially sensitive to personal nuances, to meanings within a relationship. This sensitivity, together with low status and low self-esteem, results in women's tend- ing to interpret what happens at work in personal terms. Women are prone to entangle the personal and impersonal and to look in the imper- sonal work situation for signs that they are liked. In a personalized situation there is the delicious prospect of feeling liked as well as re- spected. There is also the eviscerating possibility of feeling rejected when one's work is criticized or one's opinion disputed. Women at work not only have to learn to express their opinions in an appropriately open, assertive way but, like all marginal people, have to gain enough self-esteem so that fear of rejection, especially over work disagreements, no longer dominates and controls what they do.

Sexism is also subtle. We tend to say that women err when they personalize the work situation; we can also say that men err when they do not. Personalizing a work situation can be negative when people respond to criticism about their work as a critique of themselves. Personalization can be positive when those who work together develop richer and more honest exchanges.

I recently spoke with the president of a large corporation, an unusually self-confident and intuitive man who is more introspective than most people. He had been thinking, he said, about how men relate in ritual ways and as a result do not have intimate friends in the same way that women do. He finds that he really enjoys the company of the women he is now hiring, not only because they tend to be extraordinarily competent and interesting but mostly because these confident women have a tendency to push work relationships into personal friendships. Since they want to be friends with at least some of their co-workers, the women are pushing him into a kind of friendship he did not know before, with men at work.

From the perspective of male and female deficiencies, we can say that many women lack the skills to behave assertively. We can also see that more men than women lack the ability to express positive feelings. Such a negative perspective includes the judgment that women's lack of certain skills is more important than men's lack of other skills. Such a judgment is based both upon sexism and a hierarchical, competitive work place in which winning or losing, competing itself, is part of the stereotypic masculine role.

But the same situation can also be seen from a positive perspective. The data that attests to women's discomfort with being assertive does not have to be interpreted to mean women are deficient in competitive work situations; it may be that *women are more comfortable with a work style that is cooperative rather than competitive.* As long as success has depended on successful competition, women have been penalized. But it is an assumption, not a fact, that a competitive situation is usually best for those who are working within it or yields highest productivity.

As men are socialized to be competitive and women supportive, as masculine styles and values dominate in the marketplace and are the essential criteria of effectiveness, then men who are exploitive are seen as more effective than women whose accommodative strategies are designed to result in an outcome fair to everyone.[7] Women's preference for friendships at work and their discomfort with exploitation is in accord with their traditional values. When their behavior is determined primarily by feelings of insecurity, inadequacy, and low self-esteem, then women will see only its weaknesses. When women are able to act with the confidence that they have a right to do so, they may redefine the issues and state that the feminine style—cooperative, supportive, and trusting—is the preferable way to work.

I am not really being overly idealistic and impractical. The academic department in which I work has developed a style in which everyone is assumed to be responsible and to work to their fullest extent. Everyone is also assumed to be an able professional. Cooperation is not only necessary, it is cherished. I do not know anyone who would not help a colleague or someone else's student. While some competition exists, it is displaced to the field as a whole. Overall, what goads people to produce is not competition, it is the pursuit of excellence.

The Fear of Success

It is easy to document that very few women have achieved outstanding professional success, and that a high percentage of women train for and work in low-status, mostly female occupations. The reason this is true is not as discernible as it first appears. As far back as 1949, Margaret Mead wrote, "The more successful a man is in his job, the more certain everyone is that he will make a desirable husband; the more successful a woman is, the more most people are afraid she may not be a successful wife."[8] Matina Horner made this idea more specific in the publication of her first paper in 1969; and ever since psychologists have been wondering whether a major source of women's lack of success lies in their fear that success is in opposition to, or jeopardizes, feminity.[9]

Horner's original method for measuring fear of success asked people to write a story that began, "At the end of first-term finals, Anne finds herself at the top of her medical class." Females wrote stories about "Anne," males about "John." The stories were then examined for themes indicating a negative consequence for the medical student's success. Women's stories were found to reflect the following themes: (1) being socially rejected and losing one's friends, (2) experiencing fear and other negative feelings, (3) bizarre or hostile responses or a denial of the facts of the original cue.

Hormer said that the reason women do not respond like men in studies of people's need to achieve or avoid failure—and the basic reason they do not achieve in the marketplace—is that, unlike men, women are afraid of success. While femininity and success are both desirable, women have learned that they are mutually exclusive. Because women are therefore afraid to really achieve, they avoid roles in which significant success could be accomplished; or when in these roles they do not work full-out; or they enter "women's fields," where success does not carry the same weight.

Although Horner later said that the motive to avoid success is aroused by women's expectations about the *consequences* of success, the focus in her research was on *internal* causes. The motive to avoid success was seen as a stable—that is, a permanent—personality quality. Thus the need to avoid success should be characteristic of such women in all sorts of situations.

The idea that women are motivated to avoid success seemed a logical and very powerful explanation of why women made the role choices they did. Psychologists accepted the idea astonishingly quickly. I did too. It appealed to us because we were still emphasizing internal, stable personality qualities, especially as they developed in childhood, in our explanations of behavior. And it appealed to those of us who were professional women in 1969 because we remembered our own ambivalence. It was easy for us to accept the basic idea that the core of a feminine identity is achieved by being chosen by a male. It was also very easy for female psychologists to be comfortable with the even more basic premise that since feelings of masculinity are marvelously fragile and vulnerable, men are threatened by competent women and therefore pick women whom they can dominate and who are not their professional peers. (Whether or not this is really true is much less important than whether women believe it to be true and choose accordingly.) Women's fear of success was thus thought to be based ultimately on their fear of never being chosen and loved by a man.[10]

While this is a perfectly reasonable explanation, we should ask if it is the only logical one. Very different things would be implied if the focus was changed from women's fear that their competence threatens men to women's anxiety about being deviant. "Deviance" refers to being or behaving in ways which are significantly different from expectations based on the sex norms and the gender stereotypes. People who behave or have traits or preferences which are very different from the norms for their gender jar us, and we tend to reject them.

If gender discordance is the crucial variable, we would also be upset when men choose occupations that are not "men's work" or that require supposedly feminine personality qualities. When, for example, I ask male corporate executives to finish a story that begins, "At the end of first-year finals, Paul finds himself at the head of his nursing school class," the stories are filled with anxiety and usually reject the basic premise that Paul will be a nurse. In the stories we learn that Paul entered nursing school in order to become a hospital administrator or, somehow, to become a physician. For obvious reasons, it is hard to accept the idea of a nursing man.

While men would also be punished socially for being very different from what we expect them to be, the large shift has been for women to engage in activities or develop personality styles that have been traditionally male. The social trends promise that far more women than men will shake our stereotypes and provoke us, even though there are as yet very few prominently successful women. It is a reasonable idea that women's fear of success may not be a psychological trait, but an expectation that if they come close to the male stereotype, they will be deviant and punished for it. Women's fear that significant success will result in anguishing feelings of loneliness or rejection may be based on realistic observation or exaggerated expectations. It is not, however, an inappropriate or neurotic anxiety.

Women who are secure in their sense of femininity but very traditional in their values may consider outstanding work achievement inappropriate and the personality characteristics necessary for success unfeminine. Secure in their identity and values and satisfied by their traditional role accomplishments, they may be honestly unmotivated to achieve occupationally. We cannot assume that their disinterest in work success is motivated by anxiety. Other women, especially those without a secure sense of femininity, may act on the basis of such insecurity and thus avoid competitive success. These women would best be understood in terms of Horner's thesis. But other, less traditional women, who do not associate gender and achievement and who are not anxious about their own femininity, are equally likely to express a fear of success as they imagine what it would be like to achieve, especially in a traditionally masculine field. The last description probably fits the largest group of women who write stories displaying a fear of success—because that response is given most often by female students with the highest grade point averages in the most prestigious schools.

When we shift the explanation of the fear of success from a stable internal trait to a consequence of being deviant, we have changed the explanation from an internal variable, which is assumed to be permanent and enormously difficult to change, to external reality, which is easier to alter. The optimistic consequence is that if a significantly increased percentage of women were to succeed, then achieving women would no longer be deviant and would no longer have to fear the results of being successful.

When I do management consulting I find that women in certain middle management positions do not give fear-of-success responses, no matter how cleverly I try to elicit them. These women are usually middle aged, have a long work history, and tend to be chiefs of nursing or dietetics, head librarians, or federal employees. Their stories generally are realistic, deal with the logistics of managing the responsibilities of work and their families, and usually state explicitly that work takes a lot of their time but is worth it. Unlike students, who are the subjects in most of the research on people's motive to achieve or fear of success, these women are not *anticipating* the consequences of success. Relative to most women, they are already successful. In addition, they are not really deviant. They have succeeded in fields where there are large percentages of women; or if they are in corporations, they are just entering middle management. In large high-pressured corporations I find that the few women who have achieved middle management express feelings like the men who give fear-of-success responses. These women wonder if the effort is worth it.

Something unexpected has happened since Horner's original work. At least among college students, men are tending to give as many fear-of-success responses as are women, frequently more.[11] Since men's masculinity is surely not jeopardized by success as women's femininity might be, the fear-of-success response means something different when given by men. While both female and male students tend to write stories describing social rejection for successful women, male students, who are writing about men tell stories that denigrate the goal. That is, these young men, like the unusually successful women who give the fear-of-success response, seem to be asking if the effort and risk are worth it. Their stories seem to ask, How wise is it to invest one's self-esteem in occupational achievement? How many other interests and commitments does one have to give up in order to be very successful?

Female students who have not yet experienced career success and have few relevant role models of achievement express anxiety about the consequences of success. Men, whose tradition ties masculinity to work success and who have many role models, are far more prone to wonder whether success is worth pursuing.

Perhaps a large number of men have become aware that traditional men who are obsessed with their work—like traditional women preoccupied with their families—can become too narrow and vulnerable. In the recession of 1973 and 1974, middle-class and professional men who faced prolonged unemployment were described as having a sense "of not being the men they once were," as losing the feeling that they were in control of their lives, as beginning to believe in the determinism of luck. Unemployed, these previously competent, energetic, confident men resembled unemployed unskilled workers. Both were cynical and felt powerless and uneasy.[12]

Whenever we lose the anchorage of basic commitments, we lose a part of ourselves and of our self-esteem. No loss is more profound than that. People are especially vulnerable if their range of commitments is narrow and their anchorages few. Americans have a special vulnerability. We are more preoccupied with success and with work than other people; since we are easily seduced by success or its possibility, we are prone to lead lives dominated by work. Like successful men, outstandingly successful women will be preoccupied with work—perhaps even more so than men. Success is a gratifying and a dangerous lifestyle. Achieving success is costly in terms of energy, relationships, and the freedom to make other commitments. It is also risky, because one may fail in the competition. Never having been shut out from the possibility of trying for success, males seem to grasp these costs more than females do.

Success

Several years ago I interviewed 20 men who had been selected by others as extremely successful.[13] There were six corporate executives, two banking executives, one president of a foundation, three academicians, three entrepreneurs, one physician, one academic administrator, and three lawyers. Work was an extension of themselves—it was what they did, what they could talk about, what they were fascinated by. Work was the very core of their lives and determined how they lived, how they related to others, and especially how they felt about themselves. It was the sector where life was exciting. When work was especially difficult and risky and they succeeded, that was fun. In comparison, everything else was muted. They made work engulf their lives by continuously creating big changes in their responsibilities so that they had to grapple happily, full-out.

How did I characterize them? They were productive, ambitious, decisive, and often creative. Equally, they were confident, assertive, and responsible. Most of all they were egocentric, inner directed, active, asocial, autonomous, risk takers, *risk creators*.

Ogilvie found the same sort of qualities in athletes of national and international caliber. At this extreme competitive level, women and men had almost identical personality structures. They sought risk, excelled in tests of abstract thinking, were tremendously motivated to achieve success and recognition, were extremely autonomous, needed to dominate, saw themselves as people others trust and depend on, and assumed that they would lead and others would follow. They were self-assertive, and forthright; they made their own decisions; and they were loners, emotionally detached from others.[14]

Few people are that ambitious, competitive, autonomous, confident, inner-directed, and assertive. Few people are so motivated to gain responsibility and power, so exhilarated by controllable risk, and so preoccupied and egocentric that the value of success far outweighs any costs. Yet these are the characteristics that outstanding success seems to require. People who do not have these qualities are more likely to be competent than outstanding. In addition to gaining education, experience, and opportunity, women who want to lead will have to succeed in the competition by becoming extraordinarily assertive, independent, confident, and egocentric.

The question I end with is the question with which I began. What is the level of your ambition? This is an old question for men but a palpably new one for women. People who want outstanding success must be willing to be respected rather than liked, criticized rather than supported; and they have to put most of their energies into work. If we really want success and we get it, the gratifications are great, but so are the costs. We have always acknowledged this when we talked about men. In today's feminist political climate the cost of success to women is usually ignored or denied.

The first efforts by women will be to enter the institutions of work and governance as they exist. But the data on unemployed, underemployed, and retired men, and the fear-of-success responses of young men all signal the dangers to women who subscribe to the masculine model of what a successful person is or what a successful lifestyle ought to be.[15]

Thus, I believe that the second phase of women's participation should be directed toward modifying the priorities and changing the institutions' unquestioned, unchallenged sexist presumptions of what they ought to be like. With confidence gained from numbers, women could assert the legitimacy of traditionally feminine values as a guide to changing the institutions. Many men would agree.

I found it revealing that when a group who were planning community changes were asked how they would improve the performance of city police and fire fighters, their long-range goals were all objective and easily counted, such as "an increase in the number of arrests sustained by the court." The ways by which these objective goals were to be achieved included decreasing racial friction, increasing morale, solving housing problems for minority employees, decreasing boredom, and so on—all involving creating better harmony between people. But the justification for making people happier had to be stated in terms of how it increased their work output. Why is it so unacceptable—dare I say "unmasculine"—to say that work takes up most of our day and determines a lot of how we live and how we feel about things, and that the work organization has the responsibility of making labor as harmonious and pleasant and worthwhile as possible?

It would be paradoxical but not surprising to see a shift toward women's traditional values lead to increased productivity. People who are freed from the draining effort and loneliness of endless competition and from anxiety about failing in the competition, or who are given increased support and cooperation, may simply be better able to focus on mastering whatever they are supposed to accomplish. And it would be equally paradoxical but not surprising to learn that many people would enjoy a life modeled on that of women, in which the extent of one's commitment to work changes as other aspects of one's life change. This would not only help people to protect themselves from the loss of an existential anchor that work provides, but would also enable them to bring something more to work, and indeed to life.

As Douvan and I have written:

> It has been our personal experience, and it is our theoretical stance, that people grow when they are involved in more than one set of significant commitments. People become complex as they extend themselves coping with the different sorts of demands of diverse spheres and integrating among them. People living complex lives become richer and more complex. As they shift from one set of obligations and investments to another they are also able to clarify for themselves aspects of the roles that are beneficial from those that are costly. In the process they are better able to clarify their own sense of self, their knowledge of who they are.[16]

Women who have married and had children and worked have generally not pursued a career success with the same single-minded ambition as have men. But is this necessarily a loss? In a society devoted to work and success, we swiftly assume that it is.

The assumption that women's complex lives, in which they participate to varying extents in different roles, result in lower work productivity is based on the judgment that commitments other than paid work are less meritorious, significant, or maturing. This is another manifestation of sexism in a work-centered society. We may reverse the assumptions and ask instead, What experiences, skills, and qualities do people lose when they devote themselves wholeheartedly to any role, including that of work? People who lead complex lives with varying commitments are more likely to have new perspectives, enthusiasm, and creativity.

Women in this sexist society are likely to see only the personal costs of their complex role history and their marginal work position. Instead, women should reject the sexist presumption and ask what have they *gained* from such complex involvements. It is not difficult to imagine that there could be a further shift in social values so that only a relatively small percentage of people would be engrossed in work success. If such a shift should occur, "successful" people would be those who are able to find pleasure in leisure, in relationships, and in work—with no one commitment overriding the others.

Today, women and men approach work with somewhat different perspectives. For women who are just beginning to take this commitment seriously or who have been working but are now seeking to pioneer in new fields or at new levels of accomplishment, the effort is risky, the routes are uncharted, and the consequences are unknown. Men, who have always worked, are facing issues of recession and unemployment, of bureaucracies and divided responsibilities, of routinized work. In conditions where men can achieve security but not heroism, can experience competition but rarely courage, work no longer provides feelings of "masculinity." When women's reality forced them to examine the origins of their unhappiness and led them to broaden their goals and therefore their roles, women redefined femininity. Men's reality may well force them to redefine masculinity.

Our ideas of masculinity have come from efforts to survive in a subsistence economy. In a subsistence economy people experience themselves as successful, responsible, and worthy of respect basically because they have survived. The question of meaning or challenge is provided by the task of surviving; when survival is no longer an issue for a large sector of the population and success provides only the increased accumulation of things, then issues of meaning replace those of survival.

Like many women, many men are not happy. Affluence provides us with freedom of choice and the burden of finding new goals. As technology deprives more people of a self-sufficient self-esteem and as more people are made aware of the costs to their humanity by an achievement-circumscribed life, then men, like women, will have to redefine their sexual identity within a broader idea of human identity. The lives of too many men signal that, for society's sake, women must not subscribe to the sexist assumption that a work-preoccupied life is intrinsically more worthy and gratifying than the complex of role commitments that increasingly characterizes women's lives.

Of course, women must now learn to compete and use power and succeed within the Establishment. Thus far, only a few women are in positions of significant power, and their objectives and style do not seem much different from those of their male counterparts. I look forward to that time when women who want to enter the system will be able to do so in quantum numbers and, from the normalcy such numbers create, will be able to think innovatively and not defensively, creatively rather than in conformity. Because marginal people—those who have never really been members of the Establishment—are likely to have developed priorities which are different, the way they perceive important problems and the solutions they develop may also be somewhat different. We can hope that their marginality will supply a reservoir of different perceptions, values, and coping styles that women can tap to lead in creating needed changes. When minority people—meaning all those who can never take acceptance for granted—are freed from anxiety about being deviant and from the emotionally draining reality that they are visible for the wrong reasons, they will be able to stop conforming to the ongoing norms. When their presence is normalized they will be able to bring their perceptions to the tasks and thereby increase the possibility of new, creative solutions.

While it is idealistic, I hope that from a confident position women will initiate changes designed to enable their supportive and humanistic style to become a normal quality in our work life. It is possible to encourage cooperation, friendship, even compassion, at work.

The values that women have emphasized outside the work situation should be brought into it. Unending striving in an unending competition is enormously stressful. People cope with this struggle by distancing themselves from others and ultimately from themselves. When the stress is extreme—when they are without any power or when they are the leaders—they tend to mentally transform themselves and others into things. This transformation makes it easier for them to bear what is done to them or makes their manipulation of others less difficult. It is easier for them to become whatever the organization wants. People can give up too much.[17]

When women discern and reject sexist values I hope that they will see that they have the opportunity and the awful responsibility of being in the vanguard of those who will formulate new values and thus new norms. It is possible to encourage people to value diverse commitments, helping them to emphasize now one and then another in different phases of their life. Our goal has to be nothing less than the humanizing of society. Women are in a special position to know that when we value commitments other than those of work, these alternatives are able to give us important gratifications.

Maternity: From Duty to Choice

4

When I returned to the United States after a year in Latin America I was struck by the fact that I saw so few children. In the Latin countries children were everywhere—carried on someone's back or in someone's arms, toddling or running. Wherever members of the family went, children went too. Not only were children everywhere, but they seemed to be adored and indulged. It was unusual to see a child cry.

In contrast, in the United States it is not unusual to see children cry or parents angry. More than that, we segregate children and protect ourselves from having too much to do with them. I was jarred by the difference, and it occurred to me that, regardless of what we say, we are at heart an anti-child people in terms of what we do. Since we have also been a coercively pronatal society, as we have also assumed that all healthy adults will have children, a basic reason exists for parental and especially maternal conflict.

In terms of what we consider important, the people we respect, the achievements we honor, the institutions we develop, and the time we spend with children, we are an anti-child culture. *It is not so much what we do as what we do not do.* Since child rearing is difficult, a society that is not explicitly supportive is effectively negative.

We have been so forcefully pronatal that almost everyone who could, has had children; but as an anti-child culture we have denied our responsibilities and made child rearing, especially in the child's first five years, the responsibility of individuals. We have not created the institutional supports or the emotional climate to help and sustain those whose duty is to care for the children. We have created the setting in which parental, and especially maternal, resentment and guilt and anxiety are almost inevitable.

No issue provokes more emotion among young feminists than that of maternity. Even when the discussion seems to be tough-minded and factual, there is often an undercurrent of anger and intense emotionality that are symptomatic of the conflict. Somehow, the emotionalism always takes me by surprise. Since my children are already adolescent, maternity is not an emotional issue for me. It has been a long time since I had to find baby-sitters or cope with people's disapproval when my children were young and I was in school. Most of all (and to my relief), I never had to wrestle with the question of whether I wanted to have children. In the 1950s that was not a question we asked. We wondered how many children we would have and how far apart they ought to be —but in that extraordinarily pronatal, family-centered period, we did not have the psychological freedom to even imagine that we had choices.

In contrast, in the late 1960s and the early 1970s the population explosion had led many to decry childbearing. At the same time feminists were challenging the values of and coercions resulting from women's traditional responsibilities. Feminists were indicting women's maternal responsibilities as the core of the bond that smothered. In a revulsion from the saccharine piety of the selfless mother of the feminine mystique, maternity was designated the quicksand of women's individuality and ambition. As the divorce rate continued its climb and the counterculture and young dropouts provided the specter of a dotingly reared generation repudiating their parents, the image of happy families went tumbling like a deck of cards in *Alice in Wonderland*.

Virtues in extreme form are often vices. In the 1950s the ideal mother had been someone whose devotion to her children was so selfless that in the extreme, she had no separate sense of herself. As maternal selflessness had been glorified, by the 1970s it was degraded. With this reversal of values, a life in which a woman's self-esteem came from contributing to the welfare of other people was now seen to result in a woman who was self-less, and selflessness was seen no longer as a virtue but as a vice.

Extreme self-preoccupation and healthy parenting of young children are fundamentally antithetic. Egocentric gratification is in conflict with caring for young children, unless the parental role is perceived as one in which accomplishments are important, pleasures are possible, and the self is enriched. At the height of the feminine mystique we believed that maternity was creative and extraordinarily significant. But as values shifted and women focused on achieving success in "masculine" spheres, women's traditionally most difficult and symbolically important role was downgraded. On one level this reflected the pragmatic, logistical difficulties involved in rearing children, without significant help, while employed. On another level, the downgrading of maternity reflected the entire culture's shift to a focus on achieving autonomy and personal growth, especially in work.

Now, when many men are taking a more active role in rearing their children and are discovering that it can be a source of profound pleasure, radicalized women are venting anger at the same responsibility. As women assess the costs to their careers which are exacted by child care responsibilities, the emphasis on the right to work implicitly shifts priorities from the welfare of the child to that of the mother. While feminists correctly assert that a child's best interests are fulfilled when the mother is satisfied with her life, the feminist insistence that others share the responsibility—fathers, neighbors, cities, the state—is not motivated as much by consideration of the child's welfare as by concern for the mother's. The implicit anti-child ethos of this culture is thus made explicit.

I am sometimes afraid that in this generation of children some large number will feel guilty because they exist—because their existence got in the way of their mother's pursuit of more "important" and pleasurable things. It is sad that in an increasing number of divorce cases, neither parent wants custody of the children.[1]

Coercive Pronatalism

Our norms have been coercive in that we have expected everyone who married to rear children. While couples had the option of not becoming parents, those that had no children took on the psychological burden of being judged as not normal. That is, being a parent was defined as normal behavior for all psychologically competent married adults, and those who chose not to have children were stigmatized as irresponsible, selfish, and neurotic. Since parenting was perceived as the essence of normalcy, it was also prescribed as a way to become normal. People with personal or marital problems were (and sometimes still are) told that such difficulties would be solved by having children. The vast majority of people had no choice about becoming parents.

Am I exaggerating the coerciveness of the norms? The following are quotations from the social sciences in the period from the late 1950s to mid-1960s:

> Childlessness is perceived to be associated with irresponsibility, unnaturalness, immaturity, emotional instability, marital unhappiness, divorce proneness, psychological maladjustment, and generally unsatisfactory mental health however that may be defined.[2]

... the great majority of Americans want two to four children. Having no children is considered a tragedy and having one is considered very undesirable. Two, three, and four are the number wanted, expected, and considered ideal by the great majority.[3]

Childlessness now results mainly from fecundity impairments. Few of our couples with no fecundity impairment will be voluntarily childless.[4]

The major cause of [this] childlessness is the existence of fecundity impairments. Voluntary childlessness is nearly extinct.[5]

"Looking at the total pattern of rationales for large and small families, we can abstract one central norm; one shouldn't have more children than one can support, *but one should have as many as one can afford.* To have fewer is regarded as an expression of selfishness, ill-health, or neurotic weakness; to have more is an expression of poor judgment or lack of discipline."[6]

These quotations reflect the values and the norms of the period. How many obeyed them? In 1970, among women aged 40 to 44 who had been married, only 11.9 percent of the nonwhite women and 7.2 percent of the white women had never had a child.[7] In other words, among this population roughly 9 out of 10 women had at least one child. Since 10 to 12 percent of all marriages are estimated to be involuntarily barren, these figures mean that virtually every fertile couple had at least one child. This percentage makes it obvious why all women were presumed to be mothers and why we assumed the personality characteristics of any woman would be identical with the characteristics of the role of mother.

Today's rejection of mandatory maternity by feminists is partly political. As long as the pronatal norm is coercive and the major responsiblity for taking care of children remains the mother's, the extent of social change is less. The role of mother is a conservative force in each woman's life; in the collective, it is a major conservative element in society. But most of all, feminists validly reject this norm because it had become conscripting.

Not only the pressure to have children but also the norms for child rearing were coercive. These norms declared that mothers could have no other major interests or involvements until their children were old enough to be self-sufficient. Deviation from this rule was, and to some extent still is, judged to be clear evidence of unbounded selfishness and inadequate mothering. All of these conditions meant that almost everyone married and had children, and those who did not had to explain. Of course, women worked; but they entered the labor market before they had their first child and left it to stay home when the infant was born. There was really no option about becoming a mother, and a devoted one at that. Moreover, no one thought about what would happen to all these mothers when their kids grew up and left home and the women faced the long second half of their lives unprepared to do anything else.

In addition, feminists were appropriately furious at the hypocrisy of a culture in which "motherhood" is holy but mothers are unpaid and unpraised.

I recently visited some friends who have small children. The first morning I was awake before anyone else, and I stumbled into the kitchen to make coffee. As the water began to boil, I heard the two-month-old infant stirring. Ignoring the coffee, I made formula instead. Then the infant started screaming. I poured the water into the coffee filter anyway. As I started for the howling infant, the two-year-old came in. His pajamas were sopping. He had wet his bed, his clothes, himself. Gambling that the infant would not go from howl to hysterical, I got the two-year-old changed. The infant was getting close to the point of no return. I swooped up the infant with one hand, poured a cup of coffee with the other, and told the two-year-old to eat a banana. Then the five-year-old came into the kitchen and announced that she *needed* Rice Krispies. Keeping the baby's bottle steady with one hand, I got the cereal with the other and then the milk and then the spoon ... and I thought, with momentary intensity, that when fathers manage, we applaud; when mothers cope we say, "Well, OK, sure," as though it were some kind of feminine instinct.

Given the coercive pronatalism and the adoration of motherhood in a society that reveres career achievements, it was inevitable that where maternity was once cited as the route to fulfillment and happiness, it would now be condemned as the role that blocked crucial gratifications and smothered individual growth. In the angrier feminist rhetoric of the late 1960s the ideal mother of the 1950s was seen as a patsy, as someone who had stupidly given up self-gratifications in order to be loved and who ended up neither loved nor liked, with her children gone. Most of all, the feminists indicted a life dominated by taking care of others, in which identity was derived from being in a family, because they saw it as a life which ultimately results in the death of the real, the actualized self. Being a mother precluded achieving a sense of *Me!* Overtly, feminists called for more child care centers and more sharing of parental responsibilities. Less overtly, they contributed to a new idealization of a life free of children.

If that were all, if values had simply reversed, then people, especially those who have no children, would not experience significant conflict. While those who have children can feel ambivalent—torn between self-centered and family-centered values—and can feel resentment if their responsibilities are not shared, the conflict is sharpest for those who are childless. The values of these people are, of course, influenced by the new visibility of everything bad about being a parent. Yet they must wonder, because the older values still exist and are important, whether it is true that having children is the essence of adulthood, perhaps of creativity, surely of generativity. Conflict about whether to have children is predictable even for those who embrace a more radical stance, because they did grow up learning the earlier values.

(In this chapter I am using the past tense to refer to the traditional norms. My married students who have no children tell me that they are under enormous pressure, especially from their parents, to have children. In this sense one might use the present tense, implying that parental norms are still coercive; but while the values of their parents remain traditional, the values of the students are not. These young people are clearly aware that they have a choice about having children.)

Women who decide not to have children do not achieve what historically has been the single most important symbol of adult femininity. The decision by women and men not to have children means giving up the generativity that transcends one's death. For most people this is a conflicted decision, appropriately so.

It is therefore not surprising that most people drift into childlessness. J. E. Veevers, for example, found in a study of childlessness that only 17 of the childless women he interviewed had made their decision before marriage; the other 35 had first postponed having children for a definite length of time, then postponed it for an indefinite period, then realized after a while that they might remain childless, and finally acknowledged that they had, in fact, made that decision.[8]

Changes in Values and Behavior

While the media present images of great change, the crucial question is always the extent to which behavior and attitudes have actually changed. To what extent are people choosing not to have children or to have smaller families? Is the trend toward the rejection of a child-centered family; and if there is such a trend, does it seem related to feminist values?

In general the answer is Yes. After World War II we had a baby boom. Women were having an average of 3.5 children. That rate started to decline in 1960, and by 1972 it had fallen to 2.08. In 1976 it was 1.8—the first time an industrialized society had reached zero population growth. The birthrate is now lower than it was during the Depression in the 1930s.[9] Among those who still want children, the number desired is now 2. The trend, especially among the young, is to adopt more modern values. The more modern the values held, the lower the number of children intended, the higher the probability the wife is employed, and the longer the time between marriage and the first birth. While the birthrate has fallen among women of all classes and ethnic groups, it has fallen most sharply among middle-class, educated women. The implication is that young women who have been to college are pursuing a career, and whether or not they call themselves "feminists," their priorities are the same as feminists'. The overriding characteristic of college women who declare themselves pro-liberationist tends to be their desire for independence, self-sufficiency, and freedom from external control. They are not interested in raising children because they associate motherhood with women's dependence, loss of options, deference to others, and low status.

A study at the University of Michigan in 1972[10] and another at Stanford in the same year[11] found that 10 percent of the undergraduates wanted no children. Linda Wolfe reports that of the 70 percent who responded to a poll, only 3 babies were born among Bryn Mawr graduates who graduated between 1971 and 1975. Among those who graduated between 1966 and 1970, more than 70 babies had been born to the 70 percent of respondents. In five years the rate of those who had had a child went from over 10 percent to under 1 percent.[12]

Demographers and others are wondering whether the low birthrate is a result of the new ideal of the smaller, two-child family, and whether it is the result of delaying a first child rather than deciding never to have a child. Still, it seems reasonable to conclude that there has been a real increase in the number of people, especially women, who will not have children. After all, the extremely high birthrate of the 1950s was abnormal. Any decline in the birthrate is therefore a return to more normal rates. It seems most unlikely that 90 percent of women would want to become mothers and would flourish in the role. Of course, the coerciveness of the pronatal norm resulted in some percentage having children who were unwilling and therefore unable to mother. Becoming a good mother requires, at a minimum, wanting to be a good mother.[13] When maternity is based on real choice, fewer women will find themselves rearing children when they really don't want to. That result will obviously be constructive.

But there is a less benign aspect to this change. The low birthrates, especially among middle-class women, imply an important percentage of agreement with the feminist position that women have to be free to achieve individually. This goal is attained much more easily with few or no children. Maternity became a psychological option when its value was rejected. That is, the basis for women's new choice about maternity is a focus on all of the negative and personally costly aspects of child care.

Besides frustration and ambivalence and resentment, enormous pleasure was gained from being a mother in the 1950s. We were quite certain that maternity was creative and entailed an enormously significant set of responsibilities. When our children did well and were happy, so were we. Betty Friedan recently wrote about how she felt then:

> And, to be honest, those years were not all self-delusion. The reality of the babies, the bottles, the cooking, the diapering, the burping, the carriage wheeling, the pressure cooker, the barbecue, the playground, and doing-it-yourself, was more comfortable, more safe, secure and satisfying—that year and for a lot of years thereafter—than that supposedly glamorous "career" in which you somehow didn't feel wanted, and no matter what you did, knew you weren't going to get anywhere. . . .
> At home you *were* important, you were the boss; in fact, the mother—and the new mystique gave it the rationale of career.[14]

Helena Lopata found in her sample of basically ordinary housewives that women with young children were quite clear about their problems and their feelings of frustration. It is a familiar list that includes increased responsibility, the need to plan and organize a great deal of work, a tremendous decrease in free time, a decrease in opportunities for mental stimulation, and a feeling of being isolated from other adults. While these housewives feel "tied down," they also experience satisfaction as they see that they can manage, have the right and opportunity to make decisions, and are competent. Most of all, Lopata found these women very much aware that they had created new human beings, which they knew was an important accomplishment.[15]

In the 1950s, mothers were not allowed a legitimate sense of frustration. Today we are dwelling on maternity's frustrations and denying its gratifications. Ambivalence is an inevitable result of all commitments. The sheer fact that we made the commitment, as well as the specific responsibilities or obligations that are part of it, means that we have lost some options and gained some opportunities. Aside from the constraints imposed by the real tasks in the obligation, our judgment of whether we have made a gain or suffered losses is also a result of what we expect things to be like and of our past attitudes about the commitment that we bring to the present.

When we think that alternative choices in roles or commitments are mutually exclusive—that one has to choose between two or more roles or commitments—the chances are very good that we will ameliorate the ambivalence we feel when confronted with important choices.

We do this by modifying how we value the alternatives, so that we are no longer choosing between two equally matched alternatives, which would be a very hard decision. We change our attitudes so that one choice is judged more negatively and the other more positively than is realistic. Thus traditionalists glorify domesticity and feminists idealize work and each degrades the alternative.

Especially during a transitional period, when values are changing and old and new norms coexist, people feel uncertain when they make either choice. One way to resolve this anxiety is to act very extremely and decisively. For example, a clinician told me that she is observing a new fashion in which mothers nurse children as long as 18 months. Since this is far longer than usual in our culture, we may wonder whether such behavior is an attempt to still ambivalence. One mother the clinician knows had back surgery and was immobilized for months. When she was no longer confined to bed, this mother insisted on restarting nursing with hormones. Her son was then 15 months old. The clinician met her at a party and conversationally inquired how her Ph.D. dissertation was coming along. The mother burst into tears.

It should be clear that maternity may involve experiences and responsibilities that enable people to grow and increase their sense of self-esteem. The crucial question is, When is maternity enhancing or depleting? In an effort to explore how maternity effects women's self-esteem, Eleanor Lewis and I studied a group of 73 women who were 35 to 45 years old, had been married at least 10 years, and had none, one, or three children.[16]

Women with three children, we found, had typically grown up in traditional homes and had created a traditional family. Their values and interests were predictably traditional and their identities were based on the roles of wife and mother. While they were educated, only a few were employed. They described the ideal woman as someone who was employed in a traditionally feminine field when family circumstances permitted but who continued to be primarily concerned with the welfare of the family even then. They believed themselves successful in the traditional roles and, with one exception, were basically satisfied with their lives, which were complex and involved personal, home, community, and work interests. They described themselves as very competent, perceived child rearing as important, and were relaxed and realistic about the effects of children. While they gained great satisfaction from their children, they were well able to recognize that children also created problems.

This group, relative to the others, had lives closest to those they imagined as ideal and which society said was best. They had high self-esteem and enough confidence to become involved in diverse activities.

Those who *involuntarily* had zero or only one child were also basically traditional. Like those who had three children, these women were eager to marry and create a family by their late teens. Feeling competent and confident would normally have been derived from marriage and especially maternity. For them, maternity was very limited or was never achieved. Since these women had wanted to adopt children, the decision to limit the size of their family was actually made by their husbands, who refused adoption. It was also interesting that in every case the women went for physical testing because of infertility, while very few husbands went for a diagnosis and none for treatment. The anxiety of the men regarding their fertility or potency is certainly implied, as is the terrible dependence of the women who, although extraordinarily conflicted, went along with the husband's decision. These women led the most constricted and least involved lives we saw. They were frustrated by their idealization of the crucial significance of maternity and were not able to develop enough self-confidence to develop different goals. Because they did not get involved in other activities they valued, they had no way to achieve any sense of esteem. They were more than frustrated—they were truncated in terms of developing a sense of self, confidence, esteem.

In contrast, those who voluntarily had zero or one child grew up in nontraditional homes. Their fathers did not dominate, their mothers were educated, and many had known divorce or the death of one parent. They had rarely been asked to take care of children and said that they had not enjoyed doing it. As girls they were seriously involved in doing well in school and had anticipated having a career. Among the three groups, they were least dependent upon others for feelings of esteem. They were usually employed, had hobbies, and were involved in the community. Like those who had three children, those who chose to have zero or one were leading lives that were in agreement with their values. But while they did not experience the pain of those who involuntarily had zero or one child, they described themselves as less fulfilled or satisfied than the mothers of three.

At least in 1971, when the study was done, the women who had voluntarily limited the number of their children had the lowest feelings of self-esteem of those we saw. We interpreted this to mean that while they were not traditional, they were still affected by traditional values. While different norms are evolving among some groups today, new ideas about what women are supposed to do or be like have not yet been broadly accepted. In addition to pressures from other people, this means that those with nontraditional values have also internalized the traditional values because they were the dominant ones. It is therefore reasonable to conclude that, in spite of their own divergent values, when people do not achieve according to the traditional criteria they will feel anxious and suffer some loss of self-esteem.

As long as traditional values coexist with emerging, modern ones, women who achieve very significantly may need reassurance about their femininity and may not be psychologically able to choose not to have children. Those who may experience the least conflict and be best able to diverge from traditional expectations may be women who are competent but not deviantly successful.

In another study, Susan Bram found that voluntarily childless wives described their childhood homes as less happy than did women who had children or were planning to have them. This is similar to our data in which the childless were more likely to have grown up in unstable or unloving families or in families in which they were not especially valued. Today it is difficult to estimate how many persons will not have children because they grew up unloved, and how many will not because they are being influenced by new values shared with their spouse and friends.[17]

In the near future there will probably be an increase in the number of people who prefer not to raise children. The majority, though, are more likely to limit their children to two. We do not have much information, but what we have indicates that women who have combined maternity and a career, like men who combine paternity and a career, are generally more satisfied with their lives than are those who chose one and either gave up or minimally participated in the other.[18]

It should be equally clear that exactly the reverse may occur. Maternal responsibilities can encourage a contraction of one's life and make one feel selfless and depressed. Whether one enjoys the role or resents it, grows within it or survives despite it, self-actualizes or self-destructs, depends on such reality factors as money and fatigue and depends on what one wants to do and what maternity makes one give up. How a woman defines herself in terms of modernity or traditionalism significantly influences how she feels about the role, because underlying the rational and logistical problems of combining motherhood and work is the fear that if she is a mother she is in danger of losing control over her own life, in danger of losing her independent self. We are well aware of all these things. We are much less aware of the effects of our ideas about what a mother ought to be like.

The Ideal Mother

Our very definition of a "good mother" makes maternity a terrible burden. We consider anything less than selfless love and total devotion to children inadequate in the ideal of parental—which really means maternal—care. This idea of the perfect mother is based on the kind of care we know that an infant or very young child needs. It also grew out of studies of the causes of psychopathology in children.

Since roughly the 1930s the studies and reports of psychiatrists, psychologists, and psychoanalysts have reinforced or constructed our image of the perfect mother. After World War I it was observed that infants who had been institutionalized and given minimal care developed hospitalism, marasmus, and anaclitic depression. That means that infants who had been perfectly healthy but who lived in an all-white, antiseptic world and received no stimulation, attention, or love, became apathetic, were stunted in mental and physical growth, and, in extreme cases, died. These findings underscored the importance of individual care, affection, and the stimulation that occurs in a one-on-one relationship.

At about the same time in England, Melanie Klein, a psychoanalyst, began to develop her theory that the significance of the mother in the development of a child's psychopathology outweighed the influence of the father. In the early 1930s Karen Horney continued in this direction and described the child as the victim of unconscious emotions transferred primarily by the mother. In the thirties the emphasis shifted from the father to the mother as the primary source of destructive influences and the main cause of a child's illness.[19] Overwhelmingly, mothers—not fathers or siblings or genes or poverty—were now considered the cause of a child's pathology. The task of the clinician was to locate the malevolent and pathological needs in the mother that led her to cause such heinous injury. In the late 1940s and the 1950s everyone was looking for—and finding—the schizophrenogenic mother, the mother who made her children schizophrenic. Led by such clinicians as John Bowlby, we looked for and found pathologies created in the vulnerable young when they were separated from their mothers.[20] No one mentioned fathers.

So the idea grew and flourished, especially after World War II, that a psychologically healthy child was the direct result of good parenting and especially good mothering, so that where to place the blame for the psychologically maladjusted child was obvious. The child's abilities, performance, health, and happiness became the responsibility of the mother. She was judged as though no one or nothing else determined what the child became. The responsibility became disproportionate; it became imprisoning. Anxiety about inadequacy and guilt because of ambivalence became too likely.

It is well established that the physical and especially the emotional needs of very young children mandate that their caretakers be expressive and warm. People who nurture very young children must be able to feel pleasure when they empathically fuse with them. The child's welfare thus takes precedence over the needs of the person caring for it. The person who nurtures the child must not feel resentful over the young child's total egocentricity and demands for instant gratification. This means that those who care for very young children have to feel fulfilled in the relationship, so that they can give of themselves in a sensitive, nonegocentric adaptation to what the child needs without feeling conflicted or resentful over this constant responsibility.

It is crucial for the emotional health of the child and the caretaker that an attachment develop between them. Without this bond the child cannot be normal. Without this bond the adult cannot give up an egocentric sense of self. Fortunately for both, babies—like kittens and puppies and all other young—are adorable and we are attracted to them because of their physical configuration. In addition, from shortly after birth babies cuddle, suck, nuzzle, and smile, and we are thus rewarded. To the extent that people are not threatened by the demands of the role, frightened by their pleasure from it, or dominated by their need for autonomy, they gain enormous pleasure when they form attachments with very young children.

But children do not respond only in ways that elicit this emotional attachment, they also behave in ways that encourage separation. As children grow, they physically explore, verbally engage, learn, remember, insist on doing things themselves, and expand their affections to people outside their family. By the age of 3 or so, the child's interests and the people important to those interests are outside—in the neighborhood or school—except when the child is in trouble and comes home. As a child grows older, the most intimate and important relationships will be with peers, not parents. Separation is as vital to the welfare of the child as is the early attachment. Lest I be misunderstood, I must note that separation does not mean rejection. It means allowing or encouraging children to explore and attempt on their own, with affection freely given by adults who retain a sense of their own priorities.

Children need to separate from those who take care of them in order to form an independent sense of self and to learn that they can cope by themselves. Separation and the transferral of attachments from parents to peers is a crucial part of the maturing process. Yet our most visible and powerful ideas about perfect parenting—especially mothering—ignore the need for separation and discourse only about attachment. Our model therefore coerces unnecessarily and destructively toward a continued infantilization of the child and the continuous interdependence of the child and mother. It is true that healthy parenting requires selfless, unboundaried nurturance—a psychological fusion between the infant and those who care for it—when children are very young. It is also true that healthy parenting requires a shift from un-boundaried nurturance to boundaried separation, to the emergence of the knowledge and the sense of separate identities, in school-age children.

Because our model of ideal mothering denies the importance of separation, it creates the setting in which even mothers of school-age children whose focus has shifted toward their own interests can be slandered as selfish. Resentment leads to martyred mothers, and no separation leads to smothered mothers. When parents are desperately harried, children are more easily brutalized. Child abuse is now a national epidemic.*

In addition, endlessly, "selflessly" nurturing mothers, who have no other interests and nothing else important to do, must make the job of parenting as big as possible, which prolongs an immature and irresponsible—and resentful—childhood. Very simply, it is much healthier for the child as well as the mother when the adult respects her own needs as well as her child's need to grow up. The stereotypic ideal of mothering is thus, paradoxically, anti-child and anti-mother.

Anti-Mother, Anti-Child

My focus is on maternity rather than parenting because child care has traditionally been the mother's responsibility and still is. For both parents to share this responsibility equally is now a visible goal, desirable but not likely to be attained. Real equality in child rearing cannot occur unless men are willing to work less and employers allow them to do that. In the early 1970s, before the recession, it was not uncommon for young academicians who were planning to have their first child to say that they would both work halftime and both take care of the baby. Since academicians have much more flexible hours than most people, part-time appointments are not unknown, and since academicians tend to be liberal, this arrangement sounded perfectly feasible. The reces-

*Figures released by the Department of Health, Education and Welfare in late November 1975 revealed that more than 1,000,000 children each year are physically abused or neglected and at least 1 in 500 children die from mistreatment. At the very least the report estimated that 2000 children die each year from abuse or neglect. There is no previous data, so we cannot know whether this represents an increase. The report estimated that the number of incidents is probably significantly greater than projected because there are likely to be many unreported cases of children who are beaten, burned, or sexually molested; who have serious physical injuries which remain untreated; or who are not adequately clothed or fed.[22]

sion and declining student enrollments made it impossible. That is, as the academic marketplace shrank, the competition for jobs became fierce. Instead of being able to cut back on the amount of time they put into work, academicians had to work much harder to be hired or retained. Until the economy prospers and skilled labor is in short supply, there is no reason for employers to moderate their demands or become flexible in terms of hours, so employees cannot work less. The idea that fathers should be actively involved in raising their children is widely accepted. But parents who are employed—and this includes far more fathers than mothers—take care of their children in their disposable time. These parents, especially the fathers, do have something to do with their children after they have worked to their own or their employer's satisfaction. This is quite different from equally shared child rearing, because it is still expected that if either parent cuts back on outside work, it will be the mother; the father does not have to lessen his ambition or shorten the hours he spends at work.

As long as we are quite certain that the mother should take care of the children, and as long as most mothers do take care of them, then everyone else can minimize or ignore what his or her responsibilities to children really are or ought to be. Our stereotype of the ideal mother allows us to deny that we have any obligation to develop social aids that will help her and benefit the young child.

Some years ago, when the economy was prospering, voters in the liberal, academic community in which I live consistently increased property taxes to fund the schools. At that time (around 1973) a special issue on the ballot asked whether the city should provide funds for preschool care, since day-care facilities were not adequate in number or quality. No one disputed the inadequacy of the facilities. Nonetheless, the issue was soundly defeated. Americans make a judgment, which has strong moral overtones, that under all conditions mothers of preschool children ought to be home, caring for their children.

The facts are that social support has become necessary because of the enormous increase in two-job or one-parent families. Aside from any changes in women's values, inflation has pushed many women into the labor force. People tend to have children when they are young and their earnings are low. In addition, since 1960 there has been a 10 percent increase in the number of white women who head their families and a 35 percent increase in black women who do.[23] One out of every six American children is being raised by a single parent; this includes at least 10 percent of children younger than 6, and most of these families are poor.[24]

In 1960, one mother out of five with preschool children worked, as did two out of five mothers whose children were of school age. By 1971 approximately one-third of women with preschool children and almost half of those with school-age children were out of their homes and in the labor force. In 1975, 57 percent of women with school-age children were working.[25] Projections by the federal government are that 70 percent of American mothers will be employed by 1980. If this trend continues, the demand for child care facilities will approach the demand for elementary schools. Almost 60 percent of the nation's children have mothers who are employed outside the home. Who will take care of these youngsters?

Robert Owen established the first English infant school in 1816 so that mothers could work. A New York hospital established nursery school programs for the children of poor women in 1854, and in the 1870s more day nurseries were opened for the children of working mothers. In spite of significant opposition, the federal government established child care centers in order to assist the mobilization of women workers in World War II. This trend serves to underline what seems to be universal in industrial societies. Child care facilities are provided and have high priority when women's labor is needed; otherwise they are a low-priority item.[26] Benefiting women and children has been an insufficient reason for child care centers to have high priority.

There are 13,000,000 working mothers, including 4,800,000 mothers who have 6,000,000 children younger than 6 who are searching for help with child rearing. The going rate for live-in help is between $5000 and $7500 a year; the cost of day care ranges from $1200 to $2300 a year. Care of very young children is expensive (or ought to be) because children under the age of 3 need a great amount of personal attention. Neither nonprofit subsidized day-care centers nor private centers operated for profit can normally afford the personnel needed for very young children. Moreover, studies show that the quality of care provided is rarely as good as the care the very young child would receive if it were home.[27]

Other countries have successfully provided widespread group care even for very young children. For example, factories in China have nurseries for children from the age of 56 days, which is when paid maternity leave ends, to the age of 3, as well as a kindergarten for children aged 3 to 7½.[28] In the kibbutzim of Israel, children move daily from friendly nonintense peer relationships to very intimate, intense, loving relationships with their parents. Studies have shown that while kibbutz infants may be temporarily slower in the development of social and language skills, in childhood and afterwards they are cognitively equal to nonkibbutz children and generally enjoy the psychological advantage of feeling secure. In Sweden day-care centers are designed specifically for children. The ratio of staff to children for infants is 2:3; for children aged 1 to 2 years, 1:4; for children aged 2 to 5, 1:5 or 1:6. People who care for children are specially trained; children's nurses and preschool teachers are popular professions.

Child care represents the interests of two low-status groups: children and women. Predictably, there was very little criticism when President Nixon vetoed a comprehensive nationwide early education program for children in 1971. There was no outcry when legislation to expand federal child care aid was stranded because President Ford said he would veto the bill. Fifteen years ago, when we were alarmed by *Sputnik,* there was an increased interest in our children; but over the last eight years the Head Start program has deteriorated and there have been major cutbacks in maternal and child health programs. We are almost the only industrialized country that has no national child or family policy and no comprehensive system of family services and supports. The inadequacy of the resources we provide for children and the choices we make about how we will allocate resources challenge the American belief that we love children.

Is the return to an extended family system, or some similar substitute, a possible solution, as some have argued? There is a persistent myth that until recently Americans lived in large extended families and child care was an easily shared joint responsibility among several adults. Studies of 16th century England and Colonial America, however, find that most households were nuclear and small. Three-generation households were not characteristic prior to industrialization and are certainly not usual post-industrialization. William Goode has called the large and extended family "the classical family of western nostalgia."[29] There is a modified extended family in the United States in which the relationship between mothers and their mothers is central. But while this family form is bound together by affection and patterns of mutual assistance, members are often physically separated. An extended family can help working mothers who need assistance every day only if they live near each other. In the United States this is not common.

Especially when there are no relatives to help; when there has been a divorce, death, or separation; when there is too little money to buy child care; when there are no friends with whom the job can be shared, no neighborhood co-op, no child center at the factory, university, or office—then the establishment of child care centers is necessary.

It seems fair to say that as a nation our priorities have not included the welfare of children and their mothers. This is partly because they are not important and powerful people. But it strikes me that something more venal is involved. I think we want to punish working mothers because we make a puritanical judgment that women who do not fulfill their material duties (which require that they remain at home); no matter why, deserve to suffer.

We know that cruelly isolated and totally deprived infants can become retarded and may die, and we know children must be stimulated and form close bonds with people who care for them. But the data does not justify the assumption that it must be the mother who cares for the child, or the child will suffer. Such evidence as we have supports the idea that group care of young children may be healthy, but for that to be the case the care must be intensive, warm, and stable. *Group child care is not equivalent to babysitting.* It must take the welfare of the child very seriously. When stable and warm people take that responsibility seriously and the parents do not feel guilty, group care of infants and young children can be adequate.

Surprisingly few studies have been made of what happens psychologically to infants when their mothers work. In general, though, we can say that the establishment of the crucial bond between the child and the mother is not simply related to whether the mother works or stays home, or whether the child is cared for by another person at home or spends the day in a nursery. Claire Etaugh concluded that "Young children can form as strong an attachment to a working parent as to a non-working one, provided that the parent interacts frequently with the child during the time they are together."[30] Jerome Kagan found that children who were in a day-care program when they were from 3 ½ to 30 months old, and who spent from 8:30 in the morning until 4 in the afternoon in the program, still showed a strong preference for their mothers. "When care is *optimal,* when you have conscientious and well-trained caretakers, then it is difficult to find any psychological differences in the children so reared."[31]

Studies of elementary school children show that the adjustment of the children is not disturbed if their mothers are employed. Rather, the best adjusted children have mothers who are satisfied with what they are doing. Studies of adolescents have similar results. The attitude of the mother—whether she is pleased with what she is doing or resentful, gratified or guilty—seems more important than whether she is employed or at home. Lois Hoffman has concluded that, "The data, on the whole, suggest that the working mother who obtains personal satisfactions from employment, does not have excessive guilt, and has adequate household arrangements is likely to perform as well as the non-working mother or better, but that the mother's emotional state is an important mediating variable."[32]

While someone other than the mother can obviously care for a child successfully, many mothers feel that it might be better in the first two or three years for a child to receive individual care rather than be put in a group situation. When my children were young I found that I was not willing to work full time. Too much happened in those early years—the development of speech and humor, mobility, and the beginnings of the sense of individuality. I could not give up being a part of that. For me and for most women I know, it felt better to work part time, so that was the option we chose. Those who do not have that choice because they are single parents or because their job or profession does not lend itself to part-time work or because they are very ambitious must find someone who will care for their children lovingly and can teach their children what they would if they were there.

For children who are 3 and older, a preschool for at least part of the day is not only reasonable but may be better than a whole day at home. Nursery schools and similar experiences provide something that children cannot get when they are home alone with their mother. The children gain interesting experiences with other children and adults, and they learn that rules of behaving are not arbitrary restrictions of a harried mother. Mostly, though, nursery school is a place with lots of kids to play with and big toys you don't have at home and grown-ups who have nothing else to do but be with children. A good nursery school is a place to learn and have fun. It ought to be available to all children. Rather than thinking of preschool primarily as a mechanism to enable women to work, we should think of it as something that benefits the child.

That all of the information we have tells us children may prosper when someone other than their mother takes care of them during a good part of the day should not be surprising. If a mother is conflicted —loving the child yet resentful, torn between the needs of the child and her own—her feelings will be communicated to the child. Others— whether relatives, friends, or people who are paid—who care for the child out of choice certainly may be less ambivalent and more loving.

As long as we pay people less money to baby-sit than we do to clean a house or run a gas pump, taking care of children will too often be a job for the least educated and the least skilled. Since most working mothers have low incomes, a standard payment to all parents—a common practice in many countries—could provide funds to increase what could be paid to the person caring for the child, or it could provide enough money to enable one of the parents not to work or to work part time.

It is crucial that those who remain at home to care for their children believe that they are engaged in something worthwhile and enjoyable; and it is important that those who leave in order to work be helped with their responsibilities so that they are not burdened with guilt and the fear that they are injuring their children. Solutions may involve cooperative arrangements between neighbors or the establishment of well-funded child care centers at work or in the community. For very young children the best solution may turn out to be a government subsidy that pays one parent to stay at home, or creative arrangements at work allowing for more part-time positions and sharing of jobs. Most of all, values must change so that children are considered truly important, and those who take care of them are respected, trained, and paid accordingly.

Children, Commitment, and Existential Anchors

It will clearly be good when people who do not want children have none and feel no pressure because of that decision. It will also be good if the feminist challenge causes us to change the way we rear children, so that there is a greater sharing of the task. And it will be good when women, like men, feel free to have a family and to work and need not choose between the two commitments.

But, as with all great changes in values, there are destructive elements too. Overtly, feminists are calling for shared child rearing so that women do not have to leave the work force when they become mothers.[33] But on a psychologically overt level the new values emphasize all the costs of being a mother and lead to increased resentment or a rejection of the role. Unless the parental and especially the maternal experience is seen as an important route to self-esteem and egocentric gratification, no role is more antithetic toward these objectives than the selfless care of young children.

I have no quarrel with those who prefer to remain childless and I am not prescribing parenthood for anyone who does not wish it. Common sense and my own research tell me that a substantial number of people's self-concept, life-style and goals are facilitated if they do not rear children.

Most people, though, do have children, and it looks as though most who marry will continue to have them. I am alarmed because I think there has been an increase in our anti-child bias, which adds to the resentment or regrets of parents. Child rearing can give a feeling of satisfaction, but not happiness. Of course, there are moments of happiness but these cannot be sustained. That is because "happiness" is a term for joy that has no connection with pain or the costs of any responsibility. In contrast, "satisfaction" means that, all in all, when we sum the account, the positive outweighs the negative. In our family we say, "51:49. Thank God the kids have 2 percent." Of course, there are personal costs to child rearing. There are costs to every commitment. An anti-child bias increases our negative set; it heightens our awareness of the toll of these responsibilities.

I am also concerned for those who have no strong feelings against having, wanting children but who, swept up in the momentum of this period, may choose not to become parents because they think that is the way to be liberated. Psychological liberation is not achieved through a lack of commitment, but is gained through growth that occurs when we cope with important commitments. Few activities, few jobs, hold the potential for psychological expansion that parenting does. As a parent, what you do matters and it matters that it is you who is doing it.

Being a parent is a unique commitment because it cannot be undone except by death. The role organizes what you do day by day and it shapes your future as you try to protect your children over the long haul. It can have a uniquely satisfying quality as you see your child grow and cope and laugh. When I see people interacting with pets, I am reminded that whenever those we take care of respond to us—whether it is a cat, a dog, or a child—we are deeply pleased and can feel love.

Most importantly, parenthood is a crucial existential anchor which makes people cope with real problems, make decisions, and adapt as the relationship changes. Being a parent defines a huge area of responsibilities and forces us to grow up, set priorities, and organize our life so that we can sustain our children. For many people—and most do not have the opportunity to do work of unusual significance—child rearing is the focus of their long-term plans, as providing for the children is the major way in which they can believe they have done something of real merit. In this sense parenting is moral; in this role we can become heroic, larger than our ordinary selves. Being parents gives people the opportunity to transform lesser motives into greater ones.

For most people being a parent is the most accessible way to gratify needs for creativity and generativity. It is a central existential anchor, a source of identity and of good feelings about oneself. It is also a source of terror, of the most wrenching fears—as well as more ordinary ambivalence and resentment. To say what is costly or difficult about the responsibility is easy, but it is enormously difficult, maybe impossible, to express the gut-level, not conscious, not-rational feelings that being a parent creates.

The joys of being a parent seem to be unique—a set of pleasures, of identifications, of *feelings* that are different, somehow, from those of other relationships or achievements. The set of emotions involved seem to be experiential and insurmountably difficult to articulate, to shape in a way that can be shared with someone who is not a parent. In this sense parenthood is like some other experiences. It is similarly difficult to verbalize a sense of panic, to share the shape of pain or orgasm or exultation. I found myself stunned by my pleasure and frightened by how vulnerable my love for my children made me. Sometimes ambivalent, occasionally romantic, but mostly realistic, I would not have missed the experience for anything.

While being a parent can be tremendously gratifying, because of the bias of our culture it is also a great burden. Feminists must denounce our anti-child and anti-mother values for the following reasons: politically, because it will appeal to a great sector of their constituency; pragmatically, because many mothers are employed; and morally, because the welfare of children and their parents, of the family itself, is a goal of great merit. We must see when being a parent deprives us of significant experience and when it holds the potential for extraordinary experience. We need to reassess our priorities and change what we do so that we sustain children and those who care for them. We should enable everyone, whether a parent or not, to know the wonder, sometimes the worry, and most often the joy that can be found in relating to children.

Feminist insistence that we support children and their parents is in accord with women's historical values. Creating life and protecting it has been women's special privilege and responsibility. While some cultures may demean the role as less significant than other, typically masculine accomplishments, it is crucial for their own self-esteem that women do not agree with this basically sexist stance.

Twenty years ago my former husband was an Air Force fighter pilot. The pilots were a self-aware elite, enormously confident in their abilities and intelligence. These sublimely confident men were unabashedly preoccupied with children. When men do not have to maintain a defensively machismo style and are not threatened by activities or feelings traditionally supposed to be feminine, men nurture and derive great pleasure from the supposedly feminine.

Women's insistence on the awesome creativity and significance of maternity will increase their sense of esteem even if they are not themselves mothers, because maternity is the essence of what is uniquely feminine. Esteeming maternity enhances the symbolic status of all women. Esteeming parenthood provides self-affirming experiences for both women and men.

Sex:
The New
Hedonism

5

A male friend, 50 and divorced, was furious. He had met a divorced woman who was about 35, and they had seemed to quickly click. They danced slowly, her legs between his conveyed an obvious erotic invitation. He took her home and she asked him in. After she hung their coats up, she said, "I want you to know I didn't invite you in for sex." He was enraged and left. At 3 in the morning she called and told him he had been very cruel. "I don't screw," she said, "I make love." When he told me this story several weeks later he was still furious at her "dishonesty," since it was obvious to him that she had been seducing him. I understood them both. From her point of view, she had been flirting in the fine-honed style of the 1950s; she felt dishonored and angry that he thought she was the kind who "put out."

Change and conflicts of choice, traditional values, and reversed values are especially clear when we look at what is happening in the relations between women and men. Today, the traditional, committed, monogamous relationship, especially in marriage, coexists with sex without involvement, open marriages, overt adultery, high rates of divorce, high rates of remarriage, tremendous numbers of unmarried couples living together, and many married couples living separately. Revolutionary, evolutionary, and traditional forms of relationships exist simultaneously.

The sexual revolution, with its theme that everyone has a right to unlimited sexual experience, arose at about the same time that feminists were beginning to attack marriage as the ultimate trap of women's autonomy, and human potential advocates were denouncing marriage as iniquitously restrictive and inhibiting. Applause for those who matured and coped within marriage was replaced by a focus on how that commitment foreclosed our egocentric development and pleasure. Nontraditional forms of relationships that did not involve legal or psychological permanence became visible—cohabitation, communes, and group marriages, for example. But most important: in terms of the numbers of us who were really influenced, was the emergent visibility of the positive aspects of sexual freedom and experimentation.

In the late 1960s and early 1970s sex became the symbol of one's liberation or inhibition. Paradoxically, as sexual pleasure seemed to become superordinately important, the sex act was simultaneously held to be insignificant and thus a commodity to be shared. Having sexual, sensual, sensate pleasures unbound by commitments of law or fidelity or emotional meaning became the model of freedom, the means to achieve the ultimate in hedonism. Enjoying an uninhibited, uninvolved, costfree orgasmic sexuality in an unrestrained lifestyle—the exact reverse of the morality and psychology of monogamous marriage —became the hallmark of chic liberation for people of both sexes.

In the sensual seventies pornography once mailed in a plain cover became available on every magazine stand and in many movie theatres. In good capitalist fashion, nonmarital sex formed an industry which provided singles bars, spouse-swapping clubs, key clubs, magazines, newsletters, massage parlors, housing complexes for single people. We seemed obsessed with the goal of maximizing our pleasure through unfettered sex.

In the 1950s and 1960s we assumed that sex involved extraordinarily powerful emotions, and we believed that sex was good when there was love or at least affection. We thought that premarital sex could acceptably precede marriage, and we were certain that psychologically healthy, mature people created permanent and essentially monogamous marriages. But in the seventies, all of us who restricted our sex lives to our spouses were forced to wonder whether we were neurotically inhibited. The impact of the new values was probably greatest on attitudes and not behavior, because the percentage who were able to experiment sexually, especially among the married, was probably small. But those who did were newsworthy.

According to the media, autonomy replaced emotional interaction, freedom replaced fidelity, and sex replaced love. In books, films, and magazines we were bombarded with the theme that restriction of sexual experience was irrational. Sex became separated from commitment, recreational sex was glorified, and the idea that sex had to be legalized by the state seemed just plain funny. Most of all, we heard, sex had no particular significance and was just another bodily function or form of pleasure.

While relatively few of us were really able to live out this Playboy fantasy, many of us were provoked to change the criteria by which we measured our own happiness. Increasingly, we wanted to experience the excitement that is characteristic of new relationships and were no longer satisfied with the contentment of an old one. Since the great majority of us were married, and relationships that are not new tend to habituate, the new criteria of exquisite pleasure became a new stress. Very few of us could avoid wondering what we were missing and how we could get it.

The gay liberation movement has also been significant in this decade, but I have not discussed it because it is not central to the themes of this book and because I have no expertise in the area. I ought to note, however, that there was not only a general emergence of homosexuality but also, among feminists, an idealization of love between women and therefore of lesbianism. Lesbians were seen as women who had made the most extreme rebellion against an oppressive patriarchal socialization, who had refused to defer to males, and whose lifestyle and choice of lover were in the vanguard of the sexual revolution. For some radical feminists, becoming a lesbian was the crucial identification of sisterhood—of feminism as love for women. In the early part of this decade bisexuality seemed the minimum compromise for acceptance by some of the radical groups.[1]

How much change in sexual behavior really occurred in the seventies and how radical were the changes? Surprisingly, the most radical period of change in American sexual attitudes and behavior took place in the 1920s, when the flapper era brought about a decisive change from the Victorian, which had preceded it. Since then there have been evolutionary changes in the sense that there has been a consistent rise in the percentage of females and males who have nonmarital or extramarital sex at increasingly younger ages.[2] In Kinsey's studies in the fifties, for example, about 8 percent of married women under the age of 25 had had extramarital sex, but Hunt's more recent data supports an estimated 24 percent.

Several very recent studies indicate that the percentage of 16-to-18-year-old girls who have experienced coitus is higher than the rate for boys of the same age.[3] This is an obvious reversal of the usual findings, and while it is too early to know whether this will be a consistent trend, several explanations have been offered. Girls' acceptance of their own sexuality, coupled with their earlier physical and social maturity, makes earlier sexual experience a logical outcome. With the decline in the double standard and its division of "good" and "bad" girls, fewer sexually promiscuous girls are available as partners for a number of males.

Instead, girls are insisting that sex occur within the context of a one-to-one relationship; and boys, who are generally less mature and unable or unwilling to make this commitment, find themselves without sexual partners.

While there has not been an abrupt change in the rates of sexual activity in this decade—which suggests that the sexual revolution was a palace revolution—the pattern of sexual behavior seems to have been especially affected by feminist values. The frequency and the age of participation of females are now much closer to those of males. It is too early to know whether the disease will be terminal, but the double standard is very ill.

Probably one of the most important changes in the 1970s is the idea that we are entitled to as much pleasure or happiness as we can get. The media gave enormous publicity to all kinds of arrangements in which people had a variety of sexual partners. It became almost embarrassing to confess to monogamy or to inexperience with trios or orgies. While the data are not terribly good, a rough estimate is that only 5 to 15 percent of adults ever engaged in swinging, orgies, and the like even once.[4] But in the glamour of airbrushed photos and in contrast to our too familiar lives, these people seemed spontaneous, liberated, free.

The apparent change in our values about sex, especially the emphasis on hedonism, was partly a revulsion from our rather puritan public morality, partly an acknowledgment of the fact that our behavior had changed in the last 50 years, and partly a rejection of a life ruled by duty. With widespread publicity given to the Pill and the IUD, sex was increasingly separated from reproduction and thus from a morality in which sex was permitted only when children would be legitimate. Most poignantly, in this decade of rootlessness, sex became a means to fill the void of not touching and not feeling; the act of love was used as a symbol of connecting, even though there was no true connection with the other or with the self.

Unlimited sexual hedonism is the reverse of our traditional values that duty is more important than pleasure, that the welfare of the family, especially of the children, is more important than the happiness of the parents; that sex requires an emotional commitment; that sexual behavior should be monogamous, because you can love only one person at a time. As most of us grew up learning a monogamous morality, conflict was predictable. Americans have never treated sex lightly, as a simple pleasure. Whether we accept the traditional values or rebel against them, we have always burdened sex with heavier meanings. We have no tradition of just flowing with our impulses, taking sensual pleasures as they come. Amoral sex and sexual license are in basic discord with our traditional values.

Some may rightfully argue that the Woodstock generation was not bound by traditional values. This seems true in some ways and not in others. A larger percentage of young people than those who are middle aged and older seem able to enjoy sex without investing it with any heavy significance or rules of participation based on obligation, expectation, and commitment. But sexual moralities are powerful and fundamental; and, for most of us, in spite of chic amorality, sex generates feelings of possession and jealousy. A new but predictable anxiety arose among those who behaved according to the new values while experiencing feelings based on the old rules.

When sex is separated from reproduction, its ties to family, religion, morality, and the law are all loosened. We are now shifting from sexual ethics designed to protect the family to sexual ethics based on love and mutual commitment. In a more extreme form we are shifting to sex as recreation, to sex as enjoyable physical fun.

Probably the most important real change has been the transition from a single sexual morality to the coexistence of three patterns of behavior, each of which is considered moral by its adherents. In the first and numerically largest pattern, people still behave according to the traditional model in which men push for sex, women for love and marriage, and there is a double standard. In the second pattern males adopt traditionally feminine values and want sex to be a natural part of a relationship in which both partners care for each other. In the third pattern women have adopted the traditional male pattern of sex for its own sake, without any emotional investment. The last pattern involves the smallest number of people, but is psychologically significant because it symbolizes women's liberation from old moralities, from the double standard, and especially from the presumption that females are sexually passive.

The double standard was based on the idea that men were sexually insatiable and that sexually unawakened women were indifferent. Thus, while female virgins were desirable, male virgins were despicable. A major change in this decade has been the development of an identical morality for both sexes, based on a fundamental revision of our ideas about female sexuality. Researchers like M. S. Sherfey and Masters and Johnson have shown that sexual arousal and orgasm are more alike than different for women and men.[5] With publicity given to the female capacity for multiple orgasms in the media, men-as-rapists shared space with haggard men made impotent by unendingly demanding women. The new ideas about female sexuality legitimated women's assertion that they owed themselves maximum sexual pleasure. This assertion was essentially an adoption by women of the stereotype of sexual behavior of young men, in which love is not as important as orgasm.

As we reversed our ideas about differences in the sexes' need to feel loved as a precondition for sex and about the importance of orgasm, magazines, books, and sex therapists encouraged women to masturbate, to use electric vibrators, to engage in fantasy, and to enjoy pornography. The obvious message was that women ought to enjoy sex and could if they would learn certain techniques and give up old inhibitions. The less obvious message was that women do not need a penis or a partner, and that sex can be separated from the context of a relationship.

As usual, opportunity and threat coexist. When the importance of the relationship is diminished, fulfillment depends less upon gratifications from feeling loved than it does upon the quality of sexual performance. Quality and quantity, technique, orgasm, and arousability become more crucial than context. But every study of female sexuality has tended to demonstrate that it is a rare woman who becomes easily aroused and does not need to feel some affection for her partner, who has several orgasms a week, reaches orgasm regularly and swiftly, and is not guilty about masturbating.[6] About a third of women have little or no sexual response, another third respond more slowly and with less intensity than do men, most of the remaining third are about equally arousable as men, and some 3 or 4 percent of women are far more arousable than men as evidenced by their ability to reach orgasm through fantasy or just by walking with their desired partner.[7] The idea of identical sexuality for the sexes serves to justify women's focus on achieving maximum erotic pleasure, but it may also become a new source of feelings of frustration and failure.

A thread of rage binds various aspects of the women's movement, an expression of outrage at having been cheated, a demand for equal experience that becomes translated into identical experience. Thus sex and orgasm have become politicized. Based on Masters and Johnson's data—which demonstrated that an orgasm is basically an edemic reaction centered in the pelvic area, with fundamental parallels at the tissue level in women and men—it was easy to take the next step and declare that there is no "male sexuality" or "female sexuality" but it is identical for both sexes.

In contrast, classical Freudians stated quite flatly that the mature woman's task was to renounce and avoid forms of sexuality which were active and clitoral and therefore "masculine," and turn to passive, receptive, "feminine" sexual modes, which would be vaginal. The Freudians perceived the clitoris as a smaller and therefore inferior penis and diagnosed protracted interest in clitoral stimulation as a symptom of immature femininity and a barrier to mature, womanly sexuality.

The long debate over clitoral versus vaginal orgasms implied a difference in the quality or nature of orgasms in women and men. This was a misplaced emphasis. Aside from whether women prefer clitoral stimulation, the emphasis should have been on the context of sex. Most women prefer some sense of themselves as unique and loved people as a precondition for arousal and thus for orgasm, while men, especially when young, are more prone to emphasize sex for its own sake.

Of course, women can be very sensual and erotically responsive. It now looks as though women's sexual appetites in the middle years may be greater than those of men.[8] But if the criteria of sexual responsiveness for women is taken from the stereotypic idea of young men's sexual performance and includes swift arousability, guaranteed orgasms, and the enjoyment of casual sex, many women will be disappointed with themselves. The idealization of sex modeled on the male stereotype reflects not only hedonism but also sexism—the conviction that the male style is better, is more fun, and has fewer costs. While women's arousability may often be slower or less automatic than young men's, I find it very hard to see why a slow, prolonged, and sustained level of arousal is less good than a fast one or why emotionally uninvolved sex is better than sex that conveys caring. It is not surprising that some feminists who initially applauded an identical—that is, an unfettered—sexual morality are now wondering if that was not the conclusive screwing, the ultimate male plot to make women sexually available.

Men can feel used as sexual objects, as penises used to provide pleasure without any respect for them as individuals. But women are much more likely to feel abused, even if they freely participate in or initiate sex, if they do not have some sense that their partner cares about them. This is because women have traditionally increased their sexual activity in order to make a man love them or to signify their love or to celebrate a love they believe is mutual. The great majority of sexually active women have learned this morality. *What is new is the number of men who are adopting it.* This is a morality which is not governed by law—that is, marriage—but by ideals that sex is moral when it is egalitarian, partner oriented, and love oriented.[9]

Nonmarital or Premarital Sex

The largest shift in terms of the number of people involved is the acceptance of nonmarital sex when there is mutual affection. This value change has been evolving since the 1920s and is signified by the term *non*marital rather than *pre*marital sex. The partners, especially the women, no longer need to assume that they will ultimately marry this lover to justify the sexual relationship.

Since 1920 there has been a gradual but steady rise in the rate of nonmarital coitus. In the 1970s, rates range from about 60 percent of males and 40 percent of females, to as high as 70 percent of both, having participated in coitus by the time they leave college. These rates vary greatly by the sector of the country. While the number of virgins is still considerable, the shift is to perceive sex as morally acceptable outside of marriage if the partners are in a continuing relationship. This change is especially clear in the increased numbers or visibility of couples who are unmarried and living together. The great majority of cohabiting couples are monogamous and live together because they love each other. Factors which appear to contribute to higher cohabitation are changed attitudes toward premarital sex, the decline in colleges' attempts to regulate morality, the availability of partners, the decrease of social disapproval, the feminist movement, and the availability of contraception.

Most of the studies of couples living together have involved college students.[10] Although the figures vary on different campuses, in 1973 it was estimated that up to about 30 percent of undergraduates had lived with someone. Many more believed that cohabitation was a good idea and would cohabit if the opportunity arose. I would guess that the percentages would be much higher today for undergraduates and for graduate students because in today's college atmosphere mutually affectionate sexual relationships in which neither partner coerces or prevails are considered moral. Living together is so common in some places that it no longer seems a symbol of youthful protest. To establish an arbitrary limit on permissible forms of sexual intimacy seems silly when couples living together are intimate in every other way.

E. D. Macklin found that students living together tended to be unsatisfied with dating, which they dismissed as a superficial relationship; they wanted a more complex and committed involvement. Some couples regarded cohabitation as a trial marriage—rather like an engagement period—but others had no thought of marriage. Some wanted to try out the relationship before marriage, others questioned the viability of marriage as an institution. But most simply felt that while they were not ready to get married, they wanted to live and sleep with someone they cared about and who cared about them. About half of the students said that they would have to be involved in a strongly affectionate relationship before they would live with someone, and then they would not date others. The majority of cohabiting students are emotionally and socially committed to their partners; very few live together solely for sex. Couples living together want to be intimate in all the ways possible, and commitment seems to be initiated equally by both partners.

The most significant aspect of the increased practice of living together is not the obvious sexual relationship. More important is the couple's clear willingness to accept household responsibilities and much greater psychological obligations, for the intimacy and commitment of cohabitation are close to those of marriage. Persons who live together instead of dating may benefit from a sense of being loved and also be more vulnerable to the pain that would result from rejection and separation.

The largest direction of change seems to be that men are adopting women's traditional morality, in which the precondition for sex is affection or love. Since these relationships are characteristically monogamous, they are essentially moral in a traditional sense. While this is still a minority pattern which involves younger more educated people, they are often a social vanguard, and their values often signify what the majority opinion will become.[11] In 1970, for instance, 65 percent of the women interviewed in the Virginia Slims poll considered premarital sex immoral; in 1974 the percentage had fallen to 53 percent. In 1974, 72 percent of the women and 68 percent of the men polled did not think that the new sexual morality would make for better, more successful marriages. But a substantial minority thought the newer patterns of sexual morality were a healthy development. The continuing increase in the percentages of young people who are sexually experienced when they marry seems to me to be a healthy development, since it is clearly ill fated to marry because lust has been confused with love.

Nonmarital sex and cohabitation can help people to not mistake sex for emotional commitment and to have more realistic ideas of what it is like to live with someone and what that person is like. But as the rates of sexual activity increase, there is the possibility that a coercive norm of sexuality will develop, so that sex becomes mandatory. Women especially seem in danger of being called frigid or of being pressured to "prove" their love. Young people of both sexes can become anxious when they think that being sexually experienced is a prerequisite for being accepted. This was clearly illustrated by a clinician who told me that her patient, a college student, kept talking about the boy she was sleeping with. Since this was clearly on the girl's mind, the clinician asked her, week after week, how she felt about sex, whether she reached orgasm, and so on. The girl was evasive and the therapy was going very badly. Finally, the clinician understood. The patient meant exactly what she said: she slept with her boyfriend. There was no sex. Both partners felt it was crucial to be able to tell their friends that they were sleeping together.

Sex and Aging

A new overtness about sexual activity exists now. When we were young
we were much more secretive about our sex lives, especially with our
parents. The open sexuality of those living together—indeed, the explicit sexuality of the young in general—is a threat to those who are no
longer young. Students and young people living together often have
elaborate procedures to hide the fact from their parents, such as maintaining two residences or at least two telephones and two mailboxes.
Although the couple may not realize it, this secretive behavior prevents
not only parental rage and interference but also parental identification
and jealousy.

Most of the publicity about changing sexual values and behavior
focuses on young people. But I think that those in long-established
marriages who are entering into or are already in middle age are painfully aware of the changes in sexual values, and have become uncertain
about what they ought to do, ambivalent about all their years of sexual
fidelity, and especially vulnerable to jealous feelings. This has probably
always been true insofar as the younger generation always seems wilder
and freer than their parents are or were when young. Besides, because
we venerate youth, adults are prone to be jealous of those who are
young. Parents may envy their own children.

Increasingly, parents are being confronted with the fact of their
children's sexual activity. After talking perhaps permissively and liber-
ally about sex as natural and good, parents are being challenged by their
own children who want to know why they can't make love in their own
bedroom. A parent's first reaction is typically shock—my *child* making
love!—and a parent's first impulse is frequently to tell the child to find
a car—if it was good enough for us, it's good enough for them. While
many of the kids seem unwilling to hide their activity and to make sex
illicit, many of the parents would prefer such secrecy.

I learned from my children that the essence of sexuality is sensuality, being at ease with one's body, and I was relieved by their normalcy.
Yet in spite of my role as an instructor in a course on human sexuality,
I was initially uncomfortable when my children were open and explicit
about what they were doing. They forced the issue by refusing to sneak
around. Along with the other parents I know, I was hoisted on the
petard of my liberal values. We searched for rational reasons why our
children should not make love at home. We talked about the potential
effects on their younger siblings; we discoursed about how sex would
make them more vulnerable if they were rejected. But since they were
behaving as mature people in loving relationships, both we and they
knew that the discussion was hollow. Finally, we were honestly able to

say that we were glad they were not unduly repressed and inhibited, were pleased with their moral sense of emotional commitment. We inquired about their use of contraception—and told them that we could live without the details.*

The present seems to be an especially stressful period, particularly for those who are over 35. This is because today's preoccupation with sexual experience and hedonistic freedom is a reaction against the narrow, family-confined lives that we sought. We were the generation who courted in the McCarthy era and proliferated under Eisenhower. We worked and married and had children. We joined the PTA and bought houses in suburbia. As the whole world and even our own children seem to be enjoying heady sensuality and excitements while we struggle to pay college tuitions, a new reality pervades our realization that our future is truncated; our marriages, work, and life in general are routinized; our bodies are sagging; our desirability is declining; and death is approaching. Time becomes an imperative, and the central realization or fear is that if we do not do something now, we never will. Everything seems to conspire to make those who are no longer young examine their morality, desires, and inhibitions. There's the rub. One would think that as people grow older, they would develop a firmer sense of self, a greater self-esteem, and a keener perspective, so that they would be independent and confident enough to play sexually for the sheer fun of it, without letting the potency of sexual engagements become eviscerating. Yet we are also a generation who learned and accepted a monogamous morality. And so ambivalence impales us; we do nothing.

The middle-aged man who comforts himself with the company of young women has always been a stock figure. What seems to be new —or at least more visible—is the increased sexual activity of middle-aged women. The rate of extramarital sex for women is now approaching that of men. Since an affair involves courtship, passion, and the reassurance of being sexually attractive and chosen for love, it is understandable that, like men, women often begin affairs when they enter their mid-thirties.[13] While the age and percentage of men with extramarital experience has apparently changed little since Kinsey reported a 50 percent frequency in 1953, for women, there has been a decrease in age and a significant increase in the number with extramarital experiences. The younger the women, the greater the percentage

*(I realize that I am being personal and generalizing from my own experiences. Unfortunately, there appear to be very few studies of middle-aged people and they do not involve these issues. I have lectured on this topic around the country and have published a paper on the subject of middle age.[12] My own generalizations are supported by the responses to the lectures and to the paper.)

of extramarital sex. Again we see evidence of the end of the double standard, with the change initiated by women.

A woman's sexual demands may please or threaten her partner. He may welcome them or may interpret them as a sign that he is an inadequate lover. But that is only part of any conflict between partners and it is probably a minor part. More important, I think, than sexual pleasure is people's desire for excitement, for the almost painfully vivid sense that they are alive, when they are in comfortable, old relationships.

Excitement versus Contentment

Besieged by images of effervescent thrills and chagrined by the predictable and repetitive minutiae of a large part of life, people are dissatisfied. After all, being dutiful and responsible sounds exceedingly pale in comparison to being impulsive and free. Feeling fulfilled and being confident enough to explore sensation in new sexual relationships and to give a partner the same freedom sound much richer than being secure and restricted. The giddiness of a new passion rings louder than some modification of a Wednesday and Saturday night routine.

A crucial question is whether our focus on exhilarating hedonistic gratification is asking secured relationships, especially marriages, to be something they cannot be. Long-term relationships are based on bonds of commitment and must be essentially stable. Anything stable is no longer uncertain. When uncertainty is lost, so is the acute awareness of feelings, whether joy or grief. Excitement, exhilaration, and fear are much more likely in a new relationship, in which one cannot be sure that one will be desired and preferred. New relationships are intrinsically risky and thus make people feel vividly. Whether or not you love the other, danger, freshness, and unpredictability always increase the sharpness of experience. Thus, relationships that are not yet stable can be romantic, consuming, and oblivious to the realities of dirty socks and who takes out the garbage.[14] Psychologist Charles Tripp, for one, is convinced that compatibility and commitment in a monogamous relationship dull erotic zest because optimal sexual feelings requires some tension and resistance between the partners.[14] Tripp also claims that of more than 1000 societies studied, fewer than 5 percent expect monogamy.

It is erroneous to talk about sex irrespective of context. In long-term relationships not only sex is routinized. Life in general habituates, so that each partner loses the keen sense of pleasure in the other's existence. When my former husband was in the Air Force and stationed on Okinawa after the Korean ceasefire, the death rate for pilots was still 25 percent of the squadron each year. In two years half the pilots were killed. Given the death rate, the continuous awareness of danger, and the frequent separations, people were sharply aware of their happiness when together. In our two years at Okinawa I heard of only one extramarital affair involving a pilot.

Monogamous relationships are always difficult, since one involvement is asked to gratify all sorts of needs and express all sorts of love. People are greedy for good feelings. Sometimes they want to flirt and play, sometimes they want a grand passion, sometimes they need a haven. Any relationship has the tendency to habituate over time, narrowing into one style, confining the partners into a smaller range of experiences. And most marriages—strained by problems of children, money, careers, and all the other stresses we are too familiar with—are likely to drift toward friendly, unpassionate, companionable security.

Psychologists have begun to distinguish different forms of love. J. A. Lee differentiates three. They are "eros," the chemical reaction of physical passion; "ludus," or pleasure in the games and style of courtship and sex; and "storage," a calm and peaceful affection established, typically, in marriage, home, and children.[15] While Lee describes individuals as manifesting one form, I think most of us feel all the forms, although the strongest form changes at times. Zick Rubin, in his *Liking and Loving,* discusses passionate versus companionate love and says passionate love either dies or turns into companionate.[16]

More people seem less willing to settle for unpassionate companionship today. But when the comfortable companionate relationship is life's major haven and the divorce statistics climb and everyone knows people just like themselves whose marriages have ended, than the dissolution of your marriage is a very vivid possibility. Needing the security of a stable relationship while desiring the excitements more characteristic of new relationships has led to social experiments including the "open marriage."

While many societies are publicly monogamous, they usually provide socially sanctioned outlets for people (usually males) to have additional sexual partners.[17] Ours is one of the very few societies that do not provide for a variety of sexual experiences. Where such formalized arrangements exist, alternative sexual partners need not threaten the stability of the family.

The conflict between wanting security based on a long-term mutual commitment and wanting the exhiliration of novel experiences, specifically in sex, is clearly expressed in today's experiments in open marriage, swinging, and mate swapping. Alternatively, we could say that these are attempts to create an acceptable social structure in which people can experiment sexually without jeopardizing their marriage or other long-term relationship. These extramarital arrangements are often explicit and formal and usually provide both partners with sex outside of their basic relationship.

In an "open" arrangement, partners do not keep extrarelationship sex a secret because they expect openness to eliminate any sense of being betrayed or rejected. Sharing one's fantasies or experiences with one's partner is supposed to strip them of any special power. In the ideal scenario each partner is able to say, "I respect and trust you so much that I am confident I will not hurt you and you will not leave me because I need more than I can get from our relationship. And, in turn, you can and must respect and trust me in the same way. If we have sex with other people and we keep it a secret, then it becomes too important. If we don't exaggerate the importance of sex, if we're secure enough so that we don't have to possess each other, and if we can have other relationships but we choose to stay together, then our relationship will be stronger."

The basic idea is that in an open and mutual arrangement, each partner can have the pleasures of sexual hedonism without betraying the other or feeling deceived or guilty. These new marital-sexual arrangements are not romantic in that they usually do not involve love. The search seems, instead, to be for new experiences and feelings, and extramarital or extrarelational sex is a kind of preventive medicine taken in order to protect the integrity of the primary relationship. It is psychologically significant that the arrangements are often explicitly sexual and specifically limit the intimacy possible with other sexual partners.

When the focus is on sex for the sake of sex in an arrangement designed to prevent the possibility of any emotional contact, the primary relationship is protected because sexual possessiveness is much easier to give up than is monogamous emotional loyalty. While it may be easy for some to engage in sex, it is much more difficult to evade the emotional consequences of making love.

Some arrangements that limit experimentation to sex and minimize the possibility of love include key clubs, in which house keys are randomly exchanged to determine temporary sexual partners; group orgies; and mate-swapping, "swinging" parties. In each arrangement, the experience is limited to the physical encounter; further contact between sexual partners is either specifically prohibited or more informally limited. The significance of the nonrelational sex is thus minimized. And the formality of these arrangements signifies that while some people can easily engage in sex for fun, most people are afraid that they or their partner cannot do that.

B. G. Gilmartin studied 100 middle-class swinging couples.[18] He reported that most attended a swinging party about once every two weeks; few went more than once a week. At a typical party the women engaged in erotic activities with three or four different partners and the men with two or three. A good deal of activity was noncoital, but most participants had intercourse at least once during the evening. Many of those he interviewed reported that swinging increased their sexual interest in their spouse; they often made love after coming home from a swinging party. The couples in his sample did tend to meet occasionally with other swingers for unerotic socializing, but the majority consciously avoided any serious emotional involvement with a swinging partner. The participants' ability to regard these sexual experiences as a physical recreation makes it easy to understand why they generally believe that they are moral and psychologically monogamous.

"Open marriage," in which intimacies are not limited to the physical, is intrinsically more threatening to the basic relationship because of the possibility of a more complex or significant relationship with someone else. In contrast to swinging or key club activities, the open marriage arrangement has no limits on one's becoming involved with others, because the goal is self-fulfillment. The achievement of a more "expanded" or complex self is supposedly helped by having diverse commitments and significant relationships with other people. People able to flourish in an open marriage do not need sexual or emotional monogamy.

Nena and George O'Neill's *Open Marriage* became a bestseller. Their basic idea is that there is less strain in a marriage when both spouses have large areas of independence and neither needs a deadening, unending togetherness. They began with the reasonable assumption that each spouse's involvement in a range of activities and other people will make him or her more complex and interesting. In addition, because nobody can be all things to someone else, everyone needs a range of friends and experiences. As each partner explores outside the marriage, each is enriched and brings something new to the marriage. Furthermore, no relationship, no marriage, should imprison those within it.[19] In short, relationships should facilitate the growth of the people in them and ensure that a destructive and pathological dependence on the other does not develop. When growth is achieved, the O'Neills state, people do not need a sick possessiveness and will have healthier and much more satisfying relationships. The O'Neills talk about openness in education, culture, and work. But as we know, the public's response to the book was focused almost exclusively on the legitimation of unlimited sexual hedonism.

An open—in the sense of unconfining—mariage is desirable: no relationship, including marriage, should incarcerate people. Those who have a range of experiences, commitments, and relationships are better able to give up possessive dependence and are more likely to evolve a sense of confidence than those whose lives are restricted. But a sexually open marriage is very difficult to maintain because there are no limitations on the amount or kinds of intimacy with others. Compared with mate swapping, for example, open-marriage sex with others is much more likely to involve affection. Extrarelational sex based on caring has much greater power than purely recreational sex to destroy a marriage. It is much easier to give one's partner permission to engage in something not so threatening. To the extent that one needs monogamous love and loyalty, it is hard to participate in a lifestyle in which one's partner has an emotional and not solely sexual relationship with others. In the last few years many graduate students I know have tried this lifestyle. At first many of the women felt torn, since the men most often pressured them to try the arrangement. And, although suspicious and resistant, the women acceded because they were curious and because there was enormous peer pressure to demonstrate their radical chic, liberation, and independence. After they had tried it, I heard from them that open marriage has been found wanting. They found that neither they nor their partner could live together or be married while one or both had a "meaningful relationship" with someone else. Except for its openness, an open marriage is a love affair.

Having an affair is the classical form of extramarital sex and is traditionally kept secret. Here the objective is to experience the crescendos of romantic passion. Affairs—intimate, secret, passionate, and delicious—are probably more threatening to established relationships than any other arrangement for extrarelational sex. A successful affair assures that one is still lovable; a discovered affair informs one's partner that there may be something seriously wrong. Affairs are the most individual and the most passionate of the sexual arrangements. Recognizing that this classic form is potentially the most destructive to long-term relationships, contemporary experiments try to dilute the significance of the sex by making the arrangement open or mutual or limited.

The more the novel arrangement is limited to sex, the less threatening and fulfilling it is. The more affection there is in the new relationship, the more gratifying it is and the more it menaces the old relationship.

When author Linda Wolfe first started studying affairs, she found that they were usually started by women who had important needs that were not being met in their marriage, but who wanted to save their marriages. These women believed that the affair would satisfy their unmet needs and thus enable them to remain satisfied in the marriage.[20] (This is a traditional pattern, especially for men, in European countries with low divorce rates, such as Italy and France.) But what happened most frequently was that the affair ended or the marriage broke up. It is not clear whether a poor marriage led to an affair which hastened divorce, or whether the affair supplanted the marriage in affection and importance and caused the divorce.[21] Since we have no tradition of affairs entered into casually, such arrangements are so powerful a destabilizing force that both relationships can usually not be sustained. Few of us will not feel betrayed and shattered when someone we are sexually and emotionally intimate with is sexually and emotionally intimate with someone else. Raised with the ideal of fidelity, we find it very hard not to be sexually and emotionally possessive.

Sex and Commitment

When sex was dirty and a rather scarce resource we never made the mistake of thinking it was emotionally neutral. When females participate in sex because of ideas about recreational sex or because sex is sanctioned by the time or movement, they are vulnerable because they underestimate its impact. They seem surprised and angry to discover that they may feel dishonored, may irrationally not protect themselves with contraception, may be afraid the male will leave—just as the male may be shocked by his possessiveness and his jealousy. For most of us, issues of self-esteem increase when a relationship is sexual.

In contrast with the current idea that we can all enjoy a variety of sexual engagements without mutual emotional commitment, there does not seem to have been much of a change in women's traditional value of wanting sex as part of a romance. And, in contrast with the new ideology of sexual license, the major real change has been men's increasing engagement in sex within a relationship of commitment. While detached sex is extremely visible in the media, the largest real change is that more unmarried people, at increasingly younger ages, are having sexual relationships because they are intimate in other ways. To the extent that that is true, sex is still embedded within a significant emotional context.

While new sexual values obviously express the rise of hedonism, they also reflect sexism. The stereotypic male pattern of sex without involvement, passion without possession, has become the hallmark of sexual liberation. Paradoxically, the most significant change is that young men have become sensitive to their needs for affection, their need to feel loved and esteemed within a relationship. More publicity surrounds women's adoption of traditionally male values; but more change involves men's adoption of women's traditional values about sex.[21]

While we have become enormously sensitive to the limitations of monogamy and its confinement of emotional and sexual experience, most of us are still plagued by old values and old vulnerabilities. Very few of us never worry about whether we are lovable or sexually desirable. Few of us are free of insecurities about whether our partner will leave us, perhaps for another. Most of us need to sense that we are unique and irreplaceable, at least to one other person. Most of us are prone to jealousy, because very few of us are really autonomous. Our vulnerability is greatest when a relationship is important to us, and in our culture relationships become more important when they are sexual.

Having become aware of limitations on all our experiences, we are trying to increase the range of our sexual experiences and preserve our core relationships. Such attempts aim to defuse sex and to isolate it from significant emotions by limiting it to episodic physical encounters or by making extrarelational sex open and available to both partners. However, our psychological vulnerability makes these experiments unlikely to succeed so that neither partner would feel injured and the core relationship would remain intact.

An anonymous student wrote in an unpublished sketch in 1976:

> A self-first hedonism combined with experience for experience's own sake for me and for my wife brought an anxiety and heretofore existential chagrin to the dilemmas of adultery, jealousy and revenge which had accompanied marriage since day one. We deluded ourselves in expecting mutual acceptance and support "of what I want, if you truly love me," of our limitless style of undenied sensuality. A vicious circle of love-seeking and separation, of anxiety and extended periods apart led finally to divorce. A series of three-day, three-week, three-month affairs had led me to a painful skepticism about the longevity of relationships. This cynicism fed the proclivity to engage in further brief, intense, illusory sensual affairs; while with friends a common topic of concern became the need for stability in relationships.

How can most people not feel lessened, insecure, competitive, and possessive when they see their partners achieving important gratifications with others? How many of us can avoid thinking that our partners are unfaithful because we are inadequate?

Of course, openness and involvement with others can occur in work, leisure, community involvement, or friendship. When our partners get involved in such nonsexual relationships we may feel ignored or annoyed—but we are not likely to feel devastated. It is a testimony to the power of sex that when the outside involvement is emotional and sexual, the possibility that we feel eviscerated or betrayed is increased. If sex were less potent and sexual relationships less ego involving, it would be much easier for us to engage simultaneously in long-term, trusting relationships and in other sexual ones as well.

Behavior is easier to change than emotion, which is not so easily legislated by logic. Reason may tell us that sex has no particular significance, that that two people can never be all things to each other, that monogamy is an arbitrary and outmoded rule, or that no one has the right to limit another's experiences. But most of us want to feel that we have the monogamous affection of those whom we love sexually. A monogamous commitment is a sign that our love is really reciprocated.

Today for those who are able to experiment, the issue is not so much sexual possessiveness as our anxiety about the loss of emotional commitment. In spite of the current assertion that commitment need not be exclusive and that love is infinitely expansive, our experience (in dating for example) is that when our partner loves another, we are loved less. It is possible, but rare, for very mature and confident people to feel little anxiety when their partner is significantly involved with someone else.

If a couple bases a relationship on mutual commitment and maintains it because it enhances their self-esteem, if partners trust each other and exchange commitment for emotional support, then certainty will be greater than uncertainty. I think that marital attempts to defuse sex of significance generally do not succeed, because uncertainty and thus jealousy and possessiveness threaten the marriage. I do not think that we can ask marriage, which must be a stable relationship extending commitment into the infinite future, to provide the passions and exhilaration of a new one. Uncertainty in marriage is more likely to lead to anxiety, not to exhilaration.

Most of us covet freedom and excitement. But most of us settle for a commitment in which we can drop our public masks. We need someone we can trust, someone who will respond to our various needs and moods and succor us when that is what we need. In spite of the divorce rate, commitment, especially in marriage, lets us belong somewhere. And since most of us cannot give our partners sexual freedom and still be certain of their emotional commitment, the advantages of marriage usually require us to give up the exhilarating kicks of sexual novelty. Even in the cynical seventies long-term relationships, especially marriage, remain a major existential anchor.

Marriage:
New Traditions

6

Judging from the media, the bell is
tolling. Marriage is dead. We hear that the burial should take place so
that we can get on with new kinds of relationships which will work. In
sharp contrast with this funereal perspective, a higher percentage
marry in the United States than in most other countries. While the rate
of marriage declined from 11.0 per 1000 people in 1972 to 9.9 in 1976,
the rate is still generally higher than it was during the 1960s.[1] In 1976
there were 2,133,000 marriages. From 1970–1976 there were 15,404,-
000 marriages.[2] In 1976 1.3 million people said that they were living
with someone while unmarried. That figure is large in comparison with
the 34,000 people living together in 1960, but it is dwarfed by the
88,000,000 who were living together in marriage that year.[3]

While we are marrying we are also divorcing. The rate of divorce
is increasing faster than the rate of marriage. From 1968 to 1973 our
divorce rate increased by 50 percent, and it is continuing to climb.[4] A
century ago there was 1 divorce for every 1234 marriages; at the beginning of this century it was 1 per 500, in 1920 1 in 20, 1 in 6 by 1940,
and today 1 in 3.[5]

What do these numbers mean? While the marriage rate is high, the
divorce rate is startling, because it is much higher than it has ever been
in our history and it is continuing to rise. Is it time for the funeral? Or
is it more accurate to say that the increase in divorce is the result of
more liberal laws in a more liberal social climate in which divorce is
acceptable and obtainable because one is not satisfied with a spouse and
wants to try again with someone else? Both answers are true, but not
equally.

While we do not have good data on why some divorced people do
not remarry, it is reasonable to assume that many of them stay single
by choice. Some are unwilling to make another marital commitment
because their experience tells them that marriage is unworkable for
them, and they are unwilling to risk the agonies of another separation

and divorce. For these people—whose number is probably increasing simply as the number of divorced persons increases—marriage may be dead. But the evidence says that theirs is a minority position.

The great majority of divorced people—about 75 percent of the women and 80 percent of the men—remarry.[6] Between 1970 and 1973 the remarriage rate climbed by 40 percent.[7] Actually, the rate of remarriage by divorced persons is higher than the marriage rate of single persons. Today, one-fourth of those who marry are remarrying.[8]

Our marriage rate, like the maternity rate, rose from a low of 73 per 1000 single women in 1930 to its highest peak of 150 per year after World War II, when about 90 percent of American adults had married at least once. This means that the norm was so coercive that there was little option about whether to marry. When I ask people who married in the 1950s and 1960s why they married, they are usually startled. We did not ask that question in the way that we do now. We married because everyone did. The question was not, Why? The question was, Who?

The divorce rate not only reflects our new criteria for success in a marriage but also demonstrates that a single lifestyle is never best for everyone. In this sense, the high divorce rate is an adjustment to our former marriage percentages of approximately 100 per 1000 single women.[9] But even beyond any normalization, the rate of divorce is higher than ever. The break-up of a marriage is very visible; many have experienced a wave of divorce in their own circles. Remaining single has become more acceptable, even chic, among some groups. Still, the marriage and remarriage rates are very high. Since a choice exists today, the question is, Why do people marry? What do they expect to gain that will be greater than the costs? Is being married different from living together?

Why Marry?

A friend in his late thirties who was bitterly divorced about five years ago finds his emotional relationships are inexplicably confusing. He is successful in work and has no hang-ups about career women. He enjoys their feminist stance, delights in their equal competence, and agrees that their ambitions and freedom take priority. His relationships with such women usually have a honeymoon period, in which he is convinced that he has found a perfect new partner because the sex and the talking and the being together are all good and she is as firm as he is about never marrying. Her position is clear from what she says, from her work involvement, and from the fact that she is very attractive, at least 30, and has chosen not to marry. The relationship progresses and he is shocked, every time, when she says that while she does not want to get married, she would like some sign that he loves her as much as she loves him, so they ought to agree not to see anyone else. He usually agrees. But he is never prepared when she later says, "Since nothing would change if we were married, why don't we?"

Wanting to maximize his pleasure, unwilling to restrict his life, and needing to protect himself from his own vulnerabilities, my friend wants to believe that these women are equally motivated by independence and freedom. He prefers (or needs) to ignore how new our idea is that being single is desirable, how thinly it is overlaid on the older assumption which we all learned that being married is better.

Why do people marry? We can answer that question in different ways, on different levels. The simplest explanation is that basic social change takes time, and since the overwhelming majority of Americans have married, marriage is "normal." In the 1974 Roper poll for Virginia Slims, 90 percent of the women and 92 percent of the men said that marriage was the preferred way to live. Only 1 percent wanted to remain single and live alone, 1 percent wanted to live in a commune, 1 percent of the women and 3 percent of the men wanted to live with someone of the opposite sex without marrying, and less than 1 percent preferred to live with someone of the same sex. Why marry? The reason remains romantic; 83 percent of the women and 77 percent of the men believed that love is the primary reason to marry. The great majority of Americans continue to put a happy home life at the top of their list of goals.[10]

Equally obvious, we organize our social lives in terms of couples, and we still tend to assume that normal people marry and neurotics and losers do not. In spite of the divorce rate the belief prevails that people are happier when married. Some marry for sex, some because they are lonely, some because marriage is an important symbol of adulthood or a way to get out of your parents' house.

But many of these gains can be gotten without the formal, legal arrangement of marriage, especially when it has become increasingly acceptable to live together. Clearly, people can be happy with a partner without being married. Why is there still a preference for the formal union?

Marriage is a sexual, economic, and usually procreative union which is assumed to be permanent, is signified by ceremony, and involves the larger social fabric of the law and the blood ties of two families. Because the commitment is public and presumably permanent, marriage establishes to a large extent who we are and with whom we belong. The legal contract underlines the seriousness of the relationship and makes ending the relationship more difficult. Entered into voluntarily, marriage is a concrete symbol that the commitment is really mutual.

Like friendship, marriage gives us the sense that another person cares. In marriage we can feel unique; we can know that we are crucially important to the happiness of the other. In marriage, as in friendship, we hope and expect that the intimacy we give will not result in betrayal, that is, in an attack in the areas in which we are most vulnerable. Not that we will never attack or be attacked—rather, there is a line, not necessarily verbalized, beyond which neither spouse will go. In this relationship some weapons will not be used.

This commitment, secured by its legality, is one in which partners can usually be honest and experiment and grow, and can sometimes be dependent, unpleasant, or sick. A spouse is the person to trust, who will ask help and give help in return. As long as the marriage exists a spouse is like a blood relation of mutual choice. A spouse is forever.

Of course, few people marry to gain a partner who will help cope with the future crises in life; most Americans, myself included, marry for romantic reasons, for love and passion and possession. Today, for perhaps half the younger population, love and passion do not require marriage and thus are not unique to marriage. In fact, ecstatic love is ill served by marriage insofar as romance, in the fantasy sense, tends not to survive repetitive and confining responsibilities.

I think the most crucial implication of the legality of marriage is that one theoretically enters this contractual relationship for a time which extends into the future. Marriage creates a specific identity and commitment forever. In spite of the divorce rate, the legal permanence of marriage increases the psychological sense that marriage is a primary existential anchor.

While marriage can provide these gains it may not. Some believe that it cannot. The institution has come under vigorous attack. People who espouse general sexual liberation, self-actualization, humanism, socialism, or some forms of feminism have denounced marriage and the traditional nuclear family as sick, oppressive, patriarchal, sexist, bourgeois,[11] "a form of emotional and sexual malnutrition," and a "condition of sexual deprivation."[12] Angrier feminists call for the end of the nuclear family, which they see as based on patriarchal inequities so that the husband's freedom and power assure permanent inequalities. Some think marriage is a sick relationship because it involves possession, and "owning" someone is intolerable. Some reject marriage because it traditionally calls for sexual monogamy, and they believe happiness would require illicit sexual variety. Those who are looking for humanistic self-actualization reject marriage as a commitment which forecloses choice and tends toward habituation. And some, very simply, think it is ridiculous for people to say that they will stay together for an endless future when both will change in unimaginable ways.

In the rhetoric of social change, values are more easily reversed than modified; in anger, extremes sound better than compromises. When traditional values are reversed, the assumption of permanence is replaced with the ground rule that the spouses will remain married only as long as it feels good; sexual monogamy is replaced with sexual variety; the child-centered family gives way to the childless family or, where there are children, to a lifestyle in which the focus is on the adults' needs. For some, whether or not to marry, have an open marriage, cohabit, live in a group marriage, or join a commune has become a political question.

Feminism and Marriage

Gestalt therapist Miriam Polster asked a group of women to close their eyes and imagine what their lives would be like if they were men. One of the women said that she imagined that "she had started walking through her house from one of the back bedrooms, all the way through the house, and how, as she walked through each of the rooms, she hadn't picked up a single toy or piece of clothing or newspaper, she hadn't closed a single drawer or closet door, she hadn't turned out a single light or mopped up a single spill, and finally she had just walked straight through the house and out the front door, closing the door behind her."[13]

Whether radical or mainstream, the feminist analysis of traditional marriage emphasizes the very real costs to women of their time-draining and unappreciated responsibilities.[14] Feminists have made very clear the enormous danger to women's own identity and self-esteem when their sense of self comes from relating to others and supporting others' efforts at the cost of their own development of independence and a sense of competence.

A significant sector within feminism adamantly claim that marriage profits the male but costs the female so that husbands become happier and healthier while wives become sickly, neurotic, and suicidal. Jessie Bernard describes wives as unhappy, frustrated, anxious, passive, and depressed because they have learned that being feminine is being dependent, that their role in marriage is to take care of the trivialities of life, and that their responsibility is to adapt to their husbands' expectations and their children's needs.[15] This is an image of frustration and powerlessness. It is a portrait of wives always vulnerable because they may be abandoned, forever fearful that their husbands may stop loving them or giving them money, passive because anger risks alienation, submissive because of fear, and helpless and hapless because initiating and making decisions is the province of the husband. This is a description of life in which direction and outcome are decided by someone else, of ambition and autonomy lost and followed by inevitable depression. Sally Kempton has described it vividly:

> Things rested there until, in the third year of our marriage, we went to live in Los Angeles because of my husband's work. During the year we spent away from home I found that I could not work, and that he was always working, and we suddenly found ourselves frozen into the textbook attitudes of male–female opposition. We fought continually, and always about the same things. He accused me of making it impossible for him to work, I accused him of keeping me dangling, dependent upon him for all emotional sustenance, he accused me of spending too much money and of keeping the house badly, I accused him of expecting me continually to subordinate my needs to his. The difficulty, I realized over and over again without being able to do much about it, was that I had gotten myself into the classic housewife's position: I was living in a place I didn't want to be, and seeing people I didn't like because that was where my man was, I was living my husband's life and I hated him for it. And the reason this was so was that I was economically dependent upon him; having ceased to earn my living I could no longer claim the bread-winner's right to attention for my special needs.
>
> My husband told me that I was grown up now, twenty-six years old, there were certain realities which I had to face. He was the head of the household: I had never questioned that. He had to fulfill himself: I had never questioned that. He housed and fed me and paid for my clothes, he respected my opinions and refused all his opportunities to make love to other women, and my part of the bargain should have become clear to me by now. In exchange for those things, I was supposed to keep his house and save his money and understand that if he worked sixteen hours a day for a year it was not more than necessary for his self-fulfillment. Which was all quite true. Except that it was also necessary for his fulfillment that I should be there for those few hours when he had time for me, and not complain about the hours when he did not, and that I should adapt myself to his situation or else end the marriage. It never occurred to him to consider adapting himself to mine, and it never occurred to me. I only knew his situation was bad for me, was alien, was in fact totally paralyzing, that it kept me from working, that it made me more unhappy than I had been in my life.
>
> I knew that I was being selfish. But he was being selfish also, the only difference being that his selfishness was somehow all right, while mine was inexcusable. Selfishness was a privilege I had earned for a while by being a writer, that is, a person who had by male standards a worthwhile place

to spend her time. As soon as I stopped functioning as a writer I became
to my husband and to everyone else a mere woman, somebody whose time
was valueless, somebody who had no excuse for a selfish preoccupation
with her own wants.[16]

Before World War II men had higher rates of mental illness than
women did, but that changed after the war when the rates for married
women rose.[17] Married women now have higher rates of mental illness
than do married men. In contrast, when single women are compared
with single men, widowed women with widowed men, and divorced
women with divorced men, women in these unmarried categories tend
to have lower rates of mental illness than men do.[18] Information on
suicide is consistent with the statistics of mental illness. In the decade
between 1952–1953 and 1962–1963, the suicide rate increased by 10
percent for American white men, for white women by 49 percent, for
nonwhite men by 33 percent, and for nonwhite women by 80 percent.
There was a similar trend in Austria, Sweden, West Germany, France,
Australia, Belgium, England, Wales, Canada, and Italy, but the rate was
significantly lower than the American figures, averaging a 17.9 percent
increase in suicide for women and a 1.7 percent increase for men.[19]

One interpretation of these significant increases in indices of stress
is that the coercive norms of marriage and maternity developed after
the war resulted in an increased percentage of women having to live
in a role they found enormously frustrating.[20]

On the other hand, writer George Gilder, in *Sexual Suicide*, coun-
ters these numbers with others: 60 percent of women with children
believe that wives have it "easier than their husbands"; married women
live longer than their husbands or single women; and 44 percent of
women who were single reported that they were happy, which is much
less than the 70 percent among those who were married.[21] Roper found
that only 2 percent of women interviewed would choose a career over
marriage and motherhood; 38 percent were willing to give up a career
but not the traditional roles; 52 percent wanted to combine marriage,
children, and a career; and 64 percent expressed a strong opinion that
"having a loving husband who is able to take care of me is more important than making it on my own."[22]

I don't think there is much point in debating whether being married or being a parent is more crucial, more satisfying, or more frustrating for women or for men. Whether the family roles of women and men
make them happy or frustrated, satisfied or confined, should not be
asked and cannot be answered by the choice of one gender or the other.
The important question is, Who are the people whose lives have enabled them or frustrated them in achieving goals important to them?

One is frustrated, angry, and depressed when one has not been able to become the sort of person that he or she expects or needs to become.

In a major study of how people feel about the quality of their lives, Angus Campbell found few differences in how satisfied or dissatisfied women and men were.[23] But a look at smaller, specific groups shows important differences between the sexes. Gender, age, level of education, marital status, number of children, age of children—all affect a person's degree of satisfaction.

Campbell found that Americans who are married say that they are happier than those who are not. All of the married people, of both sexes, with and without children, described their lives as more satisfying than did people who were single, widowed, or divorced. (Of course, the responses of a group tell us little about individuals who are miserable while married or ecstatic while single.) "It appears that marriage is still considered a woman's greatest achievement, and when she marries, the sigh of relief is almost audible."[24] Newly married wives were the most euphoric; while young husbands were also happy, they were simultaneously aware that they had taken on big responsibilities.

Alas, the brides' euphoria ended with the birth of the first child, after which the happiness and satisfaction of both spouses stabilized at an average level and did not rise significantly until the children reached 18. Mothers of young children, most of whom were between 25 and 34, were the most stressed and pressured. They were more likely than anyone else to say that they felt tied down, wondered whether they really wanted to be married, and sometimes wished they were child-free. Not that the couples did not want children—most couples were happy when their children were born but were unprepared for the economic and psychological burdens and thus the marital strain that child care provoked. Childless husbands over 30 and fathers of children older than 17 reported the highest level of satisfaction with life and the least pressure. In line with the increasing belief that a good marriage does not have to include children, Campbell found that wives over 30 who were childless were not as happy as their husbands, but were about as satisfied as women of their own age who had children. The childless women's lives were described as no less successful but with fewer emotional rewards. This finding is logical in that children are an extraordinary emotional resource, even though we know from experience as well as many studies that the birth of children is also accompanied by a decline in intimacy, communication, mutuality, and affection between spouses and thus a decline in general happiness, especially in the children's preschool years.[25]

Campbell also found that those whose spouses had died were more content than were people who were divorced or had never married.

While being divorced is certainly preferable to remaining in an un-happy marriage, divorced men and especially women were miserable. Divorced women were the least satisfied with their lives of any group, Campbell found. They were also the most stressed and pressured. Di-vorced men were not glowing with happiness either, but they felt less pressure, less awareness of life's difficulty, than divorced women did. In a word, divorced women were despondent.

In contrast with the rhetoric that divorce is a growth experience, that singleness swings and marriage oppresses, married people are more satisfied with their lives than are other people. The data of P. S. Sears[26] and E. Spreitzer[27] agree with Campbell's. Married women—whether or not they have children—are most satisfied with their lives and then in declining order come the widowed, those who remain single, and the divorced.

When one looks at how satisfied women are with their work life rather than life in general, education and not marriage is the crucial factor. (In Sears's data, single women were the most satisfied with their work patterns, followed by married women without children, married women with children, and finally, widows. Single women had gone farther in school and had achieved higher professional levels at work than the other groups.) Employment is not crucial to the satisfaction of married women who do not have a college degree. These women are likely to have a job rather than a career and to be less ambitious or less ego involved in their employment. Women with college degrees, on the other hand, are less happy or satisfied if they are not employed. Obvi-ously, employment is far more crucial to the satisfaction or frustration of people who are prepared to do high-status and fulfilling work. The latter women are likely to ask what opportunities and choices marriage and motherhood have forced them to give up.

That not every woman finds bliss in marriage and maternity is not surprising. What is surprising is evidence in direct opposition to our image of women as enormously dependent upon marriage for any feel-ing of esteem, while we think men reluctantly, even grievously, give up delicious bachelorhood to become shackled husbands. There are data which says that single women are happier than single men, and that women get along much better without a spouse than do men. Gove[28] found that men who never married have higher rates of mental illness than women who remained single; Gilder has compiled a vast array of statistics which say that unless men marry they are doomed to a Hobbe-sian nasty, brutal, short, and unhappy life.

Gilder says that singleness correlates better with poverty than does race. Married men earn twice as much as single people of either sex, and single men earn about the same as single women of the same age.[29] Single men are 22 times more likely to be committed for mental problems than are married men and are 10 times as likely to have chronic emotional problems.* Single men have high suicide rates. Single men commit 60 percent of the crimes. Interestingly, Gilder finds that men who are divorced or widowed tend to revert to the status of single men. Further, divorced upper-class males fare as badly as do those lower in the social structure. In spite of studies in which divorced women describe themselves as more stressed and unhappy than do divorced men, statistics indicate that divorced men have more psychological and physical problems and a death rate three and a half times greater than divorced women.

Can we make sense of the charges and counter-charges, of the contradictory numbers and percentages and categories in different studies, and determine which sex is better off in marriage? I think that what the data imply is that being confined only to the marital role is stressful for a significant number of women and being confined only to the achieving role is stressful for a significant number of men. Marrying, having children, and providing for a family can be a significant source of self-esteem and feelings of masculinity—just as marrying and having children can be a significant source of self-esteem and feelings of femininity. We have idealized and overestimated the gratifications possible for women from their traditional roles; we have underestimated these gratifications for men. Men without family, without marriage, tend to experience that not as freedom but as the absence of a crucial existential anchor. Indeed, Gilder's statistics imply that without a family many men are less able to succeed in work.

In a study I did of successful men I was startled by the importance their family had for them.[30] While a crisis at work became a goad to greater effort, a crisis in their marriage led to despair and sometimes to psychotherapy. I was equally struck by how easily these men seemed to transfer loyalty and affection from the first to the second wife, and especially to the second wife's children from her former marriage. The existence of the family seemed crucial, but who played the roles of wife

*An obvious selectivity factor is involved here, since it is likely that men with severe and chronic mental problems are unable to cope with the requirements of the male role, especially the support of a family. That is, one would expect a low rate of marriage or of marital durability for unstable people, and this is likely to be more true for men than women (since women's role in marriage can be more passive and demand less coping than men's role in employment). In addition to any selection factor, Gilder's data supports the idea that being in a marital relationship has an effect, since men who lose their spouses come to be more like men who have never married.

and child was much less important; the players were relatively inter-changeable. These men generally married traditional women who created a haven, literally and psychologically freeing the men to put most of their energies into work. If the family was destroyed through divorce, these men married another essentially traditional woman and the family was rebuilt with new players.

Dual-Career Marriages

Many wives face considerable psychological danger if they do not have important interests outside their family. It has become a psychological as well as a feminist cliché to observe that a wife who depends on her husband to give her a sense that she is a participant in the world outside the home, or who bases a large part of her identity on him and his work, has a bad life strategy. Some have called for the end of marriage and glorified the single state or waxed euphoric about lesbian relations or all-female communes. But the majority of feminists and a large sector of the general public (especially those with an education) have contin-ued to want to marry, insisting on a much more egalitarian partnership. While solutions to women's frustration or depression did not have to lie in women's modeling themselves on middle-class men, and these males' focus on career success, of course, that is what happened. The change occurred partly because of sexist attitudes and partly because inequity can be resolved fastest by behaving identically. That is, the swiftest or the most obvious way for educated women to achieve parity in mar-riage is for both spouses to have equal responsibilities within the family, allowing both to achieve equally in work. The most psychologically significant as well as widespread change in marriage has been the in-crease in dual-career marriages. And, as usual when fundamental changes occur, we have popularly exaggerated the gratifications and ignored the stresses in these new kinds of relationships.

In a training session for women in management I was confronted by a woman who had a very successful career but found herself bewil-dered and scared and was not sure why. She was a vice-president of a large bank. Every morning she left for the office with her attaché case filled with work she had brought home the night before; she worked hard and earned double what her husband did. She noticed that she had taken to going to a bar with some people from the office before going home, she said. Her husband, a professor of psychology, had irregular hours and worked a good deal at home. As a result he did most of the cleaning, shopping, and cooking. Recently they had both become alarmed as they realized he had begun to watch a lot of daytime television. Their lives were close enough to a reversal of the traditional gender roles that in spite of their liberal self-awareness and values, and despite their genuine commitment to the belief that individual skills, not gender, should determine what they would do, traditional ideas about normal femininity and masculinity intruded.

An ideological commitment to new values based on equality and individualism falters before the fact that one partner has a better job and earns more money—and much more stress occurs when the wife is more successful. Simply because dual-career marriage and its values are new, those within such marriages have also learned traditional attitudes and inevitably have some traditional expectations.

While traditional ideas about roles in marriage still remain common, there has been a predictable major shift among the young and educated toward the dual-career marriage, in which the responsibilities, freedom, and power of the spouses are equal. Roper found that 61 percent of women under 30 and 65 percent of those who had been to college preferred what is essentially a dual-career marriage.[31] Given these values, millions of educated women, and an inflationary economy, we can predict that marriages in which both adults pursue careers will become increasingly common. The obvious consequence will be that women who want to pursue success in work can. It is crassly unhealthy for any marriage when one spouse is free to pursue his or her own needs and objectives and the other cannot. Traditional marriage patterns are no longer functional for a large group of women. Dual-career marriages are based on the idea that no one has the right to limit someone else's development or accomplishments. These unions are relationships between equals in which, in addition to love and affection, there is respect. The basis of the mutual respect is the wife's clear perception that her husband is secure enough not to let her success threaten his self-esteem, while the husband clearly sees that his wife can accomplish in the ways that our society, and men especially, esteem most.

While solving some problems, the dual-career marriage may encounter or create others. The new social pressure on women for individual achievement can cause stress among those who have achieved status by marrying occupationally successful men. Many of these women would lose instead of gain status if they went to work. Many physicians' wives, for example have been trained as nurses, teachers, and secretaries. Since being a physician is a very high-status occupation and the professions dominated by women are not, these wives would find it very difficult to increase their status by entering the labor force.

A more subtle problem is that as women become more preoccupied with their own ambition and more heavily involved in their work, they may become less willing to keep being the partner who has

the major responsibility for the emotional needs of both partners. At a
behavioral level this may simply mean that women involved in their
own accomplishments will have neither time nor energy to listen sensitively and empathically to woe. These women may come to behave like
the familiar male figure who slogs or battles his way through a day at
the office, pecks his wife on the cheek as he returns home, calls out a
routine greeting to the kids, and hastens to his private corner to be left
alone with a drink and a newspaper. At a psychological level, in the
same way that many women achieved success vicariously through their
husband, many men have depended on women not only to help them
express their feelings but also have needed their wife's emotionality in
order to vicariously feel their own emotions.[32] One of the hardest problems I remember when my children were young was that as soon as I
returned from work and entered the door they came running for hugs
and kisses and stories and wanted to tell me all about their day. They
knew what a mommy was and so did I. Tired and still preoccupied with
what I had been doing, I tried to attend to my children, but was not
spontaneous. A work-preoccupied, self-centered lifestyle makes it
harder to be emotionally giving and sensitive to the needs of others.

Dual-career marriages generate problems because we do not know
the rules yet. Some people have tried to solve this by writing marriage
contracts in which obligations are spelled out. Each spouse, for example, is responsible for cooking every other day and the other is responsible for cleaning up that day. While it might prevent small issues from
becoming big battles, such a contract really suggests a lack of trust in
one's spouse. Basically, a contract tries to establish rules in a form of
marriage where the norms have not yet been established. Those who
write specific and very detailed contracts seem afraid of spontaneous
compromise, because they fear that they will revert to more traditional
patterns. In my experience, they are probably right.

Of the couples I know, most who have successful dual-career marriages show the following pattern. Both spouses are professionals and
live in a community where women's commitment to a career is widespread and normal. When the couple married, both knew and accepted
the wife's ambition and ability. Couples with small children frequently
have full-time help. The fathers are active in taking care of the children,
although the mothers have accepted more of that responsibility, often
cutting back to halftime at work. Although they live at a two-income
level, the husband generally earns more money, and there is an underlying feeling that the wife has a choice about whether or not she works.
Many tasks are shared equally and tend to be done by whoever has the
time or skill to do them; if problems that seem inequitable arise, the
help of older children or outsiders is enlisted, so that an ideological

confrontation is avoided. When the rules of obligation are not clear, couples tend to compromise, so that the most important objectives are gained while some traditional vestiges remain; or they try to specify who owes what to whom in advance. The latter method does not seem to me likely to work successfully for very long because it superimposes a rigid structure on the spontaneous happenings of life.

The most fundamental problems of the dual-career marriage emerge because commitment to a career is a very energy-depleting, self-centered endeavor. It is common for the spouses to complain that they see too little of each other, but basically work priorities threaten intimacy. I find it interesting and revealing that couples in such relationships are often glib about the effects upon their children, but generally avoid any discussion of the effects upon their relationship with their spouse. While it is generally better for both spouses to be able to do what is important to them, no lifestyle is perfect. If the pursuit and achievement of self-fulfillment through a career diminishes a spouse's sensitivity to and intimacy with the other, something has clearly been lost.

Dual-career marriages seem to be open marriages, not sexually, but in the sense that both spouses lead complex independent as well as interdependent lives. Risk taking is done with work, not with interpersonal relations. Most dual-career couples seem unwilling to jeopardize their sense of security, which is centered in the marriage. Like the successful men I studied, they avoid intimacies that would add stress. These relationships seem generally low key in that the couple are affectionate and concerned with supporting and helping each other; they are not preoccupied with hedonistic kicks or sex. In general the spouses appear to have nontraditional work arrangements and traditional attitudes about sex. While they are revolutionaries in some aspects of marital change, those in dual-career marriages are unsurprisingly conservative in others.[33]

Dual-Career Marriages and Identical Roles

We do not know whether egalitarianism in the form of identical roles for women and men is possible or desirable. Only three characteristics seem to be universally true of relations between the sexes across cultures.

First, all societies recognize significant sex differences and pattern them elaborately, although the specific tasks or personality qualities assigned to either sex vary considerably.[34] Stated slightly differently, in marriage there is always a division of labor.[35] When certain tasks are assigned to one sex and prohibited to the other, the partners are competent in different things and thus are not in competition. Moreover, when partners have different and therefore complementary responsibilities, they are dependent upon each other. Mutual dependence encourages stability in the relationship.

The second universal pattern is that societies have tasks for men that are prohibited to women, define masculinity as accomplishments achieved in competition with men, and thus strongly underline the differentiation that men are not women. Masculinity is thus achieved by doing whatever men in the society do, by doing it well in comparison with other men, by doing or being whatever that society has allocated to men and prohibited to women. This often begins with a male initiation rite around puberty. The initiation marks the boy's entrance into the company of men. There is a long period of preparation, often some form of physical ordeal, always some difficult accomplishment to be achieved—and that accomplishment is reserved for males. One of the chief functions of the puberty rite is the ceremonial and psychological symbolization that a boy has loosened his ties to his mother, has forged closer bonds with men, has achieved something masculine, and will relate to women henceforward as a man. Male initiation rites are common, while female rites are rare. The first menstruation is sometimes cause for celebration, but the girl obviously does not have to accomplish anything to make it happen. This suggests that men need to construct some decisive event or achievement to signify adulthood, and women do not.

One explanation for the frequency of male rites is that men cannot create new life and give birth. Boys of a tribe are often ceremonially killed and reborn as the sons of the men of the tribe. A boy is changed ceremonially from a mother's to a father's son, so as to be born not of women but of men.[36] Masculinity is constructed as an accomplishment and most often has to be achieved, reachieved, and defended by success in competition. In contrast, the crucial achievement of femininity is often marriage and maternity, which may involve no competition and may need to be accomplished only once.

The third universal pattern reinforces the belief that male is different from female with the belief that male is better than female. In every society men compete against other men to gain the high-status roles and perform the high-status tasks. To put it another way, whatever men compete for are considered the most important accomplishments in the society. This has been described by Steven Goldberg[37] as the association of masculinity with authority and leadership outside of the family. In whatever ways a society defines authority, male dominance is reflected in the feeling that men rightly lead. Using data from 4000 cultures,

Goldberg found that the roles (and personality qualities) assigned to men are considered the most important or valuable, and men dominate the institutions that control society. While some societies give very high status to women's reproductive and maternal accomplishments and give women significant power over other women and children, Goldberg found that every society gives a higher status to male roles than to female maternal roles.

In societies that emphasize accomplishments outside the family and restrict the most powerful and prestigious areas to men, there is a high probability that men do not dominate within the family. In the United States we have a relatively low level of male dominance within the family and moderately high degree of male dominance in the political and economic spheres.

Studies of power in American marriages generally find that decision making is basically divided along the lines of instrumental or expressive responsibilities, with the former allocated to men and the latter to women. In addition, the spouse who has more resources—social status, occupation, income, education, or membership in organizations —tends to make more decisions or have more of a say in what is decided. The higher the husband ranks in comparison with other men, the more power he has and the greater the differential between the spouses; the more resources he commands in comparison with his wife, the more power he has.

The reverse is also true. The less status the husband has in comparison with other men, and the smaller the difference in resources between the spouses, the more power the wife has. Husbands in the United States do not have power simply because they are men. Instead, they have to justify their right to make decisions by virtue of their position, skills, or accomplishments in competition with other men and their wife. When wives perceive that they are equal because of equal education, equal status in work, or equal earnings, they have essentially identical resources and are prone to act as equals in making family decisions.[39]

The dual-career marriage is one in which both spouses are involved in high-status work, in which both are educated and command essentially identical levels of resources. In this relationship male–female distinctions and male dominance are minimized. Therefore, the success of this kind of marriage is probably influenced by how self-confident the husband is—whether he needs the traditional distinctions and greater power that affirm his sense of masculinity.

Psychologist L. Bailyn has found that dual-career marriages work when wives are educated as professionals and their husbands are moderately successful. When the husbands are preoccupied with succeeding in work or are not occupationally successful, the wives are not likely to be employed.[40] Men who are extremely involved in their work and preoccupied with achieving success are likely to make emotional and logistical demands that make it hard for the wife to work, especially at a professional level. What of men who are not successful? Two people who are equally trained and able to achieve are essentially in competition, although they may will that it were not so. Men who are not successful at work are more likely to need to dominate within their family. Insofar as their sense of masculinity has been undermined, they are likely to prefer that their wife not work because they could not cope with her success.

The husband is not alone in fearing his wife's greater success—she probably fears it too. Wives who feel equally powerful or perceive that they have more power than their husbands tend to feel unfeminine, to be dissatisfied in their marriages, and to place the blame for this unhappy state upon their husbands, whom they describe as weak and ineffectual. Despite any commitment to an ideology of equality, to the extent that women and men associate masculinity with strength and dominance, the man's sense of masculinity and the woman's sense of femininity are both endangered when women have equal (much less greater) power. While this situation can occur in work, the issue is much more crucial in the intimate relationship of marriage.

We know that a significant shift in values has occurred away from the traditional ones. We know that those with modern attitudes do not want to behave in accord with the values they have rejected. Yet a relationship between a woman and a man invokes the most basic issues of self-definition, gender, and normalcy; the closer they come to having identical roles or equal power, or the more they reverse the traditional because the wife has more power or status, the more anxious the partners are likely to feel.

Few of us are really free from conservative ideas of what is feminine and masculine. When our sense of masculinity or femininity is jeopardized, we will be scared and angry. If we have no relationship in which our sense of femininity or masculinity is specifically affirmed, then a vital part of our identity may be threatened.

Many people who are really oriented to achieving success seem to flourish in stable relationships. Because stability is increased when people realize that they depend on each other for some important things, I think that most Americans, including the ambitious, will continue to marry, and professional couples will continue to create dual-career marriages. While many responsibilities will no longer be divided according to traditional rules, there will still be some tasks in which the spouses' responsibilities are not the same. I also think that couples will continue to make some distinctions, which may be symbolic and subtle, in which the male is dominant.

As women and men engage in new roles and expand their range of personality styles, new definitions of femininity and masculinity are being formulated. But since the traditional sense of masculinity seems difficult to earn and easy to lose, and traditional femininity involves feelings based on a reciprocal interaction to what is masculine, I think that even self-conscious, liberal, egalitarian, dual-career marriages are very likely to have some elements of traditional male dominance. That is, in some aspects of their lives, the couple will have a preference or a sense that it feels better when they verge closer to the traditional so that the sense of femininity or masculinity is affirmed. In sex it might be a preference that the male initiate, lead, court. In other areas it might be the assumption that the husband has greater responsibility for managing their money, or a feeling that his career is a little more important. . . . The content is not as important as the form.

It is enough in this context to note that male dominance has been associated with the sense of masculinity and thus also of femininity; and because it has been the norm, we have all learned it. Those whose lives differ in important ways from gender-related traditions may need reassurance about their masculinity and femininity; such reassurance is likely to take the form of small but significant symbols of male dominance. I do not mean a boot in the nape of the neck or a metaphorical rape or a motorcycle machismo. I do mean some male initiative, some particular responsibility which conveys the message, "I am protecting you." These affirm the masculinity of the male and the femininity of the female and are therefore sexy. It is important not to let the words—"dominance" and "submission"—distort the image, because for those involved, the distinctions are much more likely to be subtle and pleasurable.

While women have always dominated and continue to dominate in certain family decision areas, this is not usually perceived as dominance insofar as women's traditional competencies are seen as nurturant and supportive. Male dominance, as used here, does not refer to oppressive power but to symbolic acts of caring, protecting, or leading, which affirm a man's masculinity in the traditional sense, and which please a woman because they speak directly to her sense of femininity in the traditional sense. This exchange need not occur in any other relationships; at work, for example, the woman might well find such gestures demeaning.

The most important change has occurred. The wife in a dual-career marriage has achieved significant power, is equal in the ways in which we gain status, and is a partner in the decisions a couple makes. It is too early to know whether we can have stable marriages without some areas of complementarity. We do not know whether we will ultimately be able to give up all gender-based distinctions. We do know, or we can logically assume, that in this transitional period, occupationally successful women are very likely to permit or want small symbols of male protectiveness. These become signs especially important when the wife's success is deviantly high or is in an atypical field, because gender deviance—one's own or one's spouse's—creates anxiety about one's normalcy. Thus, in some small ways the wife will protect the male's ego because his response will reinforce her sense of femininity. While it is marvelous to be respected and esteemed as an individual, it is also wonderful to sometimes reaffirm the specifically feminine and masculine in an intimate heterosexual relationship.

Divorce:
The Erosion
of Commitment

7

Many years ago, when we were graduate students, some of my friends were divorced after being married a few years. All have remarried and had children, and all have since stayed married. Until recently we thus had come to see marriage as stable and permanent. My divorce in 1977 was the first to startle our perceptions; since then—partly because divorced people seem to seek each other out, but primarily because of the current extraordinary frequency of divorce—perhaps one-half of my friends and acquaintances have divorced, are divorcing, or are thinking about it. A few years ago, divorce was a statistic; today, among more and more people I know, it has become a very real choice.

There were 1,077,000 divorces in the United States in 1976.[1] In 1974, there were 970,000, nearly double the 479,000 divorces in 1965.[2] Why has such a sharp increase occurred over 11 years? There are legal, social, and psychological reasons why the divorce rate is high and continuing to climb. Beginning with California in 1970, most states have passed or are considering no-fault divorce laws. Under a no-fault law, divorce is granted because of irreconcilable differences which have caused the marriage to break down. Neither spouse accuses or is accused, humiliates or is humiliated.

As divorce becomes more common, society modifies its previously strict attitudes about divorce and significantly reduces the social condemnation based on an absolute morality. The social pressures to remain within a marriage decline as the penalties for departure lessen. In the seventies, constraints against divorce have declined. The costs of marriage are described by some as extortionate. Alternative lifestyles, such as living together or remaining single, have become more acceptable. And for some people, the goal of a secure and stable family seems hopelessly old-fashioned and limiting. When the assumption that marriage must be permanent no longer holds and we see increasing numbers of people getting divorced, divorce becomes a real alternative, often the apparent solution to problems experienced in marriage.

Psychologically, our tolerance of frustration seems as low as our expectations are high. We want to be happy. Self-help books and gurus proliferate; happiness is supposed to be possible if only one finds the right way. But a goal of happiness is like something out of childhood—a mixture of wish fulfillment, a denial of responsibility and reality—all based on the immature perception that to wish and to do are the same, to want is to get. With a goal of happiness, compromise is not acceptable, so that the discrepancy between experience and expectation must be great.

The question is not whether goals of growth or happiness are achievable—sometimes they are but sometimes they are not. Unachievable expectations are partly a matter of semantics, the choice between a goal of happiness or a goal of satisfaction; "happiness" is a fantasy image which denies the constraints imposed by living. On the married and the unmarried alike, life imposes problems, routines, and compromises, because having to cope with repetitive work or school or family responsibilities is inevitable. Moreover, new criteria are emerging to determine when a relationship is good and so people's sensitivity to when it is not fulfilling has increased. Frustration is frequent when goals are unachievable; when expectations are enormously discrepant from reality, goals are unachievable.

The 1970s have been marked by a number of attitudes that, not surprisingly, increase the likelihood of divorce. We can predict a higher divorce rate when the criteria of success in marriage change from family integrity, security, and contentment to happiness in which people are to grasp opportunity and feel vital; when compromise is judged to be a sign of inadequacy; when "doing your thing" and "getting yours" are legitimized, so that relationships are continued only as long as they gratify one's own needs. The divorce rate rises when divorce is easy to obtain, marriage counselors assert that divorce is a growth experience, and parents decide that children are better off when an insufficiently satisfying relationship is ended. When the negative aspects of commitment are emphasized and the costs of dissolving the commitment are denied, when selfishness is idealized as autonomy and tolerance of frustration is no longer considered an inevitable part of reality, and moral responsibility is to the self rather than to the relationship, divorce increases. It receives further impetus when aging conjures the imperative of now-or-never and passion is superseded by habit; when lives have separated and interests diverged; when women, especially, tally the costs of traditional marriage; when happiness is seen as just a new partner away. All these factors establish unachievable criteria for what constitutes a successful long-term relationship, or they negate the idea that marriage is a necessary precondition for a fulfilling life. In either case, they make divorce more likely.

Five changes over the past decade seem especially important regarding our attitudes toward divorce. The individual can no longer assume that marriage will be permanent; one cannot assume sexual monogamy; one cannot assume that responsibilities will be allocated according to gender; one cannot assume that the traditional role responsibilities are all that will be required of either spouse; and one cannot assume that a stable partnership organized around economic survival, mutual trust, and the welfare of the children will meet one's own or one's spouse's criteria of a successful marriage.

The criteria of a successful relationship have changed from the accomplishment of known, specific tasks to feeling states, which are much harder to specify and achieve. Marital responsibilities have expanded beyond being a good provider or housekeeper and now include the provision of psychological assistance, sexual gratifications, and friendship.[3] Similarly, the criteria of a good marriage have expanded beyond mutual respect and trust to include stimulation and excitement. "Be your own person," we hear, or "realize your own potential"; become "whole" and "autonomous," we are told. "Grow!" This emphasis on individual development and gratification fosters objectives without clear-cut criteria. When, for example, has someone "grown" enough?

Commitment involves not only mutual feeling but also interdependent obligation. The sense of real obligation and the priority of responsibilities in marriage and child rearing have declined as spouses' relationships are being renegotiated because individual happiness has become so important. Not only has there been a shift toward goals of *self*-actualization but there has also been a loss of certainty of what an "adult" is and therefore what being an adult requires. We have lost the awareness that identity is affirmed and developed through meeting obligations and managing adult responsibilities. As psychologist Elizabeth Douvan points out, throughout history the older generation has declaimed the faults of the young because the young are too slow to grow up and become what the elders know adults are; but today the elders are no longer certain about what an adult is or whether it is good to be an adult.[4]

The clearest example of this trend may be the large number of young and some not-so-young people who "dropped out" in the 1960s as they tried to create lives that would be gratifying and purposeful.

They rejected the idea that being an adult means getting serious, making your mark, achieving career success, or getting married. They did not want to be "adult" if that meant becoming Establishment and leading an existentially deadening and inauthentic life. An "adult" was someone who had exchanged human potential for two cars in a suburban garage. Before the recession of 1973—which seems to have created a generation of college students scrambling for economic security and at least one car in the garage—parents, college professors, and other adults asked themselves the same questions. For a while they seemed to vacillate as, uncertain of their own values, they strove to understand those who condemned them for their phony, foolish lives.

In this period of dual careers and role transitions, people must reformulate their own obligations. At one level this is a seemingly superficial matter decided primarily by reality. Which person in a family can more conveniently take clothes to the dry cleaner? Who is better able to interrupt work and come home to take a child to the dentist? Who is closer to the food store on the way home? The issue is not solely rational because at one level doing these chores is understood as a symbolic statement that "I love you" or "I take care of you" or "I will help you because your welfare is important to me and you can count on me." Taking on responsibility is a behavioral statement that we have made a commitment to the relationship and to the people within it. By what we do, we signify that we care. An unwillingness to take on the obligations of shared responsibility means that we are unwilling to give up restrictions on our freedom. It signifies, in fact, that our commitment is conditional and self-centered.

Autonomy versus Commitment

While feminists emphasized the lack of *Me!* gratifications for women in their traditional roles, human potential therapists were less concerned with gender than with the costs to everyone of a habituated lifestyle of routinized responding. It seemed to them that people who remained within a relationship when it was clear that the relationship did not make them feel vital and happy were neurotically dependent. The costs of marriage or parenting were only a part of the general emphasis on individual growth to be achieved by giving up dependence on any crutch, whether a therapist or a spouse. Many feminists and therapists judged a need for security in a relationship as evidence of a lack of independence; furthermore, they believed that autonomy, not needing anyone else, was the hallmark of adult psychological health. The extension of this belief is ultimately a reversal of earlier values. Long-term marriages become suspect: Why are the people in them content when their lives are so predictable? Why do they remain married? Why are they so chicken? The next step is the idealization of divorce as a stimulus to growth, to feeling, to autonomy. . . .

From the point of view of those emphasizing individual growth, habituated relationships are destructive. Separating or divorcing is seen as a way to force people to examine the reasons why they felt they had to marry and remain together, why they were afraid to strike out on their own, why being alone seems so terrifying, and why panic about loneliness leads them to cling to relationships. In this perspective, a strong need for others—especially if the relationship has to be secured and legal—is seen as based on neurotic fears.

This reasoning begins with the idea that neurotic, dependent people are insatiably needy for affection and commitment, and therefore healthy people are the reverse, are independent. While independent people may enjoy relating to others, the reasoning continues, they do not *need* to be loved or remain within a relationship. Moreover, since autonomous people are secure in themselves, they do not need legal permanence and do not need to possess their partner or limit their partner's experiences. A relationship, from this perspective, is healthy when it is made up of two autonomous people, whose commitments are first to themselves and secondarily to their partner or children.

This reasoning is articulated by psychologist George Bach, who describes divorce as a facilitating experience:

> The marital condition has now been widely unmasked as a security trap which exploits in both male and female certain regressive propensities, such as possessiveness, jealousy, and dependency. The emotional harm of having a tag-along identity by living vicariously for or through another person or as "a team" has been exposed by millions of unhappily married women seeking psychotherapy. Other millions of divorcees are willing to share their hindsight about how little their marriages added to their emotional development, self-confidence and self-actualization. And the old argument "stay together for the children's sake" has lost its credibility completely due to the discovery that children are much less—if at all— traumatized by a reasonably managed divorce than their parting parents. On the contrary, the divorce may bring the child closer to its mother and father, each as persons rather than in their parental roles. Furthermore, a new level of intimacy can be attained by dating singles which more often than not is more authentic than any marriage-romance ever was.[5]

As described by Bach, divorce creates conditions for psychological growth. I do not argue with that. For most people, at least for those who do not quickly remarry, divorce creates so much change that they must look at their lives and their unexamined habits. It is always possible that the examined life may become a richer one. I do object, however, to the glossing over of the pain and the vast sense of loss.

Of course there are bad marriages; what contract can be signed "forever"? Ending a relationship that injures and constrains is a good thing. Learning that one can cope and manage by oneself can result in a surge of energy and purpose and the development of a sense of *Me!* Learning that one can make decisions, have control over one's life, be courageous, and be alone can make one happy and a more effective, competent person. Divorcing someone who makes one unhappy is a positive act. But I have never met anyone who divorced who did not mourn and did not grieve for the death of a dream of what life could be like.

Divorce involves certain obvious problems. The family's economic standing usually changes, for instance, so that an income that provided for one household must now provide for two. Even if both spouses work, they must now pay more for separate places to live. Another obvious problem, which is usually more important for the wife, is what will happen to the children when only one parent is essentially available to cope with the jobs previously divided between two people. Managing the real needs of children by oneself is hard; taking on the sole responsibility for their psychological welfare, especially if one feels guilty, anxious, or just overworked—especially if the kids are upset—can be terrifying.

Equally obvious, being divorced can be lonely. Most people are afraid of being alone forever. This is partly because it's easier to have a partner who shares whatever has to be done, and partly because not remarrying could mean missing out on important experiences, including that of having a child. Women especially can be afraid because women's remarriage rate begins to fall when they are 30, since divorced men tend to remarry younger women. For those whose marriages lasted 10, much less 20 years, the idea of dating is scary and embarrassing. It entails the hazards of the sexual marketplace and the possibility of being rejected as unattractive in a singles scene where the social rules have changed.

Most of all, divorce means losing a sense of who you belong to and who belongs to you. Without the sense of belonging and thus of commitment—without the knowledge that you are terribly important to someone else—you can feel that nothing you do is important because there is no one to do anything for. This may explain why, in the long run, divorced men seem to fare far worse than divorced women. Women, especially those with children, seem more frightened than men at the beginning of the divorce because they are appropriately scared that they may not be able to manage. But these women may well be better off because their responsibilities are specific. It is easier to manage discrete, real jobs than it is to create the uncommitted, hedonistic life of one's fantasies. While men usually have the advantage of not being burdened with child care and household maintenance, they have the greater burden of loneliness and the loss of the daily existential anchors of attachment. Women with children may find that coping with these real responsibilities leads to knowledge that they are competent. More-over, it protects them from the searing anxiety that they do not belong anywhere and are not crucial in the lives of other people.

Divorce is ultimately the failure of a romantic dream and the tear-ing apart of the anchorage of connection. Since married people nor-mally invest heavily in their relationship and pour the majority of their emotional resources into it, their vulnerability is proportional to their investment; divorce provokes all the feelings of loss, separation, aban-donment, and rejection. In addition to any social judgments of failure in a major adult task, divorced people confront their own sense of failure, wondering whether they are guilty of not doing as much as they could have or should have, along with the despair that they have been deselected as the uniquely wonderful person in their spouse's life. Those who feel most guilty and depressed are most likely to accept all the negative judgments about them that are proffered by the spouse, the children, friends, and the rest of the family. The sheer quantity of fear, guilt, rage, and depression are frightening and predictable, be-cause the inescapable fact of divorce is the loss of a central existential anchor and the spouse's rejection of oneself as a person.

I have a healthy respect for people's vulnerability, which I think can be minimized but never eliminated. I think we are all vulnerable to feelings of being abandoned, inadequate, and impotent—and this is part of the human condition. Vulnerability comes to all of us, inevitably, from childhood when we were able to know what was going on, what we wanted, what we feared, and we were able to talk and to remember —but we're too young, too small, too weak, to accomplish our aims on our own. This is a legacy that we never erase. Whether or not one initiates the separation and knows that it is in one's best interest, old terrors of abandonment and loneliness rise and add to adult feelings of fear and loss.

Intimacy, Commitment, and Cost

"Everywhere I turn today, almost everyone I know, gay or straight, has the same complaint: an inability to become intimate with another person on almost any level except sexual. There is more sexual liberation today than ever before in our history but the ability to become intimate remains a bigger problem than before."[6]

To be intimate is to reveal, need, hear, and give. With the sense of mutual intimacy we have the feeling of mutual commitment, partially because we give and receive, but mostly because our intimates let us see their dependence and vulnerability, and in doing so they signify their trust in us. They implicitly ask for help and loyalty, and they give the same gifts to us. While the accomplishment of a mutual, intimate relationship can enhance confidence, reduce anxiety, and create the sense of belonging, it creates risks at the same time. When we allow others to truly know us, we have given them the means to hurt us most. Besides that, intimate relationships are based on knowing who we really are and the pain of being rejected by someone who once loved us is the ultimate pain that we are not lovable. When people make a commitment to someone else they risk that the other person may not reciprocate. Intimacy means that we have given to another person, and indeed to the existence of the relationship, power over how we will regard ourselves.

Loving someone, needing another's love, being intimate and needing loyalty, means that we have opened ourselves to the risks of not being loved or of having our trust betrayed. If we do not love or permit intimacy but interact by surface charm, social ritual, and recreational sex, we behave as though we were intimate while we retain the barriers that protect us from our own vulnerability. We do not let others get important or close enough so that their lack of feeling for us can really hurt. And while we make ourselves safe, we habitually relate in the social styles that people respond to; we package ourselves to sell. More than that, if we keep others at a distance and do not let them get close enough to know us, we implicitly convey the message that they cannot trust us, since we will not trust them.

In some ways there seems to be a paradox. When roles were traditional and marriage seemed a relationship of endurance and compromise, it was also permanent. Today, as roles are changing and obligations become uncertain, marriage relationships can no longer be assumed to be permanent. When one assumes marriage is forever, one can feel freer to act upon one's more selfish or idiosyncratic needs because such behavior cannot dissolve the relationship. It would be paradoxical but logical if in today's climate of marital "honesty," marital impermanence and uncertainty push anxious people toward a restrained ritual of behaviors they model themselves in ways they think will offend less.

While it has become chic to emphasize the ways in which commitment, especially in permanent relationships, diminishes choice, narrows experience, and therefore truncates growth, one can argue quite the opposite. People may be far better able to grow when they are in a mutually committed relationship because, feeling secure, they are better able to take risks. The more one trusts the relationship, the more one will protect it and, simultaneously, the more one will feel free to change within it.

All relationships involve some degree of responsibility to the other person and some level of risk. We can minimize both risk and responsibility by minimizing intimacy and the level of caring and thereby diminish someone else's power over how we feel about ourselves or our freedom to choose options. If our vulnerability is very great or we need to feel in total control of our life, we will avoid intimacy and significant commitment. Since revelation is risk taking, no wonder that many people prevent or avoid intimacy or permit it only in relationships in which there are explicit symbols of mutuality.

The ideal of the autonomous self, someone so intact and mature that he or she does not need anyone else, is, in this context, an ideal of a painless existence in which one can avoid the great hope and the awful pain that become possible when one allows oneself to need another. I have never met someone so autonomous as not to need anyone; I have met many who were so vulnerable that they could not allow themselves to act on their needs for someone. Somehow it has become unfashionable—evidence of inadequacy, even of neurosis—to acknowledge that when the world seems out of control, feeling insecure or inadequate or scared is also part of human self-awareness. Finding someone with whom one creates a commitment provides some sense of security and even some measure of control.

Commitment is costly—it increases our vulnerability to hurt, constrains our options, sets limits on our experience, and means that we have to accept whatever the limitations of the other people are. Yet we seem to need commitment even more than intimacy. Without these anchorages our identity, whatever our "self" is, is uncertain, too fluid, and has too little link to reality. Without commitment and real obligations, now and extending into the future, it is difficult to have a firm sense of who or what we are, a sense that it matters that we lived. Without commitment one is free from obligation, but without obligation there is too little that matters. Psychologically healthy people know this and acknowledge their ambivalence. The existential gains from commitment seem to be so overwhelmingly significant that the price must be paid.

Neither sex needs commitment more or less than the other. People need anchorage. Of course, one always wants what one does not have; everyone has fantasies of walking out, leaving responsibility behind. It is a seductive image, youthful and composed only of beginnings. Yet most who divorce remarry and take on obligation, giving up a free life because the gain of belonging, of not being lonely, of caring and being needed, is greater than the cost. For the vast majority of people, commitment and connection must be made to a relationship in which each partner signifies by intimacy and responsibility that the other is important.

To be split off from relationships and to define ourselves solely by our separateness is as pathological as defining ourselves within our relationships, deriving our identity from the nexus of our belonging. An unhealthy relationship is one in which identity comes solely from the relationship and from the roles one plays in that relationship.

Feminists want women to cease regarding themselves as help-mates, deferring to others, and disguising their own imperatives in some external transformation that is pleasing to others. They want women to develop a sense of their own selves, because until they do, there is too good a possibility that they will be only the sum of their roles, adapting to others' expectations, consensual rather than authentic selves.

People cannot or should not live through others; there must be an anchor of *Me!* But that does not affect the simultaneous need for involvement and commitment. The emerging criteria of what is psychologically healthy are an obvious reversal of the earlier ideal of adaptation and of marriage as a place where people find wholeness in a fusion with their other half. But is there really anyone who has never said, "I need?" We all need. If we acknowledge our need and the significance of the relationship, then we need not feel diminished by the fact that commitment to the relationship sometimes requires actions that do not immediately benefit the self. With a reversal of values and in emulation of the stereotype of men, we have come to an exaggerated denial of everyone's dependence, so that mental health is often defined as autonomy.

The more extreme forms of "autonomy as health" really amount to the idealization of narcissism. A relationship between two narcissists creates a picture of two individuals trampling on each other, because obligation to the other is not significant and the welfare of the other is not salient. I think that psychologically healthy people are able to be autonomous or boundaried, not always vulnerable to others, not always needing others, and not needing many others. But they are also able to drop the boundaries, fuse, become intimate with selected others some of the time. Psychologically healthy people are also able to admit their dependence and their vulnerability and to acknowledge their ambivalence, their sense of both the positive and the negative in all commitments.

Neither extreme of dependence or autonomy ought to characterize individuals within a relationship. Raised to their extreme, all virtues become vices. Extreme attachment and extreme disengagement are both bad. Committed relationships between intimates ought to be flexible, enabling interdependent people to move in and out of periods of more neediness and dependence or confidence and independence. People ought to be able to use the relationship for sustenance and also be free not to be dependent. Self-actualization is not achieved by protective uninvolvement.

I think that marriage is a romantic involvement in a very specific sense. Relationships are romantic when each partner truly cares about the welfare of the other, and the self-esteem of each is intertwined with regard for the other as well as with the perception of how one's own needs are being met. Relationships are healthy when the individuals within them are neither solely dependent upon the relationship for identity nor so resistant that they prevent intimacy. Healthy marriages are interdependent and may remain romantic, in this sense, forever. Interdependence recognizes that people are needful. People need intimacy as well as distance, affection and affirmation as well as autonomy. Marriage is the permanent relationship in which the dependent needs of interdependent people can be met.

Interdependence does not ask that people give up their independence; it requires, instead, that sometimes they acknowledge their dependence. The most important feelings—that one exists, that one's existence is a good thing, that the future has promise—come from long-term commitment. Rejecting a restrictive past which emphasized commitment and duty, we are reversing values. The risk is that in rejecting permanent commitment we may find ourselves unconnected, uncommitted, and in danger of losing a sense of identity, the security of meaning, and the reassurance of our own significance.

Divorce and the Survival of the Family

If divorce has become so prevalent, for whom would we expect marriage and parenting to be more gratifying than frustrating? Those who are more satisfied than frustrated are people whose histories and family backgrounds have led them to want to marry or have children, who have not been frustrated by finding that family commitments forced them to give up other major interests, and who have not found that in the marriage everyone else's happiness is more important than theirs. Perhaps most crucial of all, satisfied people have realistic expectations of what these relationships require. With a healthy ambivalence, they feel that they gain more from the relationships than they lose. When commitments result in a major loss of autonomy, they will be resented. Most people will be happier if they do not have to give up their own interests when they choose to make a commitment to another person. Such people gain more than they lose in the creation of a marriage and a family because they feel loved and know they belong somewhere. While social values and the forms of marriage are changing, the need for family commitment and loyalty remain.

I think the American family will survive, mostly in the form of the nuclear family, because it is difficult if not impossible to achieve a sense of intimacy, and thus of significant connection and caring, within larger groups. But the stability of the family will require more social changes, so that we may develop specific consensual norms of freedom and obligation in marriage. Several different family patterns will probably evolve as legitimate alternatives.

A number of variations on the stereotypical American family are prevalent enough to be considered normal. Common variations include the extended family in which the couple share household arrangements or child-rearing tasks or both, with other family members. There are many single-parent, especially mother–child, families. There are families that are no longer intact because of death or divorce. There are some rural and urban communal arrangements, which have a long history in this country. And today there are a few experimental arrangements; some are variations of group marriage, others are shared households made up of friends and their children but not necessarily involving sex.[7] One of the more interesting and frequent new family forms involves a divorced woman and her children sharing their home with several unrelated single women. Also common is the sharing of one house by several divorced women and their children. This form has obvious economic and psychological advantages and is likely to become more common, since divorced men tend to remarry younger women.

A further psychological shift will also have to occur away from the one-sided priority of gratifying individualistic needs to an increased awareness of benefits derived from the existence of the relationship. In addition, since many of us have learned that it is psychologically danger-ous to be overwhelmingly dependent on any one relationship, there will be pressure upon other relationships, especially with friends and work acquaintances, to provide alternate resources for the security of belonging or the trust of loyalty. We have learned from the social changes of this decade and from recent studies of how adults change that a workable model of marriage and family in the future will have to include expectations of change and of individual flexibility.

Since the family is the institution in which we feel we have more license to act on our own needs, the panoply of anxieties and angers which arise outside are all brought into it. Thus the stresses on the family arise both from the relationship itself and from external strains. In this way the family is a reactive institution, reflecting changes which are taking place in society. The family is the most salient place to experiment with new values or compensate for losses experienced outside.

In this decade we have all become aware of limitations on our lives imposed by rules of marriage and roles assigned because of gender. Especially those younger than 30 are attempting to break out of the cage of traditional restrictions. Yet the drift of change seems reformist and not radical, aimed at modification of an essentially monogamous nuclear family. This is probably partly because of the inertia of large-scale institutions but also because in Western society the nuclear family has met psychodynamically central needs not met in other social institutions. Fundamentally, our needs for belonging are not met elsewhere. Thus, reform of family structure is intrinsically better than total dissolution, because the sense of being a partner in marriage or a child of some specific family provides the grounding of identity that none of our other institutions can. For us, the family is still a unique and irreplaceable source of satisfaction, connecting, and belonging. We do not have other connections that are permanent, indissoluble, and intimate, in which each person belongs as an individual. The passions of the family come from possession and protection and permanence; the family, nuclear or extended, is the group we are a part of, to whom we owe, and from whom we may ask—whether they like us today or not.

Until I, the oldest grandchild, left for college, my whole family lived close to or in New York City. Part of every Sunday was taken up with visiting each other, and of course holidays were family affairs including aunts and uncles, cousins, grandparents, in-laws, and close friends. The dominant figure was one grandmother, an autocratic, illiterate, shrewd woman of absolute conviction and stunning power. Family members lent money to each other, watched over each other's kids, were privy to each other's secrets, were a bastion against the rest of the world—and were also best enemies. One grandfather, after he declared that the man was a crook, did not talk to a cousin for 20 years. With all the costs of emotional turmoil, I miss such intense family involvement. Today, like many middle-class families, my generation is sprawled all over the United States. But I notice that on the few occasions when we get together we *begin* from the premise of family intimacy and belonging. Moreover, I see that even distant members of the family respond to my children, whom they have never seen, from the fact of their family membership. Somehow the connections of blood, which can never be undone, seem more permanent than those of friendship.

While the family is the source of neurosis and the pathologies that come from possession, it is also the source of individuality and the strengths that come from emotional buttressing and the permanent conviction of belonging. The family is the first source of love and the sense of one's importance. It is not only a real organization, but also an idea of place.

The family is where we can most honestly tangle with our emotional present and, especially with children, construct a future. The feminist model of marriage tends toward the stereotype of male family involvement, in which the goals are equal power, equal freedom, and equal self-gratification; there is relative silence about equal commitment, equal dependence, and equal vulnerability. It is in the family, rather than at work, in school, or in friendship, that at psychologically conscious and not aware levels, we are passionate, tenacious, caring, and possessive, as we entangle the anchorages of our total time and total being. Clearly, this is the historically feminine model of family. What we are learning is that this commitment is one that men need too.[8]

Very few families bear much resemblance to the posed portraits of togetherness, replete with fireplace and dog, that arrive at Christmas. And rather few marriages would be described as "happy," in the sense that the percentage of time that the people would describe themselves as joyful is small over the lifetime of a long relationship. But, then, "Are you happy?" is the wrong question. Marriage and thus family are where we live out the most intimate and thus powerful of our human experiences. The family is the unit in which we belong, from which we can expect protection from uncontrollable fate, in which we create infinity through our children, and in which we find a haven. The stuff of which family is made is bloodier and more passionate that the stuff of friendship, and the costs are greater too.

Women's Attitudes toward Women

8

It is, in itself, an expression of sexism that the vast majority of the literature about the feminist movement—whether in favor of the changes or alarmed and opposed—has been concerned with changes in women's relationships with men, while the equally important shifts in women's relationships with each other have received much less attention. This lack of interest exists not only because relationships with men are considered more significant—indeed, crucial—but also because women are considered less interesting. When the daughter's only adult role is to be a mother, and the task of the mother is to teach the daughter to become a mother, and the role of mother or daughter or wife is basically the same for all women, then gender is caste, and in an achieving, individualistic culture, women are judged as insignificant. Of course, all this is changing.

Mother–daughter relationships are also changing. We are now seeing a generation of daughters, both college aged and middle aged, who may be to their mothers as their brothers are to their fathers. It is bittersweet. In the American dream the girl gets ahead through marrying upward, but the son—better educated and with advantages given him by his father—becomes more successful, earns more money, achieves higher status than the father. And the father has great pride, some sense of shared accomplishment, and the disconcerting knowledge that the power in the relationship has reversed as the son's accomplishments eclipse his own. Daughters have generally not challenged their mothers in the same way. In the past, while the mother with a high school diploma was very likely to have a daughter who graduated college, just as the mother's adult status was secured solely by marriage and motherhood, so was the daughter's. While they might have fought about details, about whether children should be fed on a schedule or on demand, for instance, in essence, the life of the daughter affirmed the values of the mother. So, too, did the successful son. But unlike the son's, the accomplishments of the daughter were not much different from those of the mother and did not provoke the feeling that the child had become the parent, had come to know more, or had become more successful, wise, or powerful.

As my brother is to my father, I am both pleasure and pain to my mother. While my life is a crucial proof that she did her job well, it simultaneously makes my mother ask herself what she has done with her own.

My mother, her mother, my father's mother, my mother's sister, and my father's sisters all led basically similar lives. When my mother was young they all worked because they were scrambling for lower-middle-class security. No one entertained any idea that women were passive, dependent, inept, and decorative. It was a mark of my parents' upward mobility that when I was born my mother could stop working and stay home to raise her children. As my father prospered, my mother lived a comfortable life—reading, going to the theatre, creating a home, involving herself in the community, taking care of all of us, apparently content.

Around 1969 my parents came to visit, and my mother and I went to see a friend of mine. She had completed her residency in psychiatry and a month later had given birth to her first child. She found she was having a wonderful time with the baby and decided to stay at home. When we visited the child was a year old and my friend had not been back to work. We spent a pleasant few hours together chatting and gossiping, and my mother had fun with the baby. On the way home, my mother was silent for a long time. Then she exclaimed, "That is a disgrace. That is a disgrace! She has no right not to work, not when she has taken up so many of society's resources, not when women are struggling to get into medicine! Not when women are struggling for their rights!"

My mother's awareness has been raised but it cannot be a constant thing. Although our lives are very different, our values are more similar than dissimilar. The generation gap between us is far greater than was the case between my mother and her mother. While my mother might like to live more as I do and be more like me, it is too late and she cannot. Like my brother, I am a source of pride. More than my brother, I am a reminder of accomplishments never attempted.

Every generation in this rapidly changing society has differed and disagreed. Today this involves far more women than in the past. The traditional priorities of marriage and especially maternity, of child welfare over maternal interests, of the presumption that it is the mother who informs and serves as model for the daughter, are no longer stable and conservative. Daughters may adopt new values that challenge the values of their more traditional mothers. This conflict is not a relatively peripheral disagreement like whether or not a son goes into his father's business. It is a disagreement over basic values, and if it is personalized —as is very likely between mothers and daughters or between sisters —it can feel as if you are being rejected as a person.

In this culture, conflict between parents and children is almost inevitable, and disagreement is greater between parents and children of the same sex. That is because that parent has more responsibility for molding—that is for rewarding, punishing, and guiding—the children of the same gender. Mothers are more likely to interfere with their daughters, to chastize and empathize, and to be the source of rules to follow and regulations to break—especially in adolescence. In a more traditional time many mother–daughter disagreements were ultimately resolved when the daughter married and again when she became a mother. Thus the daughter affirmed the mother's values; and of course the two women's lives became very similar.

Increasingly, daughters are choosing not to repeat the experiences of their mothers, and mothers are not repeating the lives of their mothers. Middle-aged mothers of adolescents seem especially to have a new self-awareness that comes from the realization of age and the imperative of "If not now, never." Aggravated by the visibility of feminist values and successful women, such awareness results in an acute hypersensitivity to what has not yet been tried. While daughters who are young women may anticipate their future and wonder if they will succeed and if they will make the right choices, their mothers may poignantly look back and wonder if they made the right choices.

While every national poll demonstrates more acceptance of feminist values among younger people, other statistics—employment figures, numbers of women re-entering college, enrollment in NOW—all sorts of data—tell us that many women over 30 have been affected by the movement and are reassessing the reality of their lives. Many daughters, whether in grammar school or college, have experienced their mothers' changing from full-time to working mothers, just as many daughters have challenged their mothers by preferring a vastly more egocentric life. The psychological task is for the daughter to do what she wants without communicating the feeling that she believes her mother wasted her life, and for the mother to do what she wants without communicating the feeling that she no longer loves her daughter.

Traditionally, the direction of power was from the mother to the daughter. The mother exercised power directly by punishing and rewarding and indirectly through the influence of how she lived. In contrast, the directions of influence between mothers and daughters today are increasingly equal. While there may be a greater chance that they are in serious disagreement as they try to make decisions for their future, mothers and daughters may also discover how much they have in common. As they review the ways in which gender has affected their lives and how it will or did influence choices, as they try to resolve uncertainties in the 1970s, they are likely to be reading the same books. Each may become a source of information, even a role model, for the other. A mother who does not have to relate from the hierarchical power of the role, especially if she shares the awareness and many of the experiences of her daughter, may still clash with and challenge her daughter. But the two may also become friends in a way that traditional mothers and daughters never could.

Studies of unusually successful women tend to find that when the women were children they had close relationships with both of their parents. Characteristically, neither parent believed that competing successfully was unfeminine. Instead, both parents enjoyed their daughter's femininity and her achievements, especially those in school. Rather crucially, the father responded to the daughter's femininity and the mother respected her own.[1] Whether the mother worked or did not work was not critical. What was crucial was that the mother respected herself as an individual and as a woman. Thus two things were generally true in the experience of a woman who became successful, and were rare in the general population. First, her parents did not confound femininity with roles and did not limit what she was allowed to do on the basis of gender. Second, the mother respected herself and was thus a model of self-esteem.

Too few women in our society develop a sense of worth. Most accept the values of their society, respecting themselves to the extent that they succeed in the traditional responsibilities and not esteeming themselves to the extent that they are limited to the less prestigious roles. Others, who have succeeded in nontraditional commitments, especially in competitive areas that involve few other women, may be proud of what they have done but simultaneously anxious about whether they are feminine.

Women who do not love or respect themselves because they are women will not love their daughters in the same way they love their sons. Moreover, they are, whether consciously or unconsciously, role models of self-disparagement for their daughters.[2] Low self-esteem for women stems partially from their roles, but more fundamentally it is self-denigration based on gender itself. Increasing women's self-esteem requires more than participation in higher status roles; it requires basic pride in gender.

Feminist awareness of sexism is leading to a reevaluation of the importance of women's relationships with each other and to a new awareness that those relationships hold an enormous potential for mutual support. But women's relationships with women have not only been based on the unconscious assumption of a shared second-rate status, they have also characteristically fused intimacy and mistrust. Women have tended neither to respect nor to trust other women.

Love, Rejection, and Distrust

It is difficult to pinpoint the beginnings of the sense of mistrust between women. Many people write about girls' competition with each other for boys. But that becomes important in adolescence; I think the origins are much earlier.

A kindergarten teacher sent me the following story, which had been spontaneously dictated to her by a 6-year-old girl: "There's two girls who like each other and are best friends. There's a little girl who wants to play with them and they don't want to play with her. She's very sad. The other girls are laughing at her."

I have not seen any data in the professional literature, nor am I certain of how widespread the pattern is, but I find that the great majority of women I have discussed this with notice a similar pattern, which begins before adolescence. Two girls are best friends. After a while another girl joins this dyad and it becomes a triad. Then one girl is rejected and again there are two best friends, but now there is also one who was repudiated. I remember this pattern from my own girlhood, have seen it repeated when my daughters were growing up, and have had students tell me that they have seen it in many other countries. This pattern of compelling intimacy and the mutual deliciousness of being "best friends," along with the potential for feeling devastated if replaced by someone else, is very different from the typical play patterns of boys. Of course, boys can also have a "best friend," but this relationship rarely seems as passionate and as crucial to boys as it is to girls. To a much greater extent the boys can substitute for each other, since boys form a group, a pool of friends. Many mothers have told me that they have warned their daughters of the vulnerability to feeling rejected if they limit themselves to one or two friends. Neither I nor any of the mothers I have asked have succeeded in getting their daughters to change from the overwhelming involvement with a "best friend."[3]

By the time he enters school the typical boy prefers to play actively with other boys, frequently in something like a team organization and usually in a ritualized way in which leadership is overt.[4] This has several effects. Dominance relations determining who leads and who follows are public; boys learn that power juggling occurs among boys; changes in dominance or leadership are made according to rules of the group; and while aggression or assertion is overt, its forms are ritualized so that boys who are accepted members of the group do not find it an intensely personal issue.

Overt aggression or dominance is not sanctioned for girls. Moreover, the desire to secure an exclusive, intimate relationship with a best friend, coupled with the knowledge that they may not be selected or may end up enemies, makes girls act in the ways that are safest, in the ways to make them popular. As a result, aggression is often covert. If overt, it takes the form of gossip, of criticism of girls outside of the clique, triad, or dyad. In addition to gossiping, girls ignore or reject others. Before adolescence, when the sexes usually play separately, the recipient of this hostility is more likely another girl. The most exquisite aggression is to reject someone; the most piercing pain is to be the one rejected.

Unlike boys, who may not be chosen first for the baseball team because they cannot hit but may be chosen third because they can run, girls are rejected for themselves, for their total selves. Girls' covert aggression leads, ultimately, to rejection; the boys' more overt and ritualized style tends not to create the intensity of acceptance or rejection that girls know.

An anonymous student wrote a paper in which she recalled what the experience was like:

> It occurs to me now that when I was young I never thought of my age as part of the "best years of my life" and in retrospect I still don't think it was. I remember having friends one day and being ostracized the next. I never quite understood what I had done that could have created such tremendous fluctuation in my appeal (or lack thereof) but for some unknown reason, recess could be absolute pleasure or a twenty minute exercise in Chinese torture. The pattern is still an enigma to me but I learned something from it (although it is not the kind of lesson one brags about). At the age of twelve, I realized that it was a dog eat dog world out there and if you want to make friends you have to gossip and slander with the rest of them. "Whattsamatta, Bronstein, gonna run home to mommy?!" (God forbid we should call them by their first name in the heat of it all.) And then you'd watch her cry like you did, but this time you'd relish the power to do it to someone else.
>
> The boys, on the other hand, never seemed to have this problem. I mean, if he was not liked (a "queer" or a "fag") he was consistently ignored. There was no adjustment to make from one week to the other and he just kept

out of the way in his own group of "fags" or "queers" (funny how girls never called each other "lesbos" or "dykes"). If it did happen that one of the boys had "a bad day," they'd fight it out but twenty minutes later, they'd be best buddies again. But the girls, even among the best of them, we all went through a time period when we were the victims of group animosity enjoyed only by the other girls.

I suppose one developed the art [of] forseeing a bad day, out of self-preservation. Certain clues seemed evident by the end of the first class such as: 1) two girls would stare at you and then giggle to each other; 2) you see a note passed around and you're the only one who doesn't read it; 3) the girl who sat next to you at study hall for the last three days, sits with another girl who you know *despises* you; 4) you are one of the last picked for a team in gym. Whether these cues were subtle or obvious, you picked them up and shuddered through the rest of the day.

To a twelve year old mind one message seems fairly clear: you don't trust other girls. Last week's confidante is next week's gossip and you had better be judicious in what you say and to whom you are saying it. In the end, you were safe with no one.

While girls' aggression can be more subtle than that of boys, it can also be more potent.[5] If a pattern of alternating intimacy and repudiation is characteristic of relationships between girls, then girls will learn that they can be seriously hurt by other girls. Anticipating rejection, they will be acutely sensitive to innuendo as they constantly scan for anything negative. Many girls will learn that they are awfully vulnerable to incursions from other girls, that they may be ostracized even by their closest friend. Not every girl need have this experience to learn its lessons. If it is common, it will be a real possibility in most girls' minds. We talk a great deal about mistrust between male and female. What I am suggesting is that many girls experience or anticipate a pattern of being chosen and then rejected as the special friend, and this establishes a core sense of mistrust which has a powerful impact on women's relationships with each other.

Power Relationships between Women

What would we expect relationships to be like between people who are afraid of each other's manipulations or who are reluctant to be obviously assertive because they're fearful of rejection and need to be liked? What would we anticipate in a relationship in which one person feels vulnerable and the other does not?

Psychologists usually describe these interactions in terms of people's needs for affiliation, their need to be liked. It might be more accurate to think, instead, in terms of power—getting power, wielding it, protecting oneself from it, or manipulating those who seem to have it. We do not think of women in terms of power. Few women are in positions of significant power. Women themselves rarely think of themselves in terms of power. Many women feel powerless. Subject to the manipulations of those with power, those without it respond in any way they can to prevent others' intrusions into their lives—which is the fundamental coercion of power.

Obviously, there are many different kinds of power. The most common is associated with a role, so that anyone in the role has its power. A chairperson or a president, for example, has role power. Most role power is in the hands of men, and women associated with these men tend to derive some authority as a spin-off from the man's power. Power also comes from superior skill, even when no specific role would assign leadership. In this case, there is consensus that the expertise of one person is greater than that of others; and, as others give her or him more weight in making decisions, this "expert" assumes the responsibility of leadership. For reasons which do not have to be repeated, few women have role or skill power, at least outside their traditional responsibilities. Within the latter responsibilities women have considerable control, but because neither the role nor women themselves are thought of in terms of power, women are prone not to perceive that they have any. Another kind of power is compensatory manipulation intended to diminish another's control, exercised in order to protect oneself. Still another type is aggressive authority enjoyed by those who like to dominate and make decisions. Charismatic power is a quality that enables people to create authority by virtue of their appeal, because they are responded to. And there is the power of the weak who manipulate to make the strong feel guilty.

There is also personal power, which is the sense of confidence that resides in oneself, that comes from one's maturity and self-respect. Personally powerful people are strong because their sense of self is based on acceptance of themselves. Not afraid, they do not need to gain at the expense of others. Not dominated by the need to be liked, not measuring themselves by others' responses, they do not need to conform to or rebel against others. Abraham Maslow terms these people "self-actualized." I prefer to call them strong or powerful, simply to remind us that women can have power and that they can have personal power.

Those who have achieved personal power are also very likely to occupy positions of role authority or to have significant skills. Those without personal power are less likely to occupy a legitimized power position. In this way an individual's position parallels his or her internal psychological dynamics, with the combination tending to one extreme or the other.

People who are self-actualized, who are personally powerful are at once envied, feared, and hated. Maslow wrote:

> The commonly seen hatred or resentment of or jealousy of goodness, truth, beauty, health or intelligence ('counter-values') is largely (though not altogether) determined by threat of loss of self-esteem, as the liar is threatened by the honest man, the homely girl by the beautiful girl, or the coward by the hero. Every superior person confronts us with our own shortcomings.[6]

Powerful people can make others uncomfortable. They can be a special threat to peers who see themselves as victims—to those who have found comfort in a conviction that they are not individually responsible for their vulnerability because they are members of a group victimized by social forces over which they never had control. Many women are threatened by the self-actualized woman because, although she is a victim of the same external forces, in her case the outcome has been bitterly different from their own. While social forces *are* hugely powerful, a distorted emphasis on *only* these factors enables individuals to cling to a denial that they have any responsibility for what they have become. Thus personally powerful people, especially personally powerful women, threaten women simply because they exist. I think that power is probably thought of very differently by those who have it and those who do not. Those without power seem to think that having it is the opposite of not having it. They seem to imagine power as being able to coerce others, as being potent, as being free from the incursions of others. In a sense, they are right. But those with role, skill, or personal power are likely to have learned that having it means making decisions and taking on responsibilities. If they seek to avoid the authority coveted by weaker persons, the powerful may seem untrustworthy to these people, especially because those without power think of it as infinite. In their experience, when someone else dominates they are impotent.

Women who have never had the sense that they are heard, who have never learned that they can be potent, will fear being manipulated by those with power, because stronger people can move into their psychological lifespace. The psychological dynamics are reaffirmed by what happens in reality: the dominant figure decides and the other follows, the stronger approves or disapproves, the weaker is overshadowed and feels anxious or inhibited.

I think that those who are without power are preoccupied with it because they are always afraid of being victims. They have learned that others determine what happens to them, that others intrude and make them feel competent or incompetent, potent or impotent. So it is appropriate, even adaptive, that weaker people are hypersensitive to control by others and are always searching for subtle cues of coercion. On the other hand, I think that those with power may be relatively oblivious or insensitive to dominance or power issues because they are not vulnerable. Women with power may be especially insensitive to the fact that they have control over others because powerful women are very discrepant from our image of what is feminine.

I would expect vulnerable men and women, who are experienced victims, would feel very much the same way, revering and fearing the powerful; but the rules of appropriate ways of behaving are different for the sexes, and so they would probably act rather differently. More than men, women have learned that it is better to disguise their anger. They are also skilled in rejecting people. Experienced in rejecting, but afraid because they are also experienced in being rejected, women are likely to disguise their anger and express their sense of hurt. Seeking solace is acceptable for women and may, in fact, elicit support, whereas anger expressed risks anger returned. Afraid of others' power and of rejection, and needing protection, weak women are likely to ingratiate themselves and seek help by subtly asking to be liked, to be liked best of all. How ambivalent and paradoxical it is that the weaker seeks to bolster herself by expressing her dependence.

To the extent that women in general are uncomfortable thinking of themselves as being powerful or having power—and insofar as strong women become uncomfortable when others appear to say, "Protect me because I can be hurt. Indeed, you are hurting me"—we can expect strong women to be conflicted about their power. When others seek her help, the dominant woman is likely to feel ambivalent, pleased that she is not vulnerable and can help the weaker but anxious because she can injure. Perhaps the stronger woman also feels guilty, not knowing whether she has helped enough. Or, resentful of the responsibility for someone else's welfare, she may try to maintain distance and keep the relationship impersonal. The situation is conflicted for both parties. Especially if she is sensitive to what it feels like to be rejected and emotionally coerced, the more powerful woman is likely to deny her resentment of the other's dependence, to respond with support, and to withhold negative judgments. This is more likely if the weaker woman expresses her pain in inescapably feminine ways, because they are more likely to trigger nurturant responses. In this way the weaker may inhibit the stronger. While vulnerability and need are acknowledged and responded to, the basically aggressive manipulation is not. When this approach is successful, we can see the tyranny of the weak. The many hidden agendas in these interactions make mistrust between the participants very likely.

These relationships are further complicated by sexist judgments. Because women are often needy and vulnerable and because an emotional and personal style is acceptable for women, emotional needs are more likely to surface in relationships between women than they are in relationships between men. In a relationship between a mentor and a protégé, for example, the tensions and the tasks that men have are the same as those of women. But emotional needs and anxieties are not likely to surface, since the model of masculinity excludes expressing vulnerability and dependence.

Women in the same situation are more likely to operate on both a task-related, objective level and a personalized, intimate one because they have learned to increased their self-esteem through the security of knowing they are liked. I think the female mentor is, to herself and her protégé, simultaneously the objective teacher, the intimate friend, and the ambivalent mother. The closer the relationship the more true this will be. As men must outgrow their mentors, the protégé woman must relate to and then separate from the authority figure. The difference, when the relationship is between women, lies in the protégé's need to identify with the already successful woman and create the intimacy, the "best friend" relationship that she has learned will sustain her through stress. It is very difficult to create autonomy through intimacy, that is, through dependence. In addition, in a sexist society a mentor-mother is at best an exception to the rule of status, while the protégé-daughter at once disdains and needs the femaleness of the model.

Roles and Power

The roles of mentor and protégé or employer and employee are clear. When roles are specific the situation is likely to be less personal than when roles are not specified. When there is a clear role, responsibilitites and obligations are known and people's resentments or fears can be expressed in terms of the role. We can state a problem and suggest a solution in an impersonal way. We might say, for example, "The chairperson's responsibilities have become too large. Some of them must be delegated to committees." When roles are not specific, resentments cannot be expressed in terms of a role but must be directed at a person. If people become leaders and make decisions when they have no specified role or no obvious relevant skill, they are seen as powerful individuals, which is quite different from being seen as persons in a role that has power. This is because roles have not only power but also specific limitations on power.

When a role has power, everyone in the role has its authority. The nature and extent of their control is, however, defined by the obligations and the limitations of the role. If there is no clear role, limitations on power and mutual obligations are no longer consensual and clear. In this case those who have no power are appropriately anxious because they are, in fact, exceedingly vulnerable to the potentially unlimited manipulations of more dominant people.

When roles are not specified, the less powerful lose the protection that comes from role constraints. They are in greater danger of being engulfed by those who are stronger, and they are more likely to feel anxious and victimized in the ambiguous situation. When the safety valve of objective organization is lost because roles are not specified, interactions are more personal and disagreement is more likely to be experienced as rejection.

This has become an important issue within feminism. Radicals especially have attacked the traditional organizational pyramid in which leadership, responsibility, and the opportunity to initiate accrue only to the few who rise to the top. The extreme feminist solution is to have no specified roles or formal organization; when there are leadership roles there is a hierarchy, they argue, and they are unwilling to create organizations in which women are given the opportunity to victimize other women.

For feminists, the issue of organizational structure is based on ideology. But questions about organization have become extremely important as women in general and a few women in particular are gaining access to real power. Organization really refers to how power is distributed. Organizational form has become a crucial issue for feminists, because when there are no controls over power, women who become leaders may block other women in the same way as men have.

There are circumstances in which roles and specified leadership are unnecessary. In small consciousness-raising groups, for example, everyone can contribute and participate equally. Most of us have had the experience of working successfully without any formal organization, usually with a small group of peers trying to accomplish some specific goal. Circumstances in which people can work effectively with shared power and without specific responsibilities are exceptional and occur only in small groups. Large groups cannot function without organization and allocated responsibilities. No large organization has yet managed to evolve a successful system without leaders and differences in power. Nothing is gained and a great deal is lost when ideology leads people to deny the need for organization or the existence of differences in power.*

There has been an ironic outcome to the feminist idealization of a humanistic organization. While the movement has grown to include large national organizations, there is no training for leadership because that would acknowledge the fact that there are leaders and differences in power. As a result, power is gained by those who already know the politics of power, how the system works.[7]

This became clear at the National Organization for Women's convention in 1974, when there was the first real contest for the presidency. The politically experienced Chicago chapter came prepared with position papers and campaign strategies. They were attacked for their political skill. Their political professionalism was deemed by the naive or inexperienced to be a personal as well as an ideological threat. If the Chicago chapter were to win, it would be because of their effective use of despised "masculine" political strategies. In 1975 there was another tense struggle over leadership, but now two groups were sophisticated in the use of political techniques. While Shirley Bernard, a candidate for NOW president, called for "Sisterhood first, competition last," the people elected were those most skilled in political maneuvering. They removed a candidate's name from the ballot when she left the room, created delays by demanding credentials, challenged, debated the rules, and so on. As we would expect, Bernard lost. When faced with the effective use of power, a powerless ideology loses.

Feminist organizations must be structured in accord with feminist ideals. To eschew formal organization is not a feasible alternative because it provides no protection for those who are without power. This was the first lesson gained from the 1975 convention. The second was that many women want power and can and will use it.

*Feminism seems to need two organizational forms. They are not contradictory because they have different purposes and are used in different circumstances. The model of the consciousness-raising group, in which opportunity is rotated and there are neither leaders nor roles, is appropriate for small groups of equals because all experiences or insights are relevant. When the group is large, organization is necessary. Feminist organizations might adapt and modify new corporate styles of management in which roles are specific, the means of entry are clear and open, and decisions are reached by consensus instead of by fiat. Consensual decision making does not mean that decisions are not ultimately made by individuals with that particular responsibility. Characteristically, one person has to decide and is accountable, but the group concerned with the decision provides important input. This group participation has the following advantages: the authority of deciding is dispersed; as active participants, people do not feel coerced; there is direct input to the leadership; and practice in decision making can prepare group members to assume leadership responsibilities later.

In a convention calling for sisterhood but characterized by manipulation and competition, many of the delegates must have realized how the power jockeying made a lie of the feminist ideology, and many must have felt impotent. When I hear and read about the intense feelings of people who were there, it does not seem to be too much of an exaggeration to think that those who felt powerless in this ingathering of sisters were really recapitulating the awful feeling that they were being betrayed by their "best friend."

As long as the movement does not create an acceptable organizational form, it is denying the fact that there are leaders. Those who do lead cannot be held accountable as long as their leadership is not acknowledged and formalized in roles. As a result, the leaders are likely to be viewed with suspicion. Women who successfully use the overt techniques of power politics can be damned as elitists who are using the movement to dominate and thereby victimize women. But those who become leaders because they are personally powerful are equally suspect. Some leaders, like Betty Friedan, sought and became leaders in the traditional way. Others were chosen and essentially created by the media:

> A good example of both press "election" and "impeachment" is Kate Millett. She and Shulamith Firestone both published the first new feminist theoretical books within a month of each other (September 1970). Through a combination of Millett's publisher (Doubleday), her own personal predisposition, and *Time* magazine's plan for a special movement issue to coincide with Women's Strike Day (August 26, 1970) her picture appeared on *Time's* cover. This "established" her as *the* first feminist spokeswoman after Friedan, and subjected her to very severe criticism from the movement. When she subsequently, at a feminist conference, publicly declared herself to be bisexual, *Time* announced that she was now discredited as a movement leader. No movement group had a role in either her ascendancy or dismissal.[8]

The sense of betrayal and despair over leaders is clear when feminists attack their leaders on the basis of personality rather than ideology. Sometimes there is an exquisite viciousness in the attacks.[9] When there is no organization and relationships are personal, it is easier to feel coerced and rebuffed as a person. For many women, memories of betrayal by trusted best friends have left unhealed wounds.

Given a structural vacuum and an ideology that mistrusts power in and of itself, mistrusts organizations that give some people role power, and denies that leadership in large organizations is necessary and inevitable, it is predictable that those who emerge as leaders will be mistrusted simply for being leaders. Yet, it is all paradoxical. The movement cannot advance without leadership; and those who lead will have more role, skill, or personal power. Indeed, feminists are more dominant, self-confident, autonomous, and assertive than nonfeminists.[10] Those who lead will do so because they are even more self-confident, assertive and so on than the rank and file of feminists. Until feminism creates an acceptable organizational structure, women who lead will do so because they are more motivated, competitive, aggressive ... dare we say more "masculine"? The "Catch-22" is complete.

I should note that while I am discussing psychological dynamics we are also talking about real power and status. While the majority of women do not have real power, increasing numbers of women are in positions where they can create or grasp power. Whether in a feminist organization, at work, in school, or in government, this power is most likely to be over other women. Feminists are correct in believing that unless women have a commitment to sharing power with other women, an elite group will develop which will dominate and perpetuate the powerless position of the majority of women. Feminists are wrong, however, in believing that this elitism can be prevented without developing formal organizations.

While not enough women have attained positions of significant authority to make it possible to study and predict how women in roles with power act toward other women, fragments of information suggest that women who lead—especially if they do not identify themselves as feminists—feel no particular responsibility toward other women. Unless their roles are within feminist organizations or they espouse feminist values, women who gain powerful positions are not likely to be feminists; if they are, their views are likely to shift toward the more traditional, nonfeminist values of the organization.

Outside of specifically feminist organizations, women who are neutral or hostile to feminism (i.e., "traditionalists" and "loners"), are likely to be promoted to positions with power, because men control advancement and they will be more comfortable with women whose values are in agreement with theirs. Either because men feel this way or because women think they do, feminist women who are trying to enter ascendent roles will be tempted to mute their feminism because they are afraid to alienate the men who control access to the positions. Other social science data says that when people enter a group, their attitudes change in the direction of those held by members of the group. This implies that even if feminists achieve entrance into the Establishment, their initial attitudes will be modified by the more traditional attitudes of the group they have joined.[11] Especially now, when real mobility is possible, women will learn that if they compete successfully as individuals they can gain the money, power, status, and opportunity that men have monopolized. At least in the short run it is logical that women compete with each other as well as with men. There is a real danger to the movement if unstructured anti-leadership prevails, because only when women cooperate with each other will they be able to force change and place a quantum number of women in leadership positions, so that women leaders will not feel isolated and deviant. As difficult as it really is—because an individualistic, competitive, and sexist culture does not foster trust and cooperation among women—women must cooperate in solidarity. Unless they do, individuals will not be sustained and the movement will die. We may hope that when a quantum number of women in leadership positions become skilled and comfortable with power, they will effectively lead toward widespread acceptance of humane feminist values.

Solidarity and Sisterhood

During a workshop for women in middle management I was startled by the very angry response of a young woman when we were discussing "sisterhood." I had said that although the word bothers me a bit because it implies an emotional affirmation and warmth I do not necessarily feel toward all women, I still can use it comfortably because it also implies a commitment to feminism. "No!" the young woman burst out. "I don't feel that way at all! I am in no sisterhood with women. Last Saturday I went to a party and it was all doctors and their wives. I have nothing in common with those women! My husband is a doctor but all those women ever did is take care of their husbands. They treat him like God. I can't talk to them and I don't like them. I would much, much rather talk with the men. At least they're interesting."

We had been enjoying the pleasure of our unity. Now it was being attacked. The other members of the group became angry and challenged the speaker. They wanted to know why she assumed that the women were only concerned with their status as doctor's wives. Why did she assume that was all they were interested in? How did she know that that was all they could talk about? Why, in short, did she identify with the men and put all those women down? "You are," they told her, "a sexist woman." She was dumbfounded. That had not occurred to her.

Most of the time I can be oblivious, in the gut-feeling sense, of sexism. I was never forced to choose between traditionally feminine and professional roles, and many women are faculty and students in my field of psychology. But occasionally I do find myself at the raw end of prejudice. This is a good experience, because then I relearn how lucky

I have been and how angry I can be. Shared awareness of sexist experiences creates cooperation, thus sisterhood, among women.

I recently served on a university committee composed largely of male physicians. There is one other female faculty member, a female secretary, and female medical student. Since everyone is aware of sexism there are no blatant stupidities, but there are many subtle putdowns. It is not obvious that we women are being ignored, since others stop talking when we speak. But the conversation picks up, when we have finished, where it was before we began.

On this committee the female secretary has no status because she is a secretary. The same is true for the student. The female professionals have no status because we are female. As a result, the women have swiftly become a team without having to say anything to each other. If we are to accomplish anything, either as professionals or as representatives of a constituency of women, we will have to support each other. The sexism of the men makes feminist issues salient. As a result, men who would prefer to remain comfortable with their prejudices have created a situation in which their values are continuously challenged. In fact, the behavior of the men has forced the women to become more militant and thus more stereotyped and predictable. That is a dangerous turn of events, as we are now more liable to be dismissed as "just women's libbers," our competence totally ignored.

Many women (and some men) achieve emotional awareness of sexism through participating in consciousness-raising groups. It is no accident that women have created a new political tool which stems from women's style of personalizing issues and finding strength through intimate relationships. While there can be destructive results when people personalize things, in consciousness raising intimacy can be used to create intellectual and emotional awareness, cooperation, and trust.

I am continuously shocked by women's surprise when they discover that it is a pleasure to talk with other women, that they share a lot, and that they can be honest with each other. We learned the same things as kids—in camp, in dorms, especially when we lived together —in "bull sessions." Bull sessions that included boys tended to be philosophical and abstract. Those with only girls tended to be personal and funny, but were largely preoccupied with the sexual games between women and men. There was no political context. Bull sessions transformed into consciousness-raising sessions have become political acts.

Consciousness-raising groups accomplish two things. First, they bring women together so that relationships can develop. This is obvious, but in a society in which women's most important commitments are supposed to be with men, creating significant relationships between women is itself revolutionary. Second, participants become aware of how much they have in common insofar as they have been molded by sexist values. This knowledge is relieving because it transforms an individual's fear that she may be neurotically incompetent, anxious, and uncertain into a perception that her doubts are common, socially caused, normal phenomena. In a sexist world few individuals are able to perceive that sexism exists and that they are victimized by it.

Thus consciousness raising helps people to become aware of their unconscious self-denigrating beliefs. Instead of continuing to blame themselves and turning their aggression upon themselves, they turn their anger outward. If they stop there, they are solaced by their rage and can point accusingly at parents or husband or children or society and say, "You are to blame for my unhappiness." In the shared beliefs of the group it is easy to locate all responsibility outside of oneself and bask in the comforting belief that one is in no way responsible for the choices one has made and the person one has become. Consciousness raising is constructive because it enables people to become aware of sexist coercion and their unconscious self-hatred. But individuals and the movement must channel the insight and energy gained into efforts that are concrete. After achieving insight, one must set goals and accomplish them if one is to achieve real self-esteem. Toward this end, women are searching for role models.

Consciousness-raising groups tend to be made up of people of the same sex and roughly the same age. When people reject the previous norms and values of society, their parents', or their own, few role models remain to guide them. Young women today have a self-awareness older women did not have at their age. They seem more ambitious than my generation was, and more aware of sexism, internal conflicts, and external difficulties. They seem more frightened of the future than we were. Women who are experiencing the shock of changing values, of consciousness raised and uncertainties created, are searching for women who seem to know what they are doing, have a course charted, and have avoided hidden reefs along the way.

We tend to idealize role models when we are scared or uncertain because we need to feel that someone has the answer, knows the game plan. Alas, we in my generation can be role models of what we are and no more than that. We cannot escape our age, our class, or the values of our times. Those of us who have careers are examples of what a few women did and most did not. We avoided the pitfalls of a traditional life but we experienced others.

No one should attempt to pattern her or his life on the blueprint of another's. No new generation can use the last as a template. Role models of people who have become successful—whatever that means to an individual—are important because their existence says that success is possible. But women, in the process of developing new values, need many models of what success can be. We will use role models most effectively not by idealizing a few but by respecting women whose lives have been gratifying in diverse ways.

One way women have generated pride is to increase the visibility of women who have been successful in the ways that society honors the most. Women have focused on those who have competed successfully in society's arenas—in art, science, academia, business, literature, and government. But the focus has been on women who have succeeded deviantly. It has, in fact, glorified largely white middle-class women, especially those in the professions.

Since the great majority of women have not succeeded in the work places, a focus on those who have leads to a further lowering of the self-esteem of those who have not. Concentrating only on work success furthers an elitism within the movement. This elitism presumes a superiority of class, education, and ambition. It is a morally intolerable put-down of traditional women, who are already too easily despised, and it is a politically dangerous threat to many women who ought to be in the movement's constituency. Elitism is not only separatism, it is one group of women threatening others as, at the same time, they are role models of what is possible.

The women's movement cannot remain parochial. Housewives and secretaries, factory workers and volunteers and professors—all sorts of women, leading all sorts of lives, can be honorable, responsible, and esteemed. A movement whose constituency is "woman" must include all kinds of people and must broaden its commitments and goals, generating ideals and objectives that are superordinate to any splinters of vested interest. There must not be a divisiveness based on an elite who have succeeded in "masculine" terms; the ultimate absurdity would be a feminist movement based on sexist values.

In the fall of 1977 I went to Washtenaw Community College's festival in celebration of International Women's Year. I was totally unprepared for what I found. There were women of all ages and backgrounds, women from all over the world, booths displaying sophisticated political tracts and booths of earnest women showing skills of canning and sewing. All sorts of women were represented; all sorts of women were there in order to be a part of the celebration. That day "the movement" spoke to everyone and reaffirmed the ideal that this movement can embrace all its great constituency.

Divisiveness within the women's movement came about in the first place because of the diversity of women. Divisiveness is enhanced when historically powerless people mistrust each other. Divisiveness between women is increased when a commitment to women seems to require less commitment to men and to children. The anti-male, anti-marriage, anti-child posture that characterized the movement in its beginning was naturally repudiated by the majority of women, who were not willing to give up old values, old priorities, old anchors of identity.

There is a lag in people's awareness that the movement has begun to shift from an anti-male preoccupation to a pro-female one. Women are increasingly writing about the contributions that women have made to their societies. Psychologically, it is enormously different when a movement is able to grow beyond its original rage and focus on its enemies, and can turn to studying the qualities and accomplishments of its members, defining their priorities from a sense of their own needs and history. With this development women will be better able to find pride in their gender as well as in their individuality.

The women's movement has begun to create the conditions that will enable women to clarify their own values as they work cooperatively together. There is a new climate in which women's relationships with each other are judged as important. This reevaluation of women and of the importance of their commitments to each other is as profound as the reevaluation of what the relationship between women and men should be. When women are able to work together and relate to each other as individuals whom they trust and like and respect, and when this becomes an ordinary experience, women will have broken through their own sexist preferences and memories of old betrayals to achieve a major step in the direction of the great revolution. Of course, women have always been friends, but these relationships would not serve as anchors as long as they were judged less important than women's relationships with men. This is changing. Now, when traditional existential anchorages are threatened, a vast new spectrum of anchorages has become possible.

Femininity and Masculinity: Changing Perceptions

9

A couple of years ago I was at a party where a professional couple who had a 3-year-old son came over to ask my advice. They were very concerned about their son's mental health, they said. They had bought him many dolls, but he persisted in playing with toy trucks and cars. I did my best to assure them that he was probably just fine.

All around us we see evidence of anxiety over gender identity. The changes we are witnessing today do not simply involve roles and responsibilities, but instead, invoke basic reformulations of what psychologically healthy women and men should be like. Sexual identity—the sense of knowing one is feminine or masculine and the certainty of what one's adult responsibilities are because of gender—has been an existential anchor for individuals and for society. We are undergoing a generally unrecognized but fundamentally revolutionary change because we no longer know what we ought to do or be as female or male, and we are no longer sure of what being an adult involves. This is reflected in the evolution of new ideas or criteria of mental health which are essentially the reverse of those we were certain of as few as ten years ago.

Historically, the great bulk of the relevant social science literature has been concerned with differences between the sexes. As professional interest in the psychology of women developed in association with the feminist movement, and as the role responsibilities of the sexes began converging, it became a scientific and political mandate to establish the existence of gender similarities.[1] Psychologists and sociologists began to concentrate on the cultural, learned, and therefore arbitrary origin of sex differences. In this decade we can see this reversal both in the professional literature and the popular press. We emphasize the similarity of the sexes by demonstrating how they share in the distribution of any characteristic, by focusing on individualism, and by emphasizing how sex roles are learned. The currently desirable implication is that no significant behavioral differences arise from biological differences. Implicit, although rarely articulated, is an attempt to refute our former sense that the sexes had different "essential natures" which had to be gratified in different sorts of activities. We now focus more on the effects of learning on behavior rather than on physiological explanations; we want to believe that human beings have infinite capacities to learn and therefore can become anything.

Psychological theories and therapies are always based on ideas of what healthy people are like and what they ought to be doing. They always involve judgments about what will make people happy or unhappy, fulfilled or constricted. Assessments about people's mental health also involve roles, the work people do, and responsibilities they have, because we do not evaluate "health" in the abstract but in relation to how people measure up to what we expect them to do. The issue of roles also involves gender, since many roles have been assigned to one sex and essentially prohibited to the other.

Thus, basic concepts of psychological health are changing because our norms are changing, and "normalcy" is always measured by criteria derived from the rules of society. Norms are based on consensus. They define the role choices, behaviors, and personality characteristics which are considered appropriate or normal. Norms are therefore powerful guides in directing people: they define goals, influence what we expect from others, and mold our self-definitions. Specific norms are blueprints which tell us how to achieve our adult identity.

On the other hand, when the norms are specific and strict, they can exaggerate sex differences, so that we may become anxious if we think we have traits or interests which belong to the opposite sex. Specific norms thus simultaneously lay the groundwork for the pain people feel when they perceive that they deviate from the consensual rules of their society, and provide the criteria and the goals by which people feel pleasure from their normalcy.

We know that we are leaving a period of rigid gender norms. We are in a transition in which old and new, complementary and contradictory, concrete and vague norms coexist. When norms are stable, we do not notice them because we take them for granted. Now that they are changing, we are forced to examine them and analyze how they affect us. We are asking the most fundamental questions: What is feminine or masculine? What are the effects of physiological gender? How alike are the sexes?

Studies of psychological sex differences began in the early part of this century. The first work was very influenced by the theory of evolution.[2] Evolutionary theory made biological and especially reproductive differences prominent, emphasized the genetic innateness of characteristics, and stimulated an overall focus on gender *differences*—with a concomitant blindness to *similarities.*

The scientific emphasis on differences reflected society's existing norms of appropriate characteristics for each sex, which had evolved so that the rules of behavior for one sex were the literal reverse of those for the other. Women were defined essentially as tender mothers, men as assertive providers, and the responsibilities of both sexes were clearly delineated. It was easy, given these widely accepted assessments, for social scientists to accept such differentiations as T. Alcott Parson and Robert F. Bales's, which characterized normal women as "expressive" and normal men as "instrumental."[3] David Gutmann described the world of women as familiar and allocentric, men's as impersonal and autocentric.[4] David Bakan made a similar distinction when he wrote that men are egocentric, while women know who they are from their experience of themselves in their relationships with others.[5]

These differences do exist to a degree in reality as well as in the stereotype. But this typology not only exaggerates the differences and encourages us to be blind to what the sexes share but also implies that the major character traits arise from and are extensions of evolutionary predispositions toward nurturance or dominance which are associated with the different reproductive tasks of the sexes.

Masculinity—Femininity Tests

To the extent that female and male are defined by their differences, gender seems to be a variable divided into two parts: what one is, and what one is not. As masculine and feminine were seen as the opposite ends of the same parameter, it followed that the first tests psychologists devised to measure masculinity and femininity would emphasize sex differences. These tests were incapable of measuring similarities because they were composed only of items which females and males answer differently and because they were scored in such a way that a subject cannot have both feminine and masculine qualities. In addition, the healthiest people were supposed to score at either extreme of the distribution—women who scored as very feminine and men who tested as very masculine.

Until recently, then, psychologists measured sexual identity by how much one is like (or says one is like) the stereotype of one's sex and by how much one is different from the opposite sex's stereotype. The stereotyped characteristics describing feminine women include *pas-*

sive, fragile, dependent, noncompetitive, nonaggressive, intuitive, receptive, afraid to take risks, emotionally labile, supportive, maternal, empathic, having low pain tolerance, unambitious, sensitive to inner feelings and to responses from other people. The comparable stereotype of masculine men is the *reverse* of that of women. Men are described as *aggressive, assertive, task-oriented, outwardly oriented, innovative, self-disciplined, stoic, active, objective, rational, unsentimental, confident, competent, courageous, analytic,* and *emotionally controlled.* Since the tests included only questions that differentiate males from females, the gender differences that resulted were exaggerated, and could not be leavened by measures in which the sexes responded in the same way. These tests were, however, accurate reflections of the norms and assumptions used by laypeople and professionals alike.

It is very difficult to measure "femininity" and "masculinity" because the terms have several meanings. While laypersons intuitively believe that they know what femininity and masculinity are, they are abstract concepts and as such, can only be measured in a derivative form. In the absence of sophisticated theory about the origins and essence of a core gender identity, investigators have measured verbal sex-role identity, sex-role preference, and sex-role adoption. "Sex-role preference" refers to the activities or character styles one prefers, and "sex-role adoption" refers to what one does. These two measures may be consistent with each other or discrepant.

"Sex-role identity" refers to one's perception of oneself as masculine or feminine and to one's judgment of how others evaluate one. Sex-role preference and adoption are concrete and therefore relatively easily measured, whereas sex-role identity and the dimension of masculinity–femininity are not and must be inferred. Measurement of masculinity–femininity and gender identity are complicated insofar as unconscious material and processes are significant.[6]

A list of what has been measured in some of the major tests clarifies what society and psychologists have considered to be healthy femininity (and by implication, masculinity). The masculinity–femininity scale of the Minnesota Multiphasic Personality Inventory (MMPI) measures the extent of culturally feminine occupations and denial of interests in culturally masculine occupations.[7] Harrison G. Gough's original femininity scale clustered into an emphasis on white-collar work, sensitivity to social interaction, social timidity and lack of confidence, compassion and sympathy, a quality of restraint and caution instead of braggadocio, and a lack of interest in abstract, political issues.[8] H. Webster's scales are (1) a preference for conventional feminine roles and interests; (2) items that refer to passivity, modesty, and a lack of domination or assertiveness; and (3) items reflecting feminine sensitivity, emotionality, introspection, and esthetic interests.[9]

In any event, if we just look at people it is obvious that masculinity and femininity are not opposite ends of a simple, unitary variable. Commonsense observation makes it clear that most people are more complicated and more variable than can be described by the stereotypic terms "masculine" and "feminine." Furthermore, within the stereotyped descriptions we do not know how generalized the significant personality characteristics are. For example, are people who are very nurturant, nurturant all, most, or some of the time? Are they equally nurturant with everyone or are they more nurturant with the young, aged, or ill? Are they appropriately or inappropriately nurturant? Are they able to respond differently when the situation changes so that they are selectively empathic, warm, and protective—or independent, assertive, and active when that would be more appropriate? Are those who are high in nurturance necessarily low in assertiveness? Do people who have many feminine interests have few that are masculine? Are people who are conventional in their sex roles necessarily conventional in personality traits?

We really cannot answer any of these questions yet. More than that, we cannot know the answers until the measures we use allow people to be simultaneously nurturant and assertive, dependent and independent, feminine and masculine. We can only see what our measures allow us to see.

As feminism generated the awareness that psychologically healthy people were likely not to be one-dimensionally feminine or masculine, new tests were created.[10] These tests are based, first, on the assumption that femininity and masculinity are not opposite ends of the same dimension, but are two independent dimensions so that anyone can be high or low on either. What we have called masculine or feminine qualities are therefore present in both men and women. The second new assumption is that people are complex rather than simple. Complexity refers to the idea that anyone can be simultaneously feminine and masculine. It also means that while people can be well aware of the simplistic gender stereotype and describe the sexes stereotypically, they may not have accepted that as the guideline for what they wanted to and have become. A third assumption is that androgynous people, those whose scores are high on both the feminine and masculine scales, have the highest levels of self-esteem. The last assumption is made because psychologists are moving toward the view that people function best if they have both feminine and masculine characteristics, and that people who cope well should feel good about themselves. This has been borne out by the research to date. In a study by Janet Spence, those who

were high in both masculinity and femininity, and were therefore clas-
sified as androgynous, were highest in self-esteem, followed by those
who scored high in masculinity and low in femininity. Those who scored
low on both sets of characteristics were lowest in self-esteem.[11] In an
extension of the Spence study, which used college students, data from
a sample of affluent adults had the same results. Women and men who
scored high on both the feminine and masculine subscales had the
highest self-esteem, and those with the lowest self-esteem scored low
on both scales.[12]

Older measures of masculinity and femininity were basically
atheoretical and reflected a simple, static version of sex differences that
paralleled the rigidly differentiated role choices of the 1950s. We are
now in a period in which change in sex roles is the major social movement. As people take on responsibilities historically associated with the
opposite sex, and as they lead increasingly complex lives, they are encouraged by the demands of their tasks to develop characteristics traditionally associated with the other sex. While traditional roles have
always required characteristics stereotypically excluded from the role
—as housewives solve problems, innovate, and make decisions, and
even male executives hug their children and can be intuitive and empathic—participation in nontraditional roles accelerates or increases
the development of a complex personality.

Increasingly, psychologists and lay observers are making the judgment that people who score high on their own gender scale and low on
the other are not psychologically healthy because their development is
too confined. We are saying that such people have developed much too
narrow a range of their own potential. This change in the criteria of
mental health is occurring because our perceptions of the appropriate
norms for each sex have changed so much, and because both sexes
increasingly share roles. Because of these changes, by 1980 many more
people will value both feminine and masculine qualities in themselves
and in others than did in 1950 to 1965.

Our new ideas about gender-related mental health are therefore
reflections of changed reality, since healthy people are defined as those
who effectively cope with what they have to do. Half the population of
American women are employed; small families have become the new
norm; men are looking for affirmation and security in their personal
relationships. Obviously women and men are participating in areas
previously assigned to the other sex and in which effective behavior
requires characteristics previously attributed to the other. Basically the
new androgynous norm is a recognition of real changes. If well-adjusted
people are those who come closest to cultural values, we can say that

in the earlier period, those who were most extremely masculine or feminine may well have been the best adjusted, whereas today androgynous people conform most to new social norms and hence might be considered the best adjusted.

The androgynous concept of psychological health defines the ideal person as having a blend of interests, abilities, and traits which are both expressive and instrumental.[13] In an androgynous society people are not forced into roles or traits on the basis of gender. To the extent that roles are not assigned on the basis of sex and that society minimizes the importance of gender and emphasizes individual capacity for taking on any set of responsibilities, we will probably find that the interests and characters of most people do become androgynous. With more freedom and fewer rigid expectations, people will want to become secure enough to feel and act in the broadest range of imaginable experience. When sexual identity can be taken for granted, people are freed and able to take risks, even in areas where action once would have labeled them unwomanly or unmanly. In time, as the androgynous personality is recognized, gender could become irrelevant to the assignment of roles. Roles would depend overwhelmingly on individual characteristics.

Physical Gender Differences

—The concept of androgyny reminds us that most people are both feminine and masculine in their interests and traits, although not necessarily to an equal extent. But we are still left with a basic question: Does physiological gender matter? That is, are some psychological sex differences likely to occur because of biological gender itself?

——We do not really know how physical gender—the physiological fact of being female or male—tends to enhance or limit what each sex can do. We are far from having clear ideas or adequate data on the ways, if any, that men and women are turned in some directions rather than others because they are physically one sex and not the other. Indeed, we are much more comfortable with a model of human development in which the significant parameters have no connection with physiology or evolution. Because of the tendency to think in either-or categories, we usually think of anything biological as fixed, permanent, immutable, unchangeable. Thus behavior (or capacity or threshhold or tendency) is thought of as either the result of unlearned, biological givens or as the consequence of learned, nonconstitutional factors.

The either-or approach is fundamentally wrong. If a member of a species or a sex has certain characteristics or proclivities that make some responses more likely than others, the responses may develop, but always in particular situations and encounters with experience. Thus any inherent constitutional quality of the organism and the experiences of that organism intersect and interact before and especially after birth.

The nature of the human species is to learn. Any genetic or physiological tendency that we have will be, from the beginning of our lives, intertwined with learning. To say, then, that learning influences the development of a behavior is true of all of our behaviors and implies nothing about any possible biological input into the development of that behavior. For example, "although many features of human sexuality obviously are controlled if not created by social conditioning, the possibility remains that behavior essential for reproduction is built up through experience from a core of unlearned stimulus-response patterns mediated by genetically controlled mechanisms."[14]

This means that the expression of any tendency is always significantly affected by the experiences that one has been encouraged to have or has been prohibited from having. If, for example, men are not given the opportunity to nurture children, then any gender tendencies women have toward nurturance that could be attributed to physiology will be enlarged, as will any physiological gender differences between men and women. For the same reason, if women are forbidden to act dominantly or aggressively and are kept from situations in which those responses are appropriate, then, in a self-fulfilling prophecy, everyone will conclude that women do not have the capacity to act aggressively and scientific studies will confirm what everyone knows.

Although it is hard to perceive basic consistencies underneath the specific differences in style and emphasis of different cultures, some sex differences seem to be universally or almost universally recognized by widely different societies. These differences appear to be linked to physiology, are related to reproduction, and can reasonably be thought of as the the result of evolutionary selection. Some sex differences that seem to be related to the reproductive tasks characteristic of each sex are very like sex differences found in many primates, and are recognized and increased through training in the great majority of cultures.

Boys and men, for instance, are more aggressive and competitive than females. Girls and women are more nurturant and responsive to children. Almost all cultures socialize males to be more aggressive, assertive, or dominant than females; and males seem to have a greater tendency to act accordingly. Though not as powerful as that relating to aggression, the data on nurturance suggests that females have a greater predisposition (or a lower threshold of sensitivity) to respond to infants than do males. Among animals and humans, taking care of young children is most frequently the responsibility of females.[15]

Sexuality is another area in which physiological differences between males and females are apparent. For one thing, sexuality is more specifically genital in males than females. For another, although there are differences between cultures in the rates of masturbation or in the frequency that adults stimulate children's genitals, the data is very consistent that males masturbate much more than females do. While 85 percent to 95 percent of American and European males masturbate, the reported rates for females are much lower. This pattern is true for most if not all cultures, even when there are severe proscriptions against masturbation. The same pattern is true for monkeys and apes.[16] While we know that prohibitions against female masturbation are usually more severe than those regarding males, still, the anatomical difference between the penis and the clitoris-vagina makes the centrality of the penis and the high rates of male masturbation predictable.

In contrast with a specifically penile sexuality learned in earliest boyhood, females learn genital sexuality later and seem to have a more diffuse sensuality. Female sexuality involves a total body erogeneity that includes nongenital areas and a greater skin sensitivity. It is probably not too farfetched to say that the greater total body sensuality of the female includes nursing, which provides erotic as well as maternal gratifications.[17]

It is not necessary here to elaborate further on the idea that specifically genital excitation develops differently between the sexes. I would simply note, first, that this is one reason why castration anxiety is much more important in the development of males; second, that it is probably an important reason why coital gratification per se is important earlier for males than females who characteristically prefer sex in the context of affection; and, third, that the sexual gratifications provided by nursing may significantly increase women's pleasure in taking care of their young children.

There are far fewer studies of infant care than one would expect. A few recent studies compare the father's response to his newborn child with the mother's within a short time after birth. They generally report no differences between the parents' responses. These studies tend to be crude assessments, made over a very short time, of gross behaviors such as whether or not the parent holds the child and for how long. There is no question that males can take care of young children and enjoy it. Of course, they can.

The question is, are there gender differences in sensitivity to the infant, or qualitative differences in how the sexes relate to the very young; and if these differences exist, do they seem to be inborn or related in some way to physiology? That is, are there any physiological tendencies that would lead cultures toward a sexual division of some roles? Are there gender differences that result in different response preferences or thresholds or tendencies?

Some provocative new data suggests that there is a sensitive or critical period shortly after delivery when mothers are especially tuned in to the baby and most likely to become attached to it. John Kennell's team found that mothers who had had 1 hour of close physical contact with their nude infants within two hours after delivery and an extra 15 hours of contact in the first three days after delivery behaved very differently at one month, a year, and even two years later. The same results were obtained with American and Guatemalan mothers. The researchers concluded that shortly after birth there is a sensitive period which appears to have rather long-lasting effects on the extent of a mother's attachment to her child.[18]

In another study, the same team found that American mothers and half of a sample of Guatemalans all displayed the same kinds of behavior to their infants during the first 10 minutes of contact with the baby.[19] They touched the baby's extremities with their fingertips and then touched the infant's trunk with their palms. American mothers, especially, tried to make eye-to-eye contact. Mothers of premature children showed only fragments of this pattern. Observations of mothers who gave birth at home show that most mothers pick the infants up immediately after birth, stroke their face, and start breastfeeding. These data, in addition to other studies of responsivity in the infant, strongly suggest that unlearned behavior patterns in both the mother and child are activated very shortly after birth and serve to unite the mother and child. While studies of mothers tell us nothing about fathers' response capacities, the idea that females are more responsive to infants seems reasonable but the present data are inconclusive.

Few studies have observed older children who have an opportunity to take care of younger children. Still, cross-cultural studies indicate that girls between the ages of 6 and 10 often behave nurturantly. In many societies girls of these ages have the major responsibility for caring for young children. A study of the number of cultures socializing girls to be nurturant found the percentage to be very high, but not as high as the percentage of cultures training males to be aggressive and independent.[20] While one interpretation of this data is that female care of infants is not as universal as male aggression, an alternative explanation is that cultures may not have to socialize as rigorously for nurturant maternal behavior as for aggressive male characteristics because there is no threat in nurturing but there is always danger in having to be aggressive.

Most of the literature about infants is concerned with the conditions that facilitate the child's development and with the baby's inborn capacity to make responses that will elicit caring behavior from those it depends upon. The focus is on the child's behavior, not the parent's. In this literature most of the discussions are about infant–*mother* bonding rather than infant–*other*. In my experience infants attach or bond with other people (and blankets and cuddly toys) who are responsive to the child and who are around often enough to be important. In most American families the mother is most available and is the person to whom the infant turns. This implies that if the father had an equal share of the responsibility for taking care of the child, the infant would be equally likely to attach to him. Although the data does not allow us to be certain, I believe it is possible that there is a general human predisposition, even a biological readiness, to respond with protective feelings and pleasure to infancy in puppies, kittens, and babies, and that the threshold for this response is lower in the female than the male.

Eleanor Maccoby and Carol Jacklin report that the most consistent sex difference is the greater aggressiveness of males in many different forms of behavior in every culture studied.[21] In addition, boys are more competitive and more resistant to directions, while girls are more compliant. This triad of characteristics—aggressiveness, competitiveness, and resistance—would seem to add up to a greater potential for dominance in males.

In another major review of the cross-cultural data on aggression, Ronald Rohner found that gender differences in aggression are universal (with males more aggressive), but the differences are very susceptible to modification because of socialization experiences. There is greater difference in aggression levels between cultures than there is between young boys and girls in the same culture; but the direction of greater male aggressiveness is universal. Rohner found no exceptions— no societies in which girls were the more aggressive. This finding is all the more remarkable, since the great majority of societies studied did not explicitly encourage greater aggression by boys. The data for adults is less clear for several possible reasons: (1) there are fewer studies of adults than children; (2) aggression may become prohibited and be expressed, for example, as leadership or dominance; (3) the behavior of male and female adults may become more alike.[22]

Steven Goldberg has defined what is meant by "aggression" in this context.[23] It does not really refer to pugnacity, belligerence, or hostility, but to an egocentric, competitive, dominating style that includes a tendency to compete if the situation lends itself to competition; a single-minded purpose and endurance; a willingness to sacrifice pleasure and affection for the possibility of control and suprafamiliar power; a need to assert one's ego; a tendency to impose one's will on the environment; a rather great resistance to doing what one has been told to do; and a tendency to dominate in relationships with the other sex.

Aggression may be significantly influenced by the effects of the sex hormones, especially testosterone. The endocrine system is directly influenced both by internal levels of the hormones and by external factors or experience. Data supports the idea that the sex hormones increase tendencies toward particular behavior, but an equally plausible derivative hypothesis is that acting in a particular way may increase the levels of the relevant endocrine. Dominant male monkeys, for example, are sexually active and aggressive and maintain high levels of testosterone. If the dominant male is defeated by other males, both its sexual and dominant behavior and its testosterone level decrease. Placed with females, the defeated male slowly recovers both his endocrine level and the capacity to behave dominantly and sexually.

If the latter hypothesis is true, then gender differences related to endocrine differences should increase significantly at adolescence, both because the steroid levels increase significantly and because the norms of gender differences become sharply differentiated when adolescents are encouraged, far more than before puberty, to engage in behavior or demonstrate personality qualities considered appropriate to their sex.[24]

The sex hormones are influential long before puberty. Some studies support the idea that male and female characteristics result partially from effects on the central nervous system before birth. For example, boys whose central nervous systems are in some ways female rather than male because they were deprived of testosterone or insensitive to androgens prenatally, are much less assertive and much more interested in taking care of babies than are boys whose endocrine–central nervous system relationships are normal.[25] Obviously, experiences after birth are crucial in creating patterns of behavior and in establishing gender identity. Gender identity in the form of the self-aware statement that you are of one sex and not of the other is clearly the result of learning. But, as one observer notes:

> Testicular secretions ... account not only for the shape of the external genitals but also for certain patterns of organization in the brain, especially by inference, in the hypothalamic pathways that will subsequently influence certain aspects of sexual behavior. ... The central nervous system ... passes on its program in the form of behavioral traits which influence other people, and which are traditionally and culturally classified as predomi-

nantly boyish or girlish . . . it is premature to attribute all aspects of gender-identity to the postnatal period of gender-identity differentiation.[26]

Gender identity is not inherited nor directly influenced by physiology, but tendencies toward certain traits are. Some of these traits relate directly to what we expect from or attribute to one gender and not the other.

Normal boys, and girls who have been exposed to abnormally high levels of androgen prior to birth, are characterized by more assertive or dominating behavior than is generally characteristic of girls. The presence of the androgen testosterone in a brief critical prenatal period seems to result in normal males and androgenized females having a greater capacity for or a lower threshold for the release of aggressive, assertive, or dominant behavior.

In this discussion of physiology, I am not saying that women do not respond to sex genitally or that men are not nurturant to small children or that women are hardly ever aggressive. What the data implies are tendencies, perhaps relative differences, in the frequencies of particular emotions that lead to dominating or nurturing behavior, which are associated with one sex far more than the other and which the great majority of cultures expect, want, and socialize for in gender-related norms. As a result, any sex differences that exist in early childhood are greatly enlarged. This is not to say that individuals of either sex could not learn the sensitivities and behavior more typical of the other. Rather, it means that in the normal course of events more individuals of one sex would, with greater ease, tend to develop characteristics thought to be typical of that sex.

Some traditional sex differences, such as differences in dependence or self-esteem, have no apparent links to constitution or physiology; they seem to be easily explained by differences in learning experiences and social values. As women and men increasingly participate in roles once assigned to the opposite sex, and as we treat children more and more asexually or androgynously and give them all the same sorts of opportunities, I expect that gender differences in learned variables will diminish and perhaps even disappear. While identical experience may lessen differences linked to gender physiology, I do not think that such differences will disappear. Differences in the thresholds for nurturing or aggressing, for example, or in the salience of the genitals, will probably remain. If these gender differences are linked to physiology, the sexes will not begin with identical interests or response tendencies in some things.

In the beginning of this chapter I noted that earlier studies were based on the premise that the major character traits of male or female arise from evolutionary predispositions associated with the different reproductive tasks of the sexes. If tendencies to nurture or dominate do originate partly from a biological difference, then, to some extent, the early premise is true. It is not completely true, however, because people have many other personality qualities. In addition, while gender is a crucial aspect of our identity, it is hardly the only one.

What is important is that if some differences between the sexes are influenced by biology, then in general these differences will exist and be recognized and expected. Expectation of sex differences influences role assignments. Since both sexes become competent in their assigned roles, sex differences should be unimportant if competence is acknowledged and rewarded. But the differences are important because role assignments carry unequal value. The personality qualities of assertiveness or nurturance combine with norm-derived pressures to lead the sexes to commitment in very differently valued activities—to the care of children or the striving for competitive success. It is also possible that when the sexes do the same thing, there will be qualitative differences in their style. This, too, would be unimportant except that in the work sphere, the area of highest status, we most respect the essentially impersonal, nonnurturant, assertive style. In other words, sexist evaluations make these differences important.

Androgyny and Reproductive Differences

Some critics object to the term "androgyny" because it is derived semantically from gender. These critics would prefer a completely asexual word. But is the androgynous person asexual? Is gender a necessary part of identity? Would we expect gender to remain significant for people with androgynous character traits?

It is very difficult to imagine that people who have a secure sense of their own identity will not think of themselves as female or male. Many things that people do have no particular or necessary link to gender, and it makes no difference whether a woman or a man does them. "Gender identity," though, refers not only to the roles people play but also to the relationship they have with their body, especially the specifically sexual body and its reproductive tasks. Identity must include one's body; the self does not reside in the head. People must find pleasure in that body, in its sexuality, in its reproductive capacity, even if they are not sexually active, because that body is an intrinsic part of their self-concept.

While everyone in every society does not reproduce—and feminism has stressed that people must not be defined by or limited to a reproductive role—reproduction is a major human commitment. Cultures socialize their children to be sexually active and to assume the responsibility of having children. While anyone may climb trees, read encyclopedias, dance, play hookey, and become an engineer or a grammar school teacher, only females become pregnant, deliver, and nurse children; and only men penetrate and impregnate the body of another.

We can all agree that people are not their reproductive system. But this is a far cry from denying that in some respects females and males are different. Angry radical feminists' denial of significant physiological differences—especially when this is accompanied by wish-fulfilling predictions of cloning and test-tube babies—seems to me to be primarily evidence of self-hate, hate of the reproductive self. In a sexist culture, men are less ambivalent about their bodies than women and do not consider gender differences and reproduction to be issues that threaten a loss of self-esteem or identity. Women can experience their gender as threatening to the extent that they believe that gender is bondage, that the reproductive system makes them vulnerable, that maternity is a loss of the individual self.

Like all major changes, the evolution of the androgynous person as an ideal of human development has constructive aspects and some destructive possibilities. Androgyny, constructively used, informs us that character and interests are not determined only by gender and reproduction. Ill used, androgyny will deny gender differences. Such denial is harmful because reproductive differences are ineradicable and because any threat these differences might create cannot be confronted if we pretend they do not exist.

Androgyny will be most ill used if we misconstrue it to mean we should go directly from the exaggerated polarity of sex differences to an ideal of asexuality. At first glance androgyny seems to supply an answer to the question of where we ought to go, for it directs our sensitivity to how our lives have been unnecessarily constricted. Yet as androgyny frees, it also creates anxiety. We have as yet developed no historical familiarities, no particular responsibilities—and therefore no existential anchors—with androgyny. To be vaguely "a person" does not substitute for gender certainty.

There can be sex-*role* transcendence, but there cannot be a gender-*identity* transcendence. People are neither neuter nor things. While there are many other components of identity, gender is still critical. We still have to know what our sex is and what it means in our society, and those who interact with us have to know this too. Perhaps, the anchorages associated with gender are more critical than are any others because, as I mentioned earlier, sex is the only thing about us that does not change as we grow up. We are anxious when we are not secured in our gender identity, and we are made anxious by those who present a fuzzy or conflicted sex identity.

We are very uncomfortable when we interact with people who are uncomfortable with their gender. Perhaps we intuitively know that people cannot have a secure sense of themselves without a firm sense of their gender; and when we deal with people who project a confused gender identity we do not know what to expect from them. In a critical way, we do not know what they are. For instance, a young person who works in an Ann Arbor bookstore is remembered, disquietingly, by everyone who has seen him. Tall and slender, he prefers tailored shirt-waist dresses which display his tiny waist. He is remarkably feminine and his appearance would not be disconcerting if he did not also have a very bushy, very long beard.

The androgynous ideal is a literal reversal of the concepts of mental health that we all learned. Until very recently, traditionally feminine women and masculine men were regarded as paragons of psychological health. It is important to understand that insofar as their major responsibilities were significantly different, they may indeed have been the best adjusted. Traditional role divisions call for more traditional character distinctions; the more extreme the polarity, the truer this will be. The research on androgyny and mental health has been based largely on college students; we know much less about older adults who are typically more traditional. We have to be careful not to assume that people whose personality characteristics and goals are traditionally feminine or masculine are limited people and less actualized than those who are androgynous. Similarly, we cannot assume that those who continue to take on traditional role responsibilities are limited to traditional gender characteristics. We cannot assume that those who say that they are happy in the traditional roles are afraid to venture out of them. We must not confuse role with character and we must not let the androgynous norm become a substitute coercive rule.

It is not difficult to imagine that actualized, mature, competent, self-esteeming people could be very masculine or very feminine or androgynous. Our emerging criteria of mental health are based on the androgynous character which, in turn, is based on nontraditional role participation. These criteria reflect the experiences, goals, and opportunities of educated middle-class people who have rejected traditional life patterns. Lest feminism and our concepts of mental health become elitist, we must not presume that those who choose to be traditional are psychodynamically constricted. Similarly, lest the new norms become coercive, we cannot assume that traditional lifestyles have to be constricted. We must instead explore the conditions under which they are self-expanding and self-affirming.

The concept of androgyny made us specify what we had already sensed as rules of participation loosened—that many aspects of our selves, many of the things we do, are not related to our sexual identity and are neither better for nor more appropriate to one sex than the other. But since androgyny is essentially an asexual concept, which deals primarily with role behaviors rather than gender identity, it can be misconstrued if used to deny the significance of gender and to ignore our need for gender identity as a part of our self-identity.

Gender is not identical with roles, interests, nor character traits. In its meaning here "gender" refers to the physiological differences between the sexes, to finding pleasure in one's body and the reproductive consequences of that body. I do not mean, for example, that a woman has to have a child in order to be a woman; rather, she has to accept that body, which could carry a child, as her own. Such acceptance is the underpinning of the statement, "I am female" or "I am male." Reproductive differences have been essential in our formulations of gender identity. If we try for an asexual concept of "personhood," we insanely deny what is blatantly obvious. If we idealize relationships in which no commitments are based on gender, we devalue and could lose too many of the existential anchors upon which we base our sense of self. Furthermore, when used to minimize gender differences, androgyny lends itself to not confronting sexist values. Some differences *exist* and our goal ought to be to accept them, to incorporate them into whatever new norms evolve, to find pleasure in complementary as well as identical pursuits, and to strip differences of pejorative, eviscerating values so that all of us can accept and find pleasure in our gender.

Toward the
Great Revolution

10

There is a general human tendency to think in straight lines, to go from *A* to *B* to *C,* to simplify complicated things. As a result, when reality is complicated and especially when it is contradictory, we are likely to construct and cling to a point of view which is comforting because it is stripped of complexity and contradiction. This is dangerous because it leads us to perceive our problems as simpler than they are and the solutions as more limited than they must be.

Somehow, after World War II, we all managed to forget that many American women had always worked and certainly had during the war. We also managed to forget that fathers had usually been fond of their children before they left to fight. An extraordinary stereotype developed about what women and men were like. Stereotypes are cartoon exaggerations, and this hyperbole, together with a ruthless social pressure, meant that people were supposed to live in accord with norms which had become unreal and unidimensional.

Incredibly, people tried to live within these guidelines. Women smilingly strangled on their organdy aprons while men gagged on their regimental ties. As they attempted to live within these social rules, people's real lives came to resemble the stereotype.

In the 1960s people began to realize how constricted their lives were, and the women's movement evolved as part of a general stream of humanistic concern about the need to develop the entire range of everyone's potential. The first realization was of constriction, the first emotion was of rage directed against the rules that had limited each individual's life, and the first reaction was to get rid of the rules. The first new rule understandably became no more rules: "Do your own thing."

Thus the new norm among the more radical chic part of society became the elimination of guidelines, and the new value was to let people evolve their unique potential according to their own individual needs and talents.

But that does not work for most people, because while we discovered how limited our lives had become together as a culture when there are no consensual norms, it is alone, as individuals, that we have the task of experimenting and trying to design a worthwhile and workable life. When values are changing, especially when they are changing quickly, people become uncertain and feel anxious. When basic ideas of healthy femininity and masculinity are changing, when the bedrock of the criteria of healthy adulthood is shifting, when our existential anchors are lost, anxiety must increase.

Most people are not able to develop without a framework, an external structure, or guide. People do not flourish when the only criterion is individual fulfillment as evaluated from within. People need commonly agreed upon directions to help them know where to go, how to get there, and how far away the goal is. In the long run people cannot sustain the anxiety that comes from not being sure about what they want to do or not being sure about what other people expect from them or they from other people. People can bear frustration because they have not reached their objectives more easily than they can sustain the anxiety of not knowing what their objectives really are. Anxiety is not reduced by anarchy. Uncertainty leads to the exaggeration of certainty. Individuals trying to cope when they are basically uncertain grab on to another set of rules because knowing any rule can provide an anchor.

Women's Liberation

A movement has to move, to surge, to go somewhere. A movement must have a goal, an in group, and an enemy. The first phase of a movement channels the latent energy of mass dissatisfaction and changes vague discontent into focused anger. Galvanized anger leads to the phase of political action, in which the line is drawn between "us" and "them" and the goal is to get what "they" have. Thus the women's movement, which was energized by its rage against the simplistic feminine stereotype of tradition, has been striving toward an equally limited masculine stereotype. Women's problems were simplified and then diagnosed as an inability to find career fulfillment; equally simplified, the solution was to substitute traditionally masculine goals for traditionally feminine ones. "Do your own thing" became "Go to work."

The high-priority goal became the achievement of equality in occupations and before the law. Although difficult to achieve, the attainment of these goals will be the easiest part of this social revolution. We can tabulate how many women, in proportion to their absolute numbers, are managers, physicians, college professors. We can determine how many females, in proportion to their absolute numbers, are in the preparatory channels in school, in government, in industry. From this information we can generate expectations of the numbers of women who ought to be in particular positions and create the legal and economic machinery to make these expectations come true.

The movement has concentrated on achieving economic parity because economic inequities are very real and can be documented, because economic independence is a critical route for self-determination and self-esteem, and because the leaders of the movement have been educated women, able to achieve and compete. To strive for a specific goal, such as increasing the percentage of women physicians, is much easier than to attempt to achieve an amorphous goal, such as winning esteem for women's humanistic style. Self-esteem is earned when people achieve goals which the culture recognizes as important and which society rewards. In this culture the straightest line to the biggest rewards is to become successful at work. It was inevitable that occupational success became the highest-priority goal of the women's movement. Besides, the easiest answer to the question of what one should do in the future is to do whatever one has not been able to do in the past.

Let us agree that change is absolutely necessary. No society can endure so long as large numbers of its population are underutilized. A society in which a large part of the population can do nothing that it believes is important cannot be sustained. Going to work and achieving success is the most obvious and the most available solution to the dreadful emptiness of having nothing you think is worthwhile to do, of feeling that you have never developed a unique identity, of believing you are not really worthy of esteem.

Change is necessary, but there is danger when change per se provides the illusion of progress. In this era of uncertainty, those who lead and seem to provide simple answers will find willing followers. No activity, involvement, commitment, is interchangeable for another. Each asks different things from us and fulfills different aspects of our selves. Parenting does not substitute for love with an adult; friendship is not the same as marriage; and work does not replace relating. While any commitment can expand to fill time (and sometimes we need to do that because there is something missing and we must fill a large empty place in our lives), let us not make that a virtue. Our ideology for change, which was first vague and open, is becoming concrete and leading women toward a different but equally narrow range of experience. Leaders must remember that it would be no small thing to inform women that they have played a losing game, that what they have done until now has been trivial. It would be no small thing to tell traditional women that they have wasted the preceding decades, that they have sought foolish goals, that they are people without significance.

More than that, I would caution against the idea that changes in the sex roles are simple, or that feminist goals are clear. Any movement for enormous social change—and the women's movement is of great magnitude—will begin by ignoring the complexity of the changes involved. The goals of this movement and the ways to achieve them seem clear only in the short run and only when efforts are focused on achieving equality in law and work.

Women and Work

One problem is our underemployment of women. I mean "employ" in the sense that individuals are able to produce to the extent of their capacity and society derives the fullest social gain possible from their participation. Clearly this is not the case for women. We do not honor women's humanistic contributions, nor do we truly encourage their work contributions.

To increase the number of women in positions of responsibility and leadership will require changes in work institutions because custom and a real fear for their own positions will lead most men and women already in the power structure to resist implementation of feminist objectives. To increase the number of women in positions of significant responsibility and power will also require certain psychological changes. Women in leadership positions will have to be certain of their motives to succeed, willing to compete and aggress, certain of their choice of role, and unafraid of their visibility, their accountability, their success.

What personality characteristics are necessary to continuously produce, innovate, and be responsible? What is needed to pursue a life in which one's self-esteem is bound up with success in competitive work? Qualities of confidence, independence, competitiveness, ambition assertiveness, and task orientation rather than people orientation more frequently characterize men than women. These are qualities necessary for competitive success in our organizations as they now exist, and therefore these are the qualities that women will have to acquire if they want to be successful. Women who achieve outstanding success in the competitive spheres of work will be very similar to outstandingly successful men.

It is understandable but paradoxical that the great surge of the women's movement has been to get women into work that will let them attain the money and status and power that men have—at the very time when men have begun to look at the male stereotype that has guided their lives and have become aware of the things they have lost in a life dominated by competition and ambition. The second paradox is that as the effort is guided by anger and the need to tear down and replace the male Establishment, the revolution to achieve self-esteem for women unwittingly accepts the premise that not just the positions but the characteristics of men are better, are more desirable than are women's. This means that women's self-esteem will be achieved to the extent that women occupy positions men have held. But until the institutions are changed, women who succeed will conform to the stereotype of male characteristics.

When women enter the system as it stands, those who succeed will do so by adapting to it—by being competitive, by submerging their interpersonal, humanistic, and supportive qualities. We must ask if the work-driven style of the successful American male is the model of what we want to become. Is achievement of *his* lifestyle to be the goal of a great social revolution of human liberation? The great risk of the women's movement is that it will stop too short; be content with economic equality instead of human freedom; and adapt to—rather than change —the institutions, the fundamental goals, and the qualities of this society.

It was inevitable that women would first assert their right to enter the hierarchies and be allowed to compete. But this must be only the first and not the ultimate goal. Feminism has the responsibility, if not the moral mandate, to become the vanguard of a new, vastly grander humanism, with more transcendent objectives than achieving equal power. Freed from sexist values, we, as a society, could conceivably strive under the leadership of women to alter the priorities and the styles of our institutions in order to foster the psychological development of each individual, the relationships of people with other people, and the relationship of people with their institutions. What we must accomplish is the reverse of the direction in which we are sliding. The worthwhile and the extraordinary revolution would be one in which the objectives and the styles historically associated with *women* become those of society and are associated with *people*.

Human Goals

If we do not force the early closure of the women's movement, we may evolve an ethic in which psychologically healthy people are simultaneously involved in their own internal growth, in the welfare of others, and in productive achievement. Now is the time to begin to construct new guidelines. In psychological terms, What should be the objectives of this human revolution?

First, this revolution should increase the breadth of people's experience in tasks and in emotions. An increased breadth of experience results in a wider range of what is acceptable, so that people are better able to experience pleasure in differences as well as similarities. Historically, our sex roles have dictated not only what we might do but also what we were allowed to feel. Men have been forced to deny their vulnerabilities and dependencies, just as women have been led to deny their anger and ambition. Let us make a broad range of feeling and experience part of everyone's expectations about living. In the same way that we practice analysis, logic, and reason, we should develop skills of feeling, intuiting, and synthesizing—because we need to develop the senses as well as the intellect.

Second, this revolution should increase commitment both to other people and to tasks. This means being able to take seriously the involvements which are important to us and to be committed while still retaining a sense of our individual selves. Growth of individuals is achieved through responsibility and commitment; meaning is provided by working toward an objective that is worth accomplishing. Let us understand why this decade evolved goals of hedonism and let us allow ourselves to learn that purely self-centered and therefore conditional commitments deprive us of certainty in objectives and relationships. People who are liberated are not free of real responsibilities and commitments, but they are free of the psychological coercion of having to conform to or rebel against responsibilities and relationships.

Third, the human revolution should reduce alienation and loneliness by encouraging the development of community. We emphasize individuality and success in a lonely competition. We tend to ignore the alienating effect of this focus on individuality and the sustaining effect of a network of other people when there is a feeling of community and sharing. The shift of women's values to success in competitive work devalues women's traditional commitment to enhance the welfare of people. Let us make the latter commitment more significant, not less. Let us increase people's commitment to people through community, undoing the isolation of individuals through the creation of neighborhoods, networks, co-ops, and anything else that provides a sense of secure belonging.

Fourth, our goal should be to increase people's feeling that they are responsible for their own lives. We should enable people to feel that they control their lives and are their own source of energy. It is necessary to end the belief that people are the sum of external pressures from culture and school and parents and contemporary relationships. People of all ages have to be able to experience themselves as effective and having some potency by doing work that has some importance to them and making some worthwhile contribution. People must participate in the decisions that impinge on their lives and must exercise at least some control over what happens to them. Given the opportunity to be responsible for themselves, people must be held accountable for their decisions.

Fifth, this revolution should increase people's self-aware, conscious joy. Everyone should sometimes experience the feeling that "At this moment I am happy, I feel good, I am alive in my body, I feel creative." People must be helped to sense acutely what is going on and what they are feeling. To do this we must acknowledge the extent to which people are bound by situations and how often these situations are static. In order for people to experience some enjoyment in their being, lives have to become less habituated because habit dulls perception and routine dulls feeling and awareness.

Sixth, we must increase people's feelings of *Me!* People who are unable to experience themselves as *Me!* are without a clearly defined sense of self and seem to lack the confidence or assertiveness that would enable them to risk and try new ventures. When there is no sense of *Me!*, individuals experience themselves as a reflected self, derived from the sum of other people's responses to them. The *Me!* self has a sense of wholeness or integrity even when roles or relationships or tasks change. From a secured sense of self, one can respect oneself as well as others.

Seventh, we need to increase people's sense of the organic unity of all living things and of the relatedness of living things to their inorganic base. Rather than emphasizing knowledge of a set of facts, we must cultivate awareness of the unity of time past and future and of the connectedness of all things. This feeling state is the existential anchor of our belonging within the universe. Let us end our alienation from nature and our isolation from each other.

The seven psychological goals specified above aim to increase feelings of worth and reduce feelings of loneliness. This list does not specify roles or norms, but it begins to specify objectives. These goals are "feminine," yet they embody the "masculine" principle of individuality and competence. Change will require feeling and knowing, discipline and intuition, experience and organization, in the real world. A fundamental assumption of these objectives is that the optimum development of an individual and of society requires the growth of autonomy, a sense of *Me!*, and real productive accomplishment. It also requires the development of feeling and of the sense of belonging in a relationship, a society, within creation itself. Would it, then, be sufficient to more simply state that our goal ought to be the recognition of androgyny, that within every individual and within almost every role there are both "feminine" and "masculine" components?

Androgyny

As far as we know throughout history and in very varied cultures, women have had major responsibility for the care of infants and young children, and men have been expected to assume an aggressive stance. Two polarities of personality developed as a result of the two milieus in which the sexes have had to function.

The emphasis for men has been to develop ego strength, the capacity to delay acting upon impulse, an orientation toward the future, individuality achieved through strong ego boundaries, and a general quality of rationalism and objectivity. Men have been encouraged to emphasize separation, task mastery, isolation, competition, and the repression of feelings.

Women have been encouraged to focus on feelings—sharing with others, being predictable to others, being concerned with others. The emphasis for women has been on communion, contact, union, cooperation, and openness to others and to their own and others' feelings.

While neither of these polarities is sufficient to be a complete human style, the danger of the androgynous vision lies in the possibility that our goal will become the development of an asexual culture. While many of the things that we do are essentially asexual in the sense that it does not make any difference whether they are done by a woman or a man, it would be a pity if an emphasis on androgyny blurred the complementary excitements that are created from the differences in how women and men perceive and feel.

We are beginning to realize that we have accepted a mode of analyzing, thinking, and perceiving that distinguishes between the conscious and the unconscious, mind and body, rational and emotional, scientific and intuitive. We accept as information only that which can be constructed by the conscious mind as rational, logical, and scientific, and we have valued only those with strong ego boundaries who think in this style. If one perceives and experiences in only the rational and logical mode, one must limit experience. The feminine mode emphasizes feelings, synthesizing, and intuiting. It is characterized as subjective, subconscious, emotional, without boundaries, emphasizing the relationships between or the togetherness of things. While everyone can learn this style, we can wonder whether the "feminine" mode is more characteristic of women because of women's relationship with their body.

My Feelings

Communicating with feelings directly, not trying to shape them into familiar verbal channels but allowing imagery to flow as I thought about this question, I have come into unexpected places. My experience is difficult to articulate because it requires transforming sensations and images into words and ideas. Still, let me try to describe my image.

It seems to me that men and women connect with the great events of death and of birth differently. I believe that women are closer to the creation of life and to blood and thereby to dying, and that women are more prone to protect, nurture, and create bonds than are men. Women's love is more likely to involve protection, tenderness, and commitment. My image is not passive or pastoral but grand. In the garden of the Museum of Modern Art in New York there is a statue of a great, nude, heroic woman. This figure is Power, the Mother of Us All, the Knower of the Mysteries, Mother Earth. It suggests the ultimate base and the firmament; it belongs within the cycle of creation and destruction, of life and death. This figure is the opposite of rational man, who dominates nature. The power of creation it embodies may be, in fact, the source of male terror of women, for the last and best mystery is, If women create life, then do women control death?[1]

Of course, men know death too, but I think that their image is likely to be that of Icarus flying too close to the sun, an individual being struck down as he grapples with the furies and defies the gods. In the male sense, death is a severing and an ending. In the female image, death is still terrible and unknown, but it is a beginning as well as an end, a merging into creation and not a final severing. My image of women's grief is closed inward, body bent over, encircling the self, lying on the earth. Connecting.

I do not confuse the part of myself in which I know I am feminine with some shared abstract idea of humanity; this part of myself I share with women, but not with children and not with men. Biologically, in ways I do not know but intuit, I am feminine. It is in my feminine essence that I know life and I know connection. It is the feminine essence of me that creates life and celebrates that life and creates bonds and preserves and protects that life and those bonds. I have given life, and in this way I am familiar with death. This knowledge is the wellspring of my connectedness. This *knowledge* I share with men; this *experience* I share with women. This experience cannot be the same as the rational acceptance of the idea.

I am neither defining women as mothers nor prescribing maternity. Rather, it was in my maternal experiences that I came closest to the feeling essence of the feminine. In order to know oneself as creative, alive, and a part of creation, one has to feel, not think. All of the ways by which we come to this awareness will be experiences in which we *feel* with sharp clarity the sense of building and connecting—and of being lonely and dying.

Sometimes I, too, believe that I am untouched by the millennia of generations before me, untouched by the turning of the earth or the waxing and waning of the moon, untouched by human evolution. Then I, too, believe that I am different from all the creatures that have existed on this earth, and I believe that humanity is created solely by culture and humans have created themselves. Sometimes I also forget that people have used these beliefs to separate themselves from the rest of creation. From the idea of the uniqueness and the separateness of our species, human beings have created the intellectual basis of each individual's aloneness. Finding our anthropocentric megalomania to be a virtue, we deny our connectedness with all other things living and we deny our knowledge of our death.

Life holds awesome miracles and terrors that have not changed since hominids crouched in caves keening over a child inexplicably cold and silent, since a woman squatted giving birth and another lived. Those who would declare that they, alone, are sufficient; that they do not need or want the bonds of present community or the organic ties to the future which are the children, those who would raise aloneness, individuality, and separateness as the goals of human maturity, have lost their sense of awe and denied that particularly human knowledge of need and of terror.

In addition to knowing, it is necessary to feel love and tenderness, fire, rage, and passion. This sense of the existential feminine constructs a powerful image and needs no apology. Life is a very lonely enterprise. Let us not continue to maximize each individual's loneliness and isolation from others. To limit our revolutionary goals to those of competitive achievement would be to limit our humanity.

The necessary first step in this social revolution is the achievement of economic, legal, and social parity. But byond successful participation in society women must esteem themselves, honoring whatever is unique in their experiences and capacities. The movement has well articulated the ways in which feminine biology has served as a mechanism to limit women's lives. The feminine truth must also ultimately recognize the creativity and power of our biology and the values derived from it. These are the values that celebrate growth and life. Are there any which are more important?

Most of us have lost our sense of religion. I mean by that the sense of awe that comes from the mysteries of creation and the cycles of life and death. The creation of a new structure of beliefs will require changing from a journey into outer space to a journey into our own interiors. A preoccupation with material things and external events lets us avoid our own depths and encourages a shallowness that precludes real joy or despair; the sense of heroics or tragedy; the transcendence of individuality; and the urgencies of sin, guilt, rage, goodness, and exultation.

Some of us hope that in a confrontation with our essential nature —as we flow into our experiences and being to find out what they are —we shall locate some organic sense of belonging to each other and to all of creation, so that we will find meanings in our relationships with ourselves, with others, and with whatever the essence of life might be. Some believe that we will find a new system of human values because we will experience new truths. Let us call for the exploration of the feminine within all of us, and for a search for the sense of religiosity that infuses life with contexts of meanings, beliefs, and priorities. Now is the time for the establishment of new existential anchors.

A social revolution must set grand objectives, goals which transmute the dross of ordinary realities to the gold of ideals. The feminist movement needs to develop goals so extraordinary that even if they cannot be achieved in their totality, their immensity and grandeur will provide all of us who work toward them with a sense of rightness, merit, and even majesty. These are the feelings and convictions that we must have. It is enormously difficult to conceptualize grand objectives that transcend the limited ones with which we are familiar. It is made even more difficult when the values and the style of our group have never been esteemed, clarified, and legitimized.

The first phase of the movement was the clarification of frustration and rage and the generation of awareness. The specifics of the next phase are unknown, but it should come from women's own existential truths. It is realistic to expect that women, whose experiences are both like and unlike those of men, will as a marginal group have perspectives and thus priorities which are different from men's. Goals of protecting and enhancing life and qualities of sensitivity and empathy require no apology. Women's experiences have led them to connect how they see themselves and society with less rigid mental boundaries than men, so that women move more easily between reason and intuition, knowing and feeling. By esteeming reason over feeling and achievement over caring, society has most rewarded men and those women who succeed in the masculine style. But the hope for a transcendent movement comes from the belief that when women are freed from their own sexism and reach for their own truths through the dialetic of feeling and knowing, then unburdened, they will be freed to develop objectives not yet imagined. Herbert Marcuse wrote: "What is at stake in this transcendence is the negation of the exploiting and repressive values of patriarchal civilization. What is at stake is the negation of the values enforced and reproduced in society by male domination."[2]

Women are not better than men, but they are not lesser. Women are not totally different from men, but they are not altogether the same. When the women's movement moves further from its initial focus on men and is able to celebrate women, it will be freed to lead in both humanistic and rational directions. When the women's movement becomes a human movement, its objectives will affirm the ultimate priority—human welfare—and its consitituency will include all of us.

The first wave of awareness is past, and the great surge of anger is over. The momentum of the movement has slowed now; the concerns of feminists have tended to become individualistic. Thus each woman is trying to better her own position. A self-actualized life cannot be found for any long period in self-aggrandizement, in small and egocentric preoccupations. People need to see themselves as good, as contributing, as accomplishing something of value, as having a purpose. This view gives meaning to our lives. Human beings need a system of values; a sense of themselves as moral; a hope that they will be able to create, build, become part of something. When nothing is really worth doing, when nothing is really significant, then events are unremarked and accomplishments are ephemeral. When nothing is worth living for, when no meaning ennobles what we do, we become vaguely anxious and episodically hedonistic. Basically, we become chronically depressed, with no sense of a future.

At least some of the time people need to feel expanded in efforts involving a purpose greater than self-concerns, to feel transcended and heroic, and to experience themselves as larger than their ordinary selves. Too many of us have lost any sense of passion, involvement, or caring. To care intensely is to experience life. When one does not care and is not involved, life passes calmly, perhaps, but without passion. As we drift in the egocentric channel of things pleasant or annoying, we lose the sense of nobility or of tragedy.

In a sense we have lost contact with the feminine in ourselves. We are familiar with the masculine. We are well practiced in the abilities with which we deal with outside matters. But the feminine, or the subjective, of everyone is lost from experience—is untutored, undeveloped, unperceived. As long as we ignore or pay only fleeting attention to our emotional processes and internal states, in a quite real way we will not know what we are.

I do not know what truths or visions will be constructed when we permit ourselves to know the wholeness of our experience. But I am certain that the goals of revolution that we now espouse will then seem narrow, pale, and superficial.

If we are fortunate and the women's movement does not simply emulate the goals and the style of achieving men, but affirms the existential truth that is female, then we may be able to create a society, with a new emphasis on the whole and not the individual, on community rather than separateness, on feeling as well as knowing, on the person as well as the task. For men as well as women, for all of us who have been freed from issues of survival but who can never be freed from the sacred mysteries of being born and being alone and someday dying, this will be the worthwhile, the great, revolution.

Notes

Introduction

1. Demos, J. "Myths and Realities in the History of American Family Life," in Henry Grunebaum and Jacob Christ (Eds.), *Contemporary Marriage*, Little, Brown and Company, Boston, 1976, pp. 9–31.
   Banks, A. J., and Banks, Olive. *Feminism and Family Planning in Victorian England*, Schocken Books, Inc., New York, 1975.
2. Bernard, Jessie. *Women, Wives, Mothers: Values and Options*, Aldine Publishing Co., Chicago, 1975.
3. Bradburn, N. M., and Caplovitz, D. *Reports on Happiness*, Aldine Publishing Co., Chicago, 1965.
4. Van Dusen, R. A., and Sheldon, E. B. "The Changing Status of American Women: A Life Cycle Perspective," *American Psychologist*, Feb. 1976, pp. 106–116.
5. Bradburn and Caplovitz, *op. cit.*

Chapter 1

1. Platt, J. "Women's Roles and the Great World Transformation," *Futures*, Oct. 1975, pp. 420–427.
2. Mayer, Michael F. *Divorce and Annulment in the 50 States*, 3rd rev. ed., Arco Publishing Co., Inc., New York, 1975.
3. Hegner, Karen C. (Ed.). *Peterson's Annual Guide to Undergraduate Study 1978*, Peterson's Guides, Princeton, N.J., 1978.
4. *Statistical Abstract of the United States*, U.S. Department of Commerce, Bureau of the Census, Washington, D.C., 1977, p. 64.
5. La Nove, G. R., and Miller, N. L. "Accounting for Education," *Society*, Jan.-Feb. 1976, pp. 52–58. The quotation is from page 57.
6. "Faculty Pay Rose 5.2%, NCES Finds; Women Show Gains," *Chronicle of Higher Education*, April 21, 1978, *27*(16), 6.
7. Keyserling, M. D. "Economic Status of Women in the United States," *American Economic Association*, *66*(2) May 1976, 205–212.
8. Roper Organization, "A Survey of the Attitudes of Women on Marriage, Divorce, the Family and America's Changing Sexual Morality," *The Virginia Slims American Women's Opinion Poll*, Vol. 3, 1975.

9. These findings are described in Pleck, J. H. "Males' Traditional Attitudes toward Women: Correlates of Adjustment or Maladjustment?" unpublished paper, Feb. 1975, 14 pp.
10. Shaevitz, Morton H., and Shaevitz, Marjorie H. "Changing Roles, Changing Relationships: Implications for the Mental Health Professional," *Psychiatric Annals, Women In Psychiatry,* Feb. 1976, *6*(2), 11 pp.
11. Tavris, C. "It's Tough to Nip Sexism in the Bud," *Psychology Today,* Dec. 1975, pp. 58, 102.
12. Mitchell, G. "Consciousness Raising Activity for Classroom Use," unpublished paper, 1975, p. 6.
13. Harrison, B. G. "The Books That Teach Wives to be Submissive," *McCall's,* June 1975, *83,* 113–116.
14. Lear, M. W. "You'll Probably Think I'm Stupid," *The New York Times Magazine,* April 11, 1976, pp. 30–31, 107–121. The quotation is from page 114.
15. Roper Organization, *op. cit.*
16. Mason, K. O., Czajka, J. L., Arber, S. "Change in U.S. Women's Sex-Role Attitudes, 1964–1974." *American Sociological Review, 41*(4), 573–596. For a marvelous political and historical analysis of the history of the current feminist movement, the reader is directed to Freeman, Jo. *The Politics of Women's Liberation,* David McKay Co., New York, 1975.
17. Harris, L. "Changing Views on the Role of Women," *The Harris Survey,* December 11, 1975.
18. Jacoby, S. "Women's Lib Plays in Peoria," *Saturday Review,* Feb. 8, 1975, *10,* 43–44.
    Anderson, P. "Women's Organizations: It's a Whole New Scene," *Family Circle,* Apr. 1976, pp. 19–22.

Chapter 2

1. Broverman, I. K., Vogel, S. R., Broverman, D. M., Rosenkrantz, P. S., and Clarkson, F. E. "Attitudinal Factors Affecting Family Size," prepared for the Center for Population Research, NICHD, 1975.
2. Lopata, Helena Z. *Occupation: Housewife,* Oxford University Press, New York, 1971.
3. Maslow, Abraham. *Toward a Psychology of Being,* 2nd ed., Van Nostrand Reinhold Company, New York, 1968. See especially p. 136.
4. Goldberg, Steven. *The Inevitability of Patriarchy,* William Morrow and Company, New York, 1973–1974.
5. Favell, A. C., Cunningham, I. C. M., and Green, R. T. "The Liberated American Wife: Fulfillment or Frustration," unpublished manuscript.
6. Menaker, E. "The Therapy of Women in the Light of Psychoanalytic Theory and the Emergence of a New View," in Violet Franks and Vasanti Burtle (Eds.), *Women in Therapy,* Brunner/Mazel, New York, 1974, pp. 230–246.
7. Block, J. H. "Conceptions of Sex Role; Some Cross-Cultural and Longitudinal Perspectives," *American Psychologist,* June 1973, pp. 512–526.

8. Goldberg, *op. cit.*

   Spence, J. T., Helmreich, R., and Stapp, J. "Ratings of Self and Peers on Sex-Role Attributes and Their Relation to Self Esteem and Conceptions of Masculinity and Feminity," *Journal of Personality and Social Psychology,* 1975, *32*(1), 29–39.

   O'Connor, K., Mann, D., and Bardwick, J. M. "Relationships between Self-Ratings of Individual and Stereotypical Sex-Role Identification and Self-Esteem in an Upper Class Adult Population," *Journal of Consulting and Clinical Psychology,* 1978.

9. Broverman, I. K., Broverman, D. M., Clarkson, F. E., Rosenkrantz, P. S., and Vogel, S. R. "Sex-Role Stereotypes and Clinical Judgments of Mental Health," *Journal of Consulting and Clinical Psychology,* 1970, *34*(1), 1–7.

10. Fabrikant, B. "The Psychotherapist and the Female Patient: Perceptions, Misperceptions and Change," in Violet Franks and Vasanti Burtle (Eds.), *Women in Therapy,* Brunner/Mazel, 1974, pp. 83–109.

11. Douvan, E. "Higher Education and Feminine Socialization," in Trites, Donald G. (Ed.), *The Future of the Undergraduate College: New Directions for Higher Education,* 1975, Vol. 9, San Francisco, Jossey-Bass, Inc., pp. 37–50.

Chapter 3

1. Yankelovich, D. "Angry Workers, Happy Grads," *Psychology Today,* Dec. 1974, pp. 81–87.

2. "The Outlook, Review of Current Trends in Business and Finance," *Wall Street Journal,* Mar. 8, 1976, p. 1.

3. *Background Facts on Women Workers in the United States,* Women's Bureau, Workplace Standards Administration, U.S. Dept. of Labor, Washington, D.C., 1970.

4. Rohrlich, L. T., and Vatter, E. L. "Women in the World of Work: Past, Present and Future," *Women's Studies,* 1973, *1,* 263–277.

5. Bird, Carolyn. *Born Female: The High Cost of Keeping Women Down.* Simon & Schuster: New York, 1960.

6. Goldberg, Steven. *The Inevitability of Patriarchy,* William Morrow and Company, New York, 1973–1974.

7. Aronson, S. G. "Marriage with a Successful Woman: A Personal Viewpoint," in Ruth Kundsin (Ed.), *Successful Women in the Sciences: An Analysis of Determinants, Annals of the New York Academy of Sciences,* March 15, 1973, *208*.

   Vinacke, W. E. "Power, Strategy, and the Formation of Coalitions in Triads under Four Incentive Conditions," *Bulletin du CERP,* 1964, *13*, 199–144.

   Bunker, B. B. "Women in Groups," in B. E. Wolman (Ed.), *International Encyclopedia of Neurology, Psychiatry, Psychoanalysis and Psychology,* in press.

8. Mead, Margaret. *Male and Female,* New American Library, New York, 1949, p. 240.

9. Horner, M. S. "Fail: Bright Women," *Psychology Today,* Nov. 1969, *3*(6), 36.
   Horner, M. S. "Toward an Understanding of Achievement-Related Conflicts in Women," *Journal of Social Issues,* 1972, *28*, 157–175.
10. It is relevant that women who choose nontraditional fields are often in relationships with men who support their choices. See, for example, Schwenn, M. "Arousal of Motive to Avoid Success," unpublished junior honors thesis, Harvard University, 1970; and Hawley, P. "Perceptions of Male Models of Femininity Related to Career Choice," *Journal of Counseling Psychology,* 1972, *19*, 308–313.
11. Tresemer, D. "Fear of Success in Males and Females: 1965 and 1971," *Journal of Consulting and Clinical Psychology,* 1974, *42*(3), 353–358.
    Hoffman, L. W. "Fear of Success in Males and Females: 1965 and 1971," *Journal of Consulting and Clinical Psychology,* 1974, *42*(3), 353–358.
12. Powell, D. H., and Driscoll, P. F. "Middle-Class Professionals Face Unemployment," *Society,* Jan.–Feb. 1973, pp. 18–26.
13. Bardwick, J. M. "The Dynamics of Successful People," in Dorothy McGuigan (Ed.), *New Research on Women,* University of Michigan Press, Ann Arbor, Mich., 1974, pp. 86–104.
14. Ogilvie, B. C. "Stimulus Addiction: Sweet Psychic Jolt of Danger," *Psychology Today,* Oct. 1974, pp. 88–94.
15. Bardwick, J. M., and Douvan, E. "Women and Work," in Rosalind Loring and Herbert Otto (Eds.), *New Life Options: The Working Woman's Resource Book,* McGraw-Hill, New York, 1967, pp. 32–45.
16. *Ibid.,* p. 44.
17. For an eloquent account of what happens to people when they have to become a commodity which they sell, see Fromm, Erich. *Man for Himself,* Holt, Rinehart and Winston, New York, 1947. An interesting article on this subject is Maccoby, M. "The Corporate Climber," *Fortune,* Dec. 1976, pp. 98–101, 104–108.

Chapter 4

1. "The Parent Gap," *Newsweek,* Sept. 22, 1975, pp. 48–56.
2. Veevers, J. E. "The Violation of Fertility Mores: Voluntary Childlessness as Deviant Behavior," in Craig Boydell, Carl Grindstaff, and Paul Whitehead (Eds.), *Deviant Behavior and Societal Reaction,* Holt, Rinehart and Winston, Toronto, 1972, pp. 571–592. The quotation is from p. 398.
3. Freedman, Ronald, Coombs, L., and Bumpass, L. "Stability and Change in Expectations about Family Size: A Longitudinal Study," *Demography,* 1964, *2*, 250–275. The quotation is from p. 253.
4. Freedman, R., Whelpton, P. K., and Campbell, A. A. *Family Planning, Sterility and Population Growth,* McGraw-Hill, New York, 1959, p. 56.
5. Whelpton, P. K., Campbell, A. A., and Patterson, J. E. *Fertility and Family Planning in the United States,* Princeton University Press, Princeton, N.J., 1966, p. 163.

6. Rainwater, Lee. *Family Design: Marital Sexuality, Family Size, and Contraception.* Chicago, Aldine Publishing Co., 1965, pp. 150–151.
7. "Subject Report PC(2)-3A, Women by Number of Children Ever Born," *Census of the U.S., 1970,* U.S. Department of Commerce, Bureau of the Census, Washington, D.C., 1970.

   Novak, E. R., Jones, G. S., and Jones, H. W., Jr. "Infertility and Abortion," in *Novak's Textbook of Gynecology,* 9th ed., William & Wilkins, Baltimore, 1975 , ch. 29, p. 625.

   Evans, P. N. "Infertility and Other Office Gynecologic Problems," in David N. Danforth (Ed.), *Textbook of Obstetrics and Gyncology,* 2nd ed., Harper & Row, New York, 1971, ch. 41, p. 798.
8. Veevers, J. E. "Voluntarily Childless Wives: An Exploratory Study," *Sociology and Social Research,* Apr. 1973, *57,* 356–366.
9. Blake, J. "Can We Believe Recent Data on Birth Rate Expectations in the United States," *Demography,* 1974, *11,* 25–44.
10. *University Record,* "ACE on "Typical" Freshman—M. Frosh: Still Ambitious But Success Not Utmost." University of Michigan publication, April 3, 1972, p. 3.
11. Lozoff, M. M. "Changing Life Styles and Role Perceptions of Men and Women Students," paper presented at "Women: Resource for a Changing World" Conference, sponsored by Radcliffe Institute, Cambridge, Mass., Apr. 17–18, 1972.
12. Wolfe, L. "The Coming Baby Boom," *New York Magazine,* January 10, 1977, pp. 38–42.
13. Hoffman, L. W. "Effects of Maternal Employment on the Child. A Review of the Research," *Developmental Psychology,* 1974, *10*(2), 204–228.
14. Friedan, B. "In France, de Beauvoir Had Just Published 'The Second Sex,' " *New York Magazine,* Dec. 30, 1974, pp. 53–55. The quotation is from pp. 54–55.
15. Lopata, Henena Z. *Occupation Housewife.* Oxford University Press, New York, 1971.
16. Lewis, E. *Psychological Determinants of Family Size,* unpublished doctoral dissertation, University of Michigan, 1972.
17. Bram, S. *To Have or Have Not: A Social Psychological Study of Voluntarily Childless Couples, Parents-To-Be, and Parents,* unpublished doctoral dissertation, University of Michigan, 1974.
18. Birnbaum, J. A. *Life Patterns, Personality Style and Self-Esteem in Gifted Family Oriented and Career Committed Women,* unpublished doctoral dissertation, University of Michigan, 1971.
19. Osmond, H., Franks V., and Burtle, V. "Changing Views of Women and Therapeutic Approaches: Some Historical Considerations." In Violet Franks and Vasanti Burtle (Eds.), *Women in Therapy,* Brunner/Mazel, New York, 1974, pp. 3–24.
20. Bowlby, J. "Some Pathological Processes Set in Train by Early Mother–Child Separation," *Journal of Mental Science,* 1953, *99,* 265–72.
21. Bowlby, J. *Attachment and Loss,* Vol. 1, Basic Books, New York, 1969.

22. "Child Abuse Called National Epidemic," *American Psychological Association Monitor, Washington Report,* Jan. 1976, p. 18.
23. Norton, A. "Female Family Heads," *Current Population Reports,* Special Studies, Series P-23, No. 50, 1974, p. 33 (ERIC).
24. "The Parent Gap," *op. cit.*
25. Fraiberg, S. *Child Care Industries Incorporated.* Unpublished manuscript, 29 pp.
    Lewis, R. "Child Care Bill Stranded in Wake of Veto Threat," *The Ann Arbor News,* October 19, 1975, p. 8.
    Moore, P. "NAS Panel Urges Income Aid for Children and Families," *American Psychological Association Monitor,* Jan. 1977, *8*(1), 1, 9.
26. Steinfels, M. O. *Who's Minding the Children? The History and Politics of Day Care in America.* Simon & Schuster, New York, 1973.
27. Fraiberg, *op. cit.*
28. Pixler, P. "Notes from China," *Whirlwind,* no date, pp. 11–17.
29. Laslett, P. "Size and Structure of the Household in England over Three Centuries." *Population Studies,* July 1969, *23,* 199–223.
    Goode, William J. *World Revolutions and Family Patterns.* Free Press, New York, 1963.
    Litwak, E. "Extended Kin Relations in American Industrial Society," in E. Shanas and G. Streib (Eds.), *Social Structure and the Family,* Prentice-Hall, Englewood-Cliffs, N.J., 1965.
30. Etaugh, C. "Effects of Maternal Employment on Children: A Review of Recent Research," *Merrill-Palmer Quarterly,* Apr. 1974, *20,* 71–98.
31. Trotter, S., "Day Care Given a Clean Bill of Health," *American Psychological Association Monitor,* Apr. 1976, p. 4.
32. Hoffman. L. W. *op. cit.*
33. Blake, J. "Coercive Pronatalism and American Population Policy," *Preliminary Paper No. 2,* International Population and Urban Research, University of California, Berkeley, Calif., Dec. 1972.

Chapter 5

1. Abbott, Sidney, and Love, Barbara. *Sappho Was a Right-on Woman,* Stein & Day, New York, 1973.
2. Christensen, H. T., and Gregg, C. F. "Changing Sex Norms in America and Scandinavia," *Journal of Marriage and the Family,* 1970, *32,* 616–627.
    Kantner, J. F., and Zelnik, M. "Sexual Experience of Young Unmarried Women in the United States," *Family Planning Perspectives,* Oct. 1972, pp. 9–18.
    Hunt, Morton. *Sexual Behavior in the 1970s,* Playboy Press, Chicago, 1974.
    Levin, R. J., and Levin, A. "Sexual Pleasure: The Surprising Preferences of 100,000 Women," *Redbook,* Sept. 1975, *145,* 51–58.
    Reiss, I. "Premarital Sexual Standards," in C. B. Broderick and Jessie Bernard (Eds.), *The Individual, Sex, and Society,* Johns Hopkins University Press, Baltimore, 1969, pp. 109–118.

Schoof-Tams, K., Schlaegel, J., and Walczak, L. "Differentiation of Sexual Morality between 11 and 16 Years," *Archives of Sexual Behavior,* 1976, *5*(5), 353–370.

3. See citations in note 2.
4. Hunt, *op. cit.*
5. Sherfey, M. J. "The Evolution and Nature of Female Sexuality in Relation to Psychoanalytic Theory," *Journal of the American Psychoanalytic Association,* 1966, *14*(1), 28–128.

   Masters, William H., and Johnson, Virginia E. *Human Sexual Response,* Little, Brown and Company, Boston, 1966.
6. A summary of this literature is found in Ellis, A. "The Treatment of Sex and Love Problems in Women," in Violet Franks and Vasanti Burtle (Eds.), *Women in Therapy,* New York: Brunner/Mazel, 1974, pp. 284–306. See especially pp. 291–292.
7. Tripp, Charles. *The Homosexual Matrix,* McGraw-Hill, New York, 1975.
8. Kaplan, Helen S. *The New Sex Therapy,* Brunner/Mazel, New York, 1974.
9. Bauman, K. E., Wilson, R. R. "Premarital Sexual Attitudes of Unmarried University Students: 1968 vs. 1972," *Archives of Sexual Behavior,* 1976, *5*(1), 29–37.

   Maddock, J. W. "Sex in Adolescence: Its Meaning and its Future," *Adolescence,* Fall 1973, *8*(31), 325–342.

   Lewis, R. A., and Burr, W. R. "Premarital Coitus and Commitment among College Students." *Archives of Sexual Behavior,* 1975, *4*(1), 73–79.
10. Macklin, E. D. *Cohabitation Research Newsletter,* Oct. 1973, No. 3, mimeographed.

    Macklin, E. D. "Cohabitation in College, Going Very Steady," *Psychology Today,* Nov. 1974, pp. 53–59.

    Macklin, E. D. *Cohabitation Research Newsletter,* June 1974, No. 4, mimeographed.

    Danziger, C., and Greenwald, M. Cited in Edrich, H. *Alternatives: A Look at Unmarried Couples and Communes,* Institute of Life Insurance, New York.

    Garza, J. M. *Living Together and the Double Funnel Theory of Courtship,* paper presented at the 4th Annual Sociological Research Symposium, Virginia Commonwealth University, Richmond, Feb. 28–Mar. 2, 1974.
11. Roper Organization. *The Virginia Slims American Women's Opinion Poll,* Vol. 3, 1970 and 1974.
12. Bardwick, J. M. "Middle Age and a Sense of Future," *Merrill-Palmer Quarterly,* 1978, *24*(2), 129–138.
13. Wolfe, Linda. *Playing Around: Women and Extramarital Sex.* William Morrow and Company, New York, 1975.
14. Tripp, C., As quoted in "Can Homosexuals Change with Psychotherapy?" *Sexual Behavior,* July 1971, pp. 42–49.
15. Lee, J. A. "The Styles of Loving," *Psychology Today,* Oct. 1974, pp. 44–50.
16. Rubin, Zick. *Liking and Loving,* Holt, Rinehart and Winston, New York, 1973.

17. Constantine, L. L., and Constantine, J. M. "Marital Alternatives: Extended Groups in Modern Society," in Henry Grunebaum and Jacob Christ (Eds.), *Contemporary Marriage*, Little, Brown & Co., Boston, 1976, pp. 53–68.
18. Gilmartin, B. G. "That Swinging Couple Down the Block," *Psychology Today*, Feb. 1975, pp. 55–58.
19. O'Neill, Nena, and O'Neill, George. *Open Marriage*. Avon Books, New York, 1973.
20. Wolfe, L. "Can Adultery Save Your Marriage?" *New York Magazine*, July 3, 1972, pp. 36–39.
    Wolfe, L. "The Consequences of Playing Around," *New York Magazine*, June 2, 1975, 49–55.
21. See citations in notes 2, 8, and 9.

Chapter 6

1. "No. 74, Live Births, Deaths, Marriages, and Divorces: 1910 to 1976," *Statistical Abstract of the United States: 1977* (98th ed.), U.S. Department of Commerce, Bureau of the Census, Washington, D.C., 1977, p. 55.
2. *Ibid.* See also "Series B 214–215. Marriage Rate: 1920 to 1970," *Historical Statistics of the United States, Colonial Times to 1970*, U.S. Department of Commerce, Bureau of the Census, Washington, D.C., 1975, p. 64.
3. This was reported by the U.S. Census Bureau in *The Ann Arbor News*, Feb. 9, 1977, p. 23.
4. "No. 74, Live Births, Deaths, Marriages . . . ," *op. cit.*
5. Libman, J., and Lawson, H. "The Future Revised," *Wall Street Journal*, Mar. 18, 1976, p. 1.
6. *Ibid.*
7. Keys, M. F. *Staying Married*, Les Femmes, Millbrae, Calif., 1975. There has been a significant increase in the number of older divorced women who have not remarried since 1970. In the beginning of this decade there were 231,000 women between the ages of 40 and 65 who were divorced; by 1973 this figure had increased to 1,600,000. There were only 935,000 divorced men in 1973, a significantly lower figure than that for women because divorced men are far more likely to remarry. The remarriage rate for women begins declining at about the age of 30 and after 40, remarriage for women is rare. While some of these women presumably choose not to remarry, it is reasonable to assume that the low rate is primarily due to the fact that middle-aged men tend to remarry women who are significantly younger than their first wife.
8. Lieberman, E. J. "The Prevention of Marital Problems," In Henry Grunebaum and Jacob Christ (Eds.), *Contemporary Marriage*, Little, Brown and Company, Boston, 1976, pp. 315–332.
9. Bernard, Jessie. *Women, Wives, Mothers*, Aldine Publishing Co., Chicago, 1975.
10. Roper Organization. *The Virginia Slims American Women's Opinion Poll*, Vol. 3, 1974.

See also Yankelovich, D. *Public Attitudes toward Selected Issues*, Institute of Life Insurance, New York, 1974.

11. Bart, P. "Depression in Middle-aged Women," in Vivian Gornick and B. K. Moran (Eds.), *Woman in Sexist Society: Studies in Power and Powerlessness*, 1971, Basic Books, Inc., New York, 1971, pp. 99–117.

    Bernard, Jessie. *The Future of Marriage*, Bantam, New York, 1972.

    Gillespie, D. L. "Who Has the Power? The Marital Struggle," in Sue Cox (Ed.), *Female Psychology: The Emerging Self*, Science Research Associates, Chicago, 1976.

12. Smith, J. R., and Smith, L. G. (Eds.) *Beyond Monogamy: Recent Studies of Sexual Alternatives in Marriage*, Johns Hopkins University Press, Baltimore, 1974.

13. Polster, M. "Women in Therapy: A Gestalt Therapist's View," In Violet Franks and Vasanti Burtle (Eds.), *Women in Therapy*, Brunner/Mazel, New York, 1974, pp. 247–262. The quotation is from p. 247.

14. Vanek, J. "Time Spent in Housework," *Scientific American*, Nov. 1974, *230* (11), 116–120.

    Robinson, J. P. *Sex Roles and the Territoriality of Everyday Behavior*, unpublished manuscript, Survey Research Center, University of Michigan, 1975.

    Vanek found that the amount of time spent on housework by unemployed women in 1974 was the same 51 to 56 hours per week that was true in 1924. Preparing meals and cleaning up after meals took the most time. There was a considerable amount of travel, shopping, family care, and general management. The amount of time for cleaning had not changed, but the amount of time in laundering had increased because Americans now own more clothes and wash them more often. Women who were employed spent 26 hours a week in housework, but the difference in hours was not made up by husbands. Husbands of employed and unemployed women spent an average of 10 hours a week on household tasks, usually in shopping.

    Robinson has basically similar results. Unemployed women in his study averaged 36 hours a week on child care and housework while their husbands contributed 8 hours. Women who were employed in this study, as in Vanek's, reduced the hours given to child care and housework by 50 percent. The husbands of women who went to work were reported to have contributed 10 percent more time than husbands whose wives were not employed—but 10 percent of 8 hours spread over 7 days is hardly significant.

15. Tavris, Carol, and Offir, C. *The Longest War; Sex Differences in Perspective*, Harcourt Brace Jovanovich, New York, 1977, pp. 218–232.

    Bernard, J. "Men and Marriage," in "Letters from Readers," *Commentary*, Feb. 1975, *50*(2), 4, 6.

16. Kempton, S. "Cutting Loose," *Esquire*, July 1972, pp. 53–57. The quotation is from p. 56.

17. Gove, W. R. "Sex, Marital Status and Suicide," *Journal of Health and Social Behavior*, June 1972, *13*, 204–213.

18. Gove, W. R. "The Relationship between Sex Roles, Marital Status, and Mental Illness," *Social Forces,* Sept. 1972, *51*(1), 34–44.
19. Gove, "Sex, Marital Status, and Suicide," *op. cit.*
20. Gove, W. R., and Tudor, J. F. "Adult Sex Roles and Mental Illness," *American Journal of Sociology,* Jan. 1973, *78*(4), 812–835.
21. Gilder, George. *Sexual Suicide,* Quadrangle, New York, 1973. See also Gilder, G. "Untitled Response to Jessie Bernard's Letter," *Commentary,* Feb. 1975, *50*(2), 6.
22. Roper Organization, *op. cit.*
23. Campbell, A. "The American Way of Mating, Marriage Si, Children Only Maybe," *Psychology Today,* May 1975, pp. 37–43.
    See also Campbell, A., Converse, P., and Rogers, W. *Quality of American Life: Perceptions Evaluations and Satisfactions.* Russel Sage Foundation, New York, 1976.
24. Campbell, *op. cit.,* p. 38.
25. For a discussion of the effects of children on marriage, see, for example, Abernathy, V. D. "American Marriage in Cross-Cultural Perspective," in Henry Grunebaum and Jacob Christ (Eds.), *Contemporary Marriage,* Little, Brown & Co., Boston, 1976, pp. 33–51.
26. Sears, P. S., and Barbee, A. H. "Career and Life Satisfaction among Terman's Gifted Women," unpublished manuscript, 1975, 42 pp.
27. Spreitzer, E., Snyder, E. E., and Larson, D. "Age, Marital Status, and Labor Force Participation as Related to Life Satisfaction," *Sex Roles, 1*(3), 235–247.
28. Gove, "Sex, Marital Status and Suicide," *op. cit.*
29. Gilder, *Sexual Suicide, op. cit.*
30. Bardwick, J. M. "The dynamics of successful people," in Dorothy G. McGuigan (Ed.), *New Research on Women,* University of Michigan Press, Ann Arbor, Mich., 1974, pp. 86–104.
31. Roper Organization, *op. cit.*
32. Tresemer, D., and Pleck, J. "Sex-Role Boundaries and Resistance to Sex-Role Change," *Women's Studies,* 1974, *2,* 61–78.
33. Giele, J. Z. "Changing Sex Roles and the Future of Marriage," in Henry Grunebaum and Jacob Christ (Eds.), *Contemporary Marriage,* Little, Brown and Company, Boston, 1976, pp. 69–86.
34. Mead, Margaret. *Male and Female,* William Morrow and Company, New York, 1949.
35. Levi-Strauss, C. "The Family," in Henry L. Shapiro (Ed.), *Man, Culture, and Society.* Oxford University Press, New York, 1956, pp. 142–170.
36. Reik, Theodore. *The Creation of Woman,* McGraw-Hill, New York, 1960.
37. Goldberg, Steven. *The Inevitability of Patriarchy,* William Morrow and Company, New York, 1973–1974.
38. A discussion of the physiological argument is not germane here, but interested readers might read Goldberg, *op. cit.,* or refer to the following: Bardwick, J. M. "The Sex Hormones, the Central Nervous System and Affect Variability in Humans," in Violet Franks and Vasanti Burtle (Eds.), *Women in Therapy,* Brunner/Mazel, New York, 1974, pp. 27–50.

Gadpaille, W. J. "Research on the Physiology of Maleness and Femaleness," in Henry Grunebaum and Jacob Christ (Eds.), *Contemporary Marriage,* Little, Brown and Company, Boston, 1976, pp. 127–164.

39. Geothals, G. W., Steele, R. S., and Broude, G. J. "Theories and Research on Marriage: A Review and Some New Directions," in Henry Grunebaum and Jacob Christ (Eds.), *Contemporary Marriage,* Little, Brown & Co., Boston, 1976, pp. 229–274.

Safilios-Rothschild, C. "The Dimensions of Power Distribution in the Family," in Henry Grunebaum and Jacob Christ (Eds.), *Contemporary Marriage,* Little, Brown and Company, Boston, 1976, pp. 275–292.

Blood, R. O., and Wolfe, D. M. *Husbands and Wives: The Dynamics of Married Living,* Free Press, New York, 1960.

40. Bailyn, L. "Family Constraints on Women's Work," *Annals of the New York Academy of Sciences,* 1973, *208,* 82–90.

Chapter 7

1. "No. 74, Live Births, Deaths, Marriages, and Divorces: 1910 to 1976," *Statistical Abstract of The United States: 1977* (98th ed.), U.S. Department of Commerce, Bureau of the Census, Washington, D.C., 1977, p. 55.

2. Reston, J. "High Divorce Rate Proves Love Life Answers Needed," *Grand Rapids Press,* Mar. 17, 1975.

3. Grunebaum, H., and Christ, J. "Marriage and Society," in Henry Grunebaum and Jacob Christ (Eds.), *Contemporary Marriage,* Little, Brown and Company, Boston, 1976, pp. 1–7.

4. Personal communication, Mar. 1976.

5. Bach, G. R. "Creative Exits: Fight-Therapy for Divorces," in Violet Franks and Vasanti Burtle (Eds.), *Women in Therapy,* Brunner/Mazel, New York, 1974, pp. 307–325. The quotation is from pages 308–309.

6. "The Gay Liberator," *Mattachine Midwest News-letter,* Nov. 1972, p. 5.

7. Keller, S. "Does the Family Have a Future?" *Journal of Comparative Family Studies,* Spring 1971.

8. Gilder, George. *Naked Nomads: Unmarried Men in America,* Quadrangle, New York, 1974.

Chapter 8

1. Hennig, M. "Family Dynamics for Developing Positive Achievement Motivation in Women: The Successful Woman Executive," in Ruth B. Kundsin (Ed.), *Successful Woman in the Sciences: An Analysis of Determinants, Annals of the New York Academy of Sciences,* March 15, 1973, *208,* 76–81. See also the whole volume.

2. Menaker, E. "The Therapy of Women in the Light of Psychoanalytic Theory and the Emergence of a New View," in Violet Franks and Vasanti Burtle

(Eds.), *Women in Therapy,* Brunner/Mazel, New York, 1974, pp. 230–246. The majority of parents prefer sons; if Americans want children of both sexes they want the boy first, and if they want an odd number of children, most want more sons than daughters. This is discussed in Williamson, N. E. "Sex Preferences, Sex Control, and The Status of Women," *Signs,* 1976, *1*(4), 847–862.

3. Some discussion of these patterns is in Stanton, M. "The Concept of Conflict at Adolescence," *Adolescence,* Winter 1974, *9*(36), 537–546; and in Poveda, T. G. "Reputation and the Adolescent Girl: An Analysis," *Adolescence,* Spring 1975, *10*(37), 127–136.

4. Aspects of this are discussed in Maccoby, Eleanor E., and Jacklin, Carol N. *The Psychology of Sex Differences,* Stanford University Press, Stanford, Calif., 1974.

5. Feshbach, S., and Feshbach, N. "The Young Aggressors," *Psychology Today,* Apr. 1973, pp. 90–96.

6. Maslow, Abraham. *Toward a Psychology of Being,* Van Nostrand Reinhold Company, New York, 1968, 196.

7. For an extended discussion of this and what immediately follows the reader is directed to Freeman, Jo. *The Politics of Women's Liberation,* David McKay Co., New York, 1975.
   For an eyewitness account of the 1975 NOW convention the reader is directed to the *Syracuse New Times,* Nov. 9, 1975, especially to Scott, L. "N.O.W.: The Feminist Mistake," *Syracuse New Times,* Nov. 9, 1975, pp. 9, 16.

8. Freeman, *op. cit.,* p. 120.

9. Stimpson, C. R. "What Matter Mind: A Theory about the Practice of Women's Studies," *Women's Studies,* 1973, *1*, 293–314.
   Freeman, *op. cit.,* discusses this in terms of the political history of the contemporary feminist movement and Stimpson does the same in terms of the development of women's studies.

10. Fowler, M. G., and Van de Riet, H. K. "Women Today and Yesterday: An examination of the Feminist Personality," *Journal of Psychology,* 1972, *82,* 269–276.
    Chernis, C. "Personality and Ideology: A Personological Study of Women's Liberation," *Psychiatry,* 1972, *35,* 109–125.
    Pawlicki, R. E., and Almquist, C. "Authoritarianism, Locus of Control, and Tolerance of Ambiguity as Reflected in Membership and Nonmembership in a Women's Liberation Group," *Psychological Reports,* 1973, *32,* 1331–1337.

11. Aldous, J. "Women Leaders and the Advancement of Other Women," unpublished manuscript, no date, 20 pp.

Chapter 9

1. Maccoby, Eleanor E., and Jacklin, Carol N. *The Psychology of Sex Differences,* Stanford University Press, Stanford, Calif., 1974.

Block, J. H. "Debatable Conclusions about Sex Differences," *Contemporary Psychology,* 1976, *21*(8), 517–522.

Maccoby and Jacklin's text, which refuted the existence of many gender differences, was widely and enthusiastically reviewed in journals and the popular press. Reviewers minimized the significance of the gender differences that were reported. The first major critique of Maccoby and Jacklin was probably by Block, and in the prevailing mood, it took a lot of courage.

2. Shields, S. A. "Functionalism, Darwinism, and the Psychology of Women: A Study in Social Myth," *American Psychologist,* July 1975, pp. 739–754.

3. Parson, Talcott, and Bales, R. F. *Family Socialization and Interaction Process,* Free Press, New York, 1955.

4. Gutmann, D. "Women and the Conception of Ego Strength," *Merrill-Palmer Quarterly,* 1965, *11*, 229–240.

5. Bakan, David. *The Duality of Human Existence,* Rand McNally, Skokie, Ill., 1966.

6. Constantinople, A., "Masculinity–Femininity: An Exception to a Famous Dictum?" *Psychological Bulletin,* 1973, *80*(5), 389–407.

7. Dahlstrom, V. G., and Welsh, G. S. *An MMPI Handbook,* Minneapolis: University of Minnesota Press, 1960.

8. Gough, H. G. "Identifying Psychological Femininity," *Educational and Psychological Measurement,* 1952, *12*, 427–439.

9. Webster, H. Personality Development during the College Years: Some Quantitative Results. *Journal of Social Issues,* 1956, *12*(4), 29–43.

10. Bem, S. L. "The Measurement of Psychological Androgyny," *Journal of Consulting and Clinical Psychology,* 1974, *42*, 155–162.

Spence, J. T., Helmreich, R., and Stapp, J. "Ratings of Self and Peers and Sex-Role Attributes and Their Relation to Self-Esteem and Conceptions of Masculinity and Femininity," *Journal of Personality and Social Psychology,* 1975, *32*(1), 29–39.

11. Spence, Helmreich, and Stapp, *op. cit.*

12. O'Connor, K., Mann, D., and Bardwick, J. M. "Relationships between Self-Ratings of Individual and Stereotypical Sex-Role Identification and Self-Esteem in an Upper Class Adult Population," *Journal of Consulting and Clinical Psychology,* 1978.

13. Heilbrun has a slightly different focus; she has defined androgynous as "a condition under which the characteristics of the sexes and the human impulses expressed by men and women are not rigidly assigned." See Heilbrun, C. "Further Notes toward a Recognition of Androgyny," *Women's Studies,* 1974, *2*, 143–149.

14. Beach, F. A. "Cross-Species Comparison and Constraints on Inference," *Archives of Sexual Behavior,* 1976, *5*, 469–485. The quotation is from p. 470.

15. Aspects of this rather controversial idea are discussed more fully in Bardwick, J. M. "Evolution and Parenting," *Journal of Social Issues,* 1974, *30* (4), 39–62.

16. Beach, *op. cit.*

Miller, W. R., and Lief, H. I. "Masturbatory Attitudes, Knowledge and Experience: Data from the Sex Knowledge and Attitude Test (SKAT), *Archives of Sexual Behavior,* 1976, *5*(5), 447–467.

Schoof-Tans, K., Schlaegel, J., and Walczak, L. "Differentiation of Sexual Morality between 11 and 16 Years," *Archives of Sexual Behavior,* 1976, *5*(5), 353–370.

Asayama, S., "Sexual Behavior in Japanese Students: Comparisons for 1974, 1960, and 1952," *Archives of Sexual Behavior,* 1976, *5*(5), 371–390.

17. Newton, N., and Newton, M. "Psychologic Aspects of Lactation," *New England Journal of Medicine,* 1967, *277*(22), 1179–1188.

18. Kennell, J. H., Trause, M. A., and Klaus, M. H. "Evidence for a Sensitive Period in the Human Mother," *Parent–Infant Interaction,* Ciba Foundation Symposium 33, ASP, Amsterdam, 1975, pp. 87–101.

19. Klaus, M. H., Trause, M. A., and Kennell, J. H. "Does Human Maternal Behavior after Delivery Show a Characteristic Pattern?" *Parent–Infant Interaction,* Ciba Foundation Symposium 33, ASP, Amsterdam, 1975, pp. 69–85.

See also, Kennell, J. H., and Klaus, M. H. *Maternal Infant Bonding,* Mosby, St. Louis, 1976.

20. Barry, H. III, Bacon, M. K., and Child, I. L. "A Cross-Cultural Survey of Some Sex Differences in Socialization," *Journal of Abnormal and Social Psychology,* Nov. 1957, *55*, 327–332.

21. Maccoby and Jacklin, *op. cit.*

22. Rohner, R. P. "Sex Differences in Aggression," *Ethos,* Spring 1976, *4*(1), 57–72.

23. Goldberg, Steven. *The Inevitability of Patriarchy,* William Morrow and Company, New York, 1973–1974.

24. This is more fully discussed in Bardwick, J. M. "The Sex Hormones, the Central Nervous System and Affect Variability in Humans," in Violet Franks and Vasanti Burtle (Eds.), *Women in Therapy,* Brunner/Mazel, New York, 1974.

25. Money, John, and Erhardt, Anka. *Man and Woman: Boy and Girl.* Johns Hopkins University Press, Baltimore, 1972.

26. Money and Erhardt. See especially Chapter 4 and 6.

Chapter 10

1. See Roberts, H. "The Inside, the Surface, the Mass: Some Recurring Images of Women," *Women's Studies,* 1974, *2*, 289–307. Roberts writes:

> The desire to return to the womb has, for some, mystical ties with an age-old fertility cult, while to others it is weighed with the menace of the Freudian death wish. There are also those to whom it is the arena in which one must test his manhood and those to whom it comprises

the picturesque itinerary of an adventurous voyage. All these are based on the concept of woman's body as harbouring an inner space of immense magnitude, an inner space mysterious and inviting, threatening and compelling, an inner space that can engender and engulf, create life or destroy it.

2. Marcuse, H. "Marxism and Feminism," *Women's Studies,* 1974, *2,* 279–288.

Name Index

Subject Index

IN
TRANSITION
JUDITH M. BARDWICK

A major new work rich in wisdom and insight, *In Transition* explains how feminism has revolutionized every woman's awareness of her place in society, whether she is a staunch adherent or opponent; how the new sexual liberation movement, with its emphasis on hedonistic gratification, has forced us to rethink our notions about fidelity and commitment and reconsider what we want from relationships; and how the atmosphere of the me-decade, in which "human potential" seems infinite, has reversed traditional emphasis on duty, sacrifice, and helping others to a new focus on "What's in it for me?"

Like *The Greening of America*, this book puts into perspective a decade of puzzling and deeply uprooting change. Like *Passages*, it makes sense of our confusion and ambivalence as we shed old values and attempt to create new ones. *In Transition* is, above all, about change: about rapid, major value shifts generated in the sixties and seventies. And it is about the very personal effects these changes have had on the lives of each one of us.

In Transition measures the costs and benefits of feminism, sexual liberation, and